To the Lawyer

Happy Chanukah.

Arnold Powell

A Touch of Chutzpah

Arnold Powell

authorHOUSE®

AuthorHouse™ UK Ltd.
500 Avebury Boulevard
Central Milton Keynes, MK9 2BE
www.authorhouse.co.uk
Phone: 08001974150

First published by AuthorHouse 3/11/2010

ISBN: 978-1-4490-6946-9 (sc)
ISBN: 978-1-4490-6945-2 (hc)

This book is printed on acid-free paper.

Dr Powell extends his thanks to the directors of Springdene Nursing and Care Homes Ltd who have very generously sponsored publication of this book.

Prologue

Sophia Podguszer, a pregnant young mother with three small children, fled Warsaw in 1905, following her husband, Morris, to London, to escape the vicious pogroms in her native Poland. Living in squalid, overcrowded conditions as a penniless refugee, she soon realised that her family could not survive on her husband's meagre wages as a butcher's assistant.

Ambitiously, she set about establishing, with the help of Morris, what was to become her own successful business, at a time when to find a woman at the head of any commercial enterprise was unheard of.

She had three sons and once they became adults she schemed that they marry young women of her choosing. This led to conflict and unhappiness, which ultimately rebounded on her, in a way that she could not have predicted.

When a middle-aged widow, she was persuaded by her children, against her better judgment, to retire in order to enjoy a life of comfort and ease. In time she realised, all too late, what an unfortunate choice she had made.

Years later her grandchildren found her to be a marvellous fun-loving companion, but her latter years were often lonely, as she felt herself to have been rejected by her children. Passed, as she described it, 'like some unwanted package' from the homes of each of her children, she entered a series of residential hotels, and finally lived in a nursing home, where she died.

Sophia was my grandmother, whom I loved dearly. I wish I could turn the clock back to have been a better grandson. Now, by recording her struggles, I seek somehow to make amends.

It seems strange that many of us are often knowledgeable about persons from history books, to whom we are unrelated; yet know little if anything of any ancestor from more than four generations ago (great grandparents).

When younger I experienced an urge to trace and record some of the events in the lives of my parents and grandparents, fearing that if I failed to do so, this knowledge would be lost forever. In retirement, I have the opportunity to share these stories, particularly relating to my paternal grandmother, Sophia, with you. Hopefully one or more of my younger readers may be encouraged to embark upon a similar project to record family events for some future generation.

In my estimation, Sophia, was a remarkable woman for her time, in spite of the fact that she invariably made my mother's life hell. In this brief biography I wish to convey something of her life and to record her unrelenting struggle, as a newly arrived refugee, to escape the impoverished social background in which she found herself.

Although no such condition appears in any medical literature, I believe a "King Lear Syndrome" does exist and is easily recognisable. In its simplest form it unexpectedly strikes an older subject who has relinquished control of personal finance and assets to another, usually a close family member, in the belief that the recipient will use these resources in the donors' best interest.

Like any malady it affected my grandmother and might afflict any of us in our latter years. There is no preventive immunisation that can be given when young and no medication that can be taken later. To minimise the risk, we should resolve to treat the elderly with kindness and tolerance so that when, in the fullness of years, we in turn become frail, our children will have learned by example the respect due to the aged and will in turn be patient and understanding and conduct themselves accordingly.

While never dwelling on the past, we should honour those who are no longer among us, by recording something of their lives, so that a future generation may be more aware of their own inheritance and not just an ancestor's name, and possibly a date and place of birth.

Herein, 'warts and all', you may read something of my grandmother's life, efforts and achievements. May she rest in peace.

Arnold Powell
London 2010

The people in this book

There have been many variations in anglicizing the spelling of the Polish family name **Chisick**. They include: **Cyzyk, Czyzyk, Chiszyk, Chissick, Chishick, Chisick, Chiswick.** For the sake of simplicity the spelling **Chisick** is used in this book.

Abraham Chisick, (circa 1860-1943), a cabinet maker, the eldest brother of Sophia (née Zlata Chisick) Podguszer. Circa 1886 immigrated from Warsaw to London and in 1888 married Betty (Beila) Cohen (1863-1941). They had 7 children. Louisa 1890; Harry 1891; Annie 1896; Bertha 1898; Isadore 1900; Zelda 1903; Kitty 1904.

Annie The four main family members with this name were:

i.**Annie Podguszer** (Warsaw 1903-1978 London) third child of Sophia and Morris. Changed her name to Anne Podguszer, then by deed poll to Anne Maurice and finally Anne Veronique when she married Vincent (Jack) Veronique in 1954.

ii. **Annie Cohen** (Mlova Poland 1896-1993 London) The fourth child of Jacob and Sarah Cohen, preferred to be called Ann. Married Mark Podguszer, but was always called Annie Cohen by the Podguszer family. In 1942, by deed poll, became Ann Powell. She had five children: Peter, Maurice, Gloria, Arnold and Michael.

iii. **Annie Ginsberg** (1900-1996) married Harry Podguszer in 1925, after which she was always called Ginsy. In 1942 became Annie Podro. She had 2 sons: Murray and Maurice.

iv. **Annie Chisick** (1896-1924) third child of Abraham and Betty Chisick. In 1919 married her first cousin, Monic Zure (1899-1926) whose mother was Ryvka, the youngest sister of Abraham and Sophia Chisick. They had two children, Peter (1920) and Netta (1923) who were later adopted by Abraham and Betty Chisick.

Arnold, fourth child of Mark and Ann Powell. Married June Fraiman and had three children, the youngest named after Sophia.

i. **Betty Chisick** (Beila née Cohen) (1863-1941). wife of Abraham.

ii. **Betty** (Rebecca Podguszer London 1907-1984 Montreal) called Becky or Keggy, but preferred Betty. Married Issie Glick in 1945 and the following year had a son, Russell.

iii. **Betty Defries**, (1933) the only daughter of Essie née Podguszer and Edward (Titch) Defries. In 1954 married Ralph Levy, an Edinburgh University medical student. They had 3 children, Beverley, Hilary and Robert.

Clara, companion housekeeper to Sophia for almost 20 years.

Defries Edward (Titch) husband of Essie Podguszer and father of Betty.

Elsie (née Gershon) in 1932 married **Steve** Podguszer, later divorced.

Essie (Esther Podguszer 1905-1969) the second daughter of Morris and Sophia Podguszer. In 1930 married Titch Defries, a widower.

Ginsy née Annie Ginsberg (1900-1996). In July 1925 married Harry Podguszer. Name change by 1942 deed poll to Anne Podro.

Gitle (née Blumensohn) Chisick the wife of Pesach Chisick and mother of Sophia.

Glick, Issie (1917-2007 Montreal) The Canadian serviceman who married Rebecca (Betty) Podguszer in 1945.

Gloria Powell (London 1930-1987 Florida) only daughter of Mark and Ann Podguszer. Named after Gitle (née Blumensohn) Chisick, her great grandmother. In 1959 married Dr Ivor Moss. They had one son, Nicholas.

Hilda Podguszer (1887- circa 1950) sister of Morris Podguszer and youngest child of Marcus and Anna (née Vladoff) Podguszer. Accompanied Sophia to London in 1905. In 1913 married Solomon Schwartz, a tailor. They had four children.

Hyman Podguszer (1909-1910) the last child of Sophia and Morris Podguszer.

Hyman (Hymie) Lazarus, (deceased Mar 1952) the CEO. of HL Cabinets, employer and lover of Anne Podguszer. His wife was Bessie and his son, Leon.

Harry Podguszer (Warsaw 1902-1979 London) second child of Sophia and Morris. In 1925 married Annie Ginsberg who was always called Ginsy. They had 2 sons: Murray; Maurice. In 1942 changed his family name to Podro, by deed poll.

Lev Podguszer (1877-1943), Morris Podguszer's younger brother. Emigrated from Warsaw to Paris, France in 1922 with his children: Albert, Regine, Sylvain, Anna, Busha, Serge, Julian and Leah Podguszer. In 1942 sent to Drancy and then to Auschwitz, where the Nazis murdered him. His son Albert and granddaughter Anna Podguszer aged 19 years were likewise killed by the Nazis.

Louisa Chisick (1890), Lulu, eldest child of Abraham and Betty Chisick. In 1913 married Louis Hart.

Mark or Marcus Podguszer (Warsaw 1900-1963 London), the eldest son of Morris and Sophia Podguszer. He married Ann (née Annie Cohen) in 1923. They had five children. Peter; Maurice; Gloria; Arnold; Michael. In 1942 changed his family name to Powell, by deed poll.

Maurice.i. Maurice Podguszer (1927) later Powell, second child of Mark Powell.

Maurice.ii. Maurice Podguszer (1928) later Podro second child of Harry Podro.

Michael (1934), fifth child of Mark (Podguszer) Powell.

Morris Podguszer (Poland 1872-1926 London) called Moisheka by his wife Sophia and friends.

Murray Podguszer (1926) later Podro, eldest son of Harry and Ginsy. Early member of the 43 Group.

Pesach Czyzyk (b.1840- circa 1916) and Gitle (née Blumensohn) (b.1838) were Sophia's parents.

Arnold Powell

Peter Powell (1924-2004), the eldest child of Mark and Ann and first grandchild of Sophia and Morris Podguszer. In 1951 married Doreen Jacobs, but later divorced. They had 2 sons Philip (1952) and Jonathan (1955).

Philip Powell (1952), eldest son of Peter and Doreen Powell, Sophia Podguszer's first great grandson and Jonathan Powell (1955) Philip's younger brother.

Rebecca Podguszer (London 1907-1984 Montreal) third daughter of Sophia and Morris Podguszer; known as Becky, or Keggy but preferred Betty. In 1945 married Issie Glick. They had one son Russell.

Rosa, Housekeeper to Anne Veronique for twenty years.

Solly (Solomon)Podguszer, (London 1908-1965 Liverpool) youngest son of Sophia and Morris Podguszer. Changed his name to Steve Maurice. Twice married, his first marriage to Elsie Gershon ended in divorce. No children.

Steve Maurice (1908-1965)**,** see Solly Podguszer, above.

Sophia (née **Zlata Chisick) Podguszer** (1879-1963 London) known to her intimates as Zoshia. In 1899 married Morris Podguszer. From 1943 onwards occasionally used the name Mrs. Maurice.

Sylvain Podguzer (Warsaw 1904-1966 Paris), third child of Lev Podguzer, Morris Podguszer's brother; A furrier and nephew of Sophia Podguszer, lived in LeHavre France from 1922 until 1940 and in Paris from 1946 until 1965. Escaped to London in 1940.

Titch (Edward) Defries (1903-1986) married Essie Podguszer. Daughter Betty.

Vincent (or Jack) **Veronique** (1904-1994) in 1954 married Anne (Podguszer) Maurice.

Zelda Chisick (1882-1961) younger sister of Sophia. Married Sam Kelter and living in London had seven children.

Zlata Chisick, Sophia Chisick's Polish name.

Zoshia, the name used by Sophia Podguszer amongst relatives and close friends.

Chapter 1

London 1962

*U*nable to unlock the front door, I realised the game was up. I was trapped in the foyer and stood there with nowhere to go. It was almost 7.30 that Sunday morning when they discovered me. It was my latest attempt to break out, and it proved to be my last. As the early staff arrived for duty, first one and then another spotted me until an excited group crowded round.

"Mrs. Maurice! You're still in your nightdress! How did you get down here?"

They were talking rapidly among themselves, yet I couldn't distinguish a single word. Everything was horribly muffled and I could merely guess what they were saying. I merely stood there, like a trapped bird in a cage. With the front door locked, there was no way I could possibly escape and I certainly couldn't make a run for it with my Zimmer frame.

The carers who gathered round me were like a crowd of unruly schoolchildren. Gesticulating, they kept talking, but not one of them had the sense to move closer and speak into my ear. I supposed they were asking questions and it seemed strange to me that these highly trained people knew that I had difficulty hearing, yet they became increasingly agitated when I appeared to be ignoring them. They were treating me like a delinquent child and it was so humiliating.

Couldn't they see that I was without my hearing aid?

This was eventually noticed by one of the senior staff that knew me well. I could feel the warm blast of her breath as she placed her lips close to my face. So closely that I could even detect the pleasant whiff of the mint flavoured toothpaste she'd earlier used.

"Mrs. Maurice, you haven't got your hearing aid on, or your dentures in! Whoever brought you down like this?"

At last, although the words were soft and quiet, I could hear what someone was saying.

I knew they'd report this little incident to my daughter, Anne Veronique, as they always did whenever I stepped out of line. She's the one who pays my bills. In turn, she'll let my other children know. That way they can further justify the need to have me "looked after for my own good," which would further soothe any remaining qualms they might have about locking me away in here.

My eldest son Mark and his wife Annie Cohen with their dissenting voices would say that there's nothing wrong with me, and that I was just being my usual awkward self. They'd be quite right, but since all the others aren't on speaking terms with them, their view won't be counted.

On the other hand none of them have any idea how awful it is to be young in mind and spirit while imprisoned in a wrinkled skin, with a saggy body that malfunctions too frequently for anyone in polite society to enjoy standing up close.

I'd love to be able to walk about as I once used to, but with knees and hips that ache whenever I budge and a spine that constantly throbs with pain, I'm reduced to a slow moving, almost immobile hulk.

Oh for something as simple as a toothache, and to hell with the pain, that could then be cured with a single visit to the dentist!

My children won't have many years to wait before they'll find out what ageing is like, but I'll have long since disappeared and I won't be able to tell them;

"I told you so!" I've had the audacity to live well beyond the three score and ten years the bible allotted me, and to repay this impudence, my children have chosen this path for me, as an early foretaste of hell, should I not mend my ways.

"Leave me alone! Let go of me! I want to leave this infernal hole." I scream and yell, as I try unsuccessfully to prevent them escorting me to my room, a ward of three beds on the second floor. I realise that my behaviour is undignified, but I don't have the strength to resist and without my hearing aid, I'm unable to argue with them to explain what I want. I'm not used to other people dictating every aspect of my life and I resent being told constantly what to do.

Once I'm back in my room, with my hearing aid installed, the interrogation begins in earnest.

"How did you get downstairs Sophie, who took you down?"

Thank heavens these nurses don't use water dripping from a tap, accompanied with bright lights shining in my eyes to extract a confession. They've obviously never heard of a lift, and would never believe me if I told them I'd simply pressed a couple of buttons.

I'm a mature woman in my 80s. I've been used to making decisions for others and myself all my life and now because I've grey hair, use a hearing aid and need a walking stick, these youngsters have the nerve to ask me how I did something as simple as take a lift to go downstairs! Not only that, my name is Sophia, not Sophie.

Sophie Tucker, the vaudeville singer who used to sing 'Life begins at forty' and who I last saw in her farewell performance at the London Casino in 1948 when there was standing room only and tickets were exchanged at a premium, preferred Sophie, but I'm Sophia; Sophia Podguszer, although amongst family and those closest to me I'm called Zoshia.

My daughter registered me here as Sophia Maurice, because nobody could pronounce Podguszer, my name since 1899 when as Zlata Chisick, which in Polish means 'goldfinch', I married my late husband, Morris Podguszer, *ova sholom* (rest in peace), in Warsaw. But that was more than sixty years ago. In those years I was considered a pretty young woman, and captured many a fellow's admiring gaze as I romped through life, with few cares and little thought of what the future might have in store for me beyond the next few weeks.

"Why-ever were you downstairs so early, before dressing and even before breakfast?"

"It's Sunday and I don't want to miss my visitors when they arrive." I lied.

"We know that Sunday's the day that most family visit, but nobody ever turns up much before mid-day and anyway you know we always call to tell you when they've arrived.

"Now just you be patient and wait here. Somebody will be along with your breakfast in a few minutes and then we'll help you bath and dress."

"Just look at my arms, all black and blue. See for yourself how you and those other ruffians hurt me."

"But those bruises were there when I helped you bathe two days ago."

"That doesn't matter. When I tell my daughter how a crowd of you manhandled me, she'll believe me. She'll tell you that an old lady of my age has no reason to lie and she'll take me out of here. You'll see. I'm going to get away from here no matter what it takes."

Since I'm unable to escape, once a week isn't exactly often to see my family and I'd hate to miss any one of them even for a minute, and that's the truth. I know that many of my visitors are much too busy to be here before early afternoon, but I tell the nurses I'm worried that I might miss someone. The trouble is that I never know who'll be visiting and sometimes I have difficulty recognising some of the younger ones. With six children and nine grandchildren, you'd never believe how I could have so few callers. During the week there are rarely any and seldom more than one or two on a Sunday afternoon. I know there's never any on Sunday morning, but I have this compulsion to wait by the door, just in case somebody might arrive unexpectedly and I'd somehow miss them.

Of course other residents have family who visit and there's always the possibility that I may recognise someone I once knew, or they might acknowledge me, but that seldom occurs; certainly never since I've been held here.

When they visit, none of my family seem to appreciate that I'd welcome going out for a drive in the country, dining in a fine restaurant, or even visiting a theatre or cinema with them, as in the old days. They all tell me of their love and devotion, but heaven forbid they should take me out for a few hours! Perhaps they're afraid that once outside, I'll make a run for it. Imagine the local newspaper headlines:

Zimmer Toting Octogenarian Runs Off.

Maybe it's my need for a little help in going to the bathroom that makes them feel embarrassed, but I'm the one who should feel uncomfortable, not them. There's hardly one of them who I've not had to take a dozen times to the toilet when they were young and whose smelly bottoms I cleaned and whose soiled clothes I washed by hand. Yet they're the ones who are afraid that they might need to help me in the lavatory.

It seems so much longer than two years ago when my children had their bright idea of placing me in a nursing home;

"It's for your own good," they told me repeatedly, as each of them tried to salve their own conscience. To me their remedy felt more like curing an ingrowing toenail by cutting off my leg! So far as I'm concerned this place feels more like a penal institution, where once you're in, it's for good and they never let you out. It's detention for life, with no review of sentence.

A small army of staff regularly assesses me and makes reams of notes. They record when I have a bath, how I sleep, whether I'm sociable and have I been to the toilet. Yet I'll never be given any time off for good behaviour, so why should I or anyone else care whether I've peed once or a dozen times in a day.

I begged them not to leave me here, but in spite of all my entreaties, nobody would listen. And believe me I entreated plenty.

My children constantly ignore my pleading that they take me home.

"Please, just take me out of here and let me get on with my life, like I once used to do." They persistently do the old 'deaf ear act' when I tell them how miserable and lonely I feel, which is every time I see one of them. Now you can understand why, whenever possible, I spend my time trying to find a way to break out from here.

The matron says that my repeated attempts to run off must be evidence of a confused state of mind and are a nuisance, but what does she know? It's because I'm rational and sane that I want to leave this place to regain my independence.

Who in their right mind would want to stay in what feels like a top security jail, where they lock all the main doors and have a guard escort me, whenever I attempt to take a short walk in the garden by myself?

I'm too old to dig tunnels, like they did in the prisoner of war camps. That's why I've decided to be as difficult as possible in the forlorn hope that they'll just say;

"We've had enough of the old biddy!" and show me the door.

I've always been self reliant, because I've always had to fight for what I needed for my family and myself. That's how I gained a reputation for being independent. My children might even say difficult, and many of the staff would probably agree, but that's hardly a crime.

To make matters worse I've found that my memory hasn't been so good lately, and being unable to read or write English properly I'm not able to keep a proper diary. This has started to worry me, because what are we without our memories? Just you try to keep track of events and appointments when you can't write things down; it's difficult at the best of times. At least my recollection of events of long ago remains good, which is some consolation.

I never had much of an education, but I'd heard of William Shakespeare often enough. He wrote a play called 'King Lear'. It's about that old King, who, just like me, had three daughters. Mind you he had a lot more to give away than me, but I also have three daughters in law, which probably evens things up a bit.

Somehow we both landed up in the same kind of mess. I could have warned him, had he been prepared to listen, but then, that would have been impossible because he lived hundreds of years ago. I'd have told him how these girls could be as sweet as meringue pie until you give them control of your assets and then watch out!

Just see how they change, no matter how much you've given them, and how much you beg and implore afterwards.

"Let me live with you and Ginsy." (rhymes with quinsy) I pleaded with Harry, my second son, and his wife.

"You know nothing would have given us more pleasure than to have you live with us, but after the boys married and decamped we moved from a spacious house in Golders Green to a one bedroom flat with a box room, in Kensington. You've seen it for yourself; comfortable and stylish, but just enough room for two adults. It's the price we pay for moving up in the world from North West 11 to South West 1, to live amongst the smarter set. There's not only very little room, but now we both have to go out to work just to pay for the larger Kensington council tax, which means the place is empty all day."

Of course I couldn't ask Becky, my youngest daughter, because she's lived in Montreal since 1945. My youngest boy Solly, or Steve as he now prefers to be called, is out of the question, since he works as a steward on the Cunard liner, Queen Elizabeth. He lives in Birkenhead with his second wife, Sophie, which is too far from London and in any case he's seldom home.

That leaves only three of my children.

There's Essie, and her husband Titch, who lived for several years after the war in my old home in Stamford Hill, but who now have their home in Brighton. Essie was by far the prettiest and most vivacious of my daughters. Unfortunately, she hasn't been at all well lately. She keeps forgetting things from one moment to the next. The doctors describe it with a name that when anyone ever dares speak about it, it's only in a whisper, in case by saying 'dementia' out loud, it's something to be ashamed of and might mean that they'll somehow catch it, like typhus.

We all forget from time to time where we leave something, particularly when we're in a hurry. I've always had difficulty remembering people's names and constantly can't find my glasses, but not only has she been doing that for ages, she forgets that she's left the gas on without lighting it and puts dirty crockery back in the cupboard as though it was clean. She doesn't remember from one minute to the next whom she last saw, or spoke to on the phone and gets lost whenever she leaves the house when unaccompanied. Anyway, they're too far away for me to stay with them, which leaves only my elder daughter Anne with her husband Vincent and my eldest son Mark and his wife Annie Cohen.

"Anne, I'm imploring you, and a mother shouldn't have to beg. Let me stay with you and Vincent."

"We've been down this path a thousand times. When Daddy, *ova sholom*, (rest in peace) passed away, I gave you a solemn undertaking that I'd always care for you. Nobody can ever point a finger and say that I haven't gladly lived up to that obligation every day of my life since then, and you have my word, that I'll continue to do so."

"I didn't say you've been anything but a fantastic daughter. It's just that I don't want to be discarded like some piece of unwanted furniture that no longer has a place in your home."

"Darling, how can you say such a thing? What a suggestion! Nobody's throwing you out; heaven forbid! You're not being discarded by me or any-one else, but you really can't live with Vincent and me."

"I've never had to sleep in a room with total strangers before and all of them *alte kakas* (old shit bags), which is putting it mildly. I know I'm a grey haired old lady with a few wrinkles, but inside I feel young and full of vitality."

"There's no way I can personally supervise your care, while I'm running a business at the same time. I have to work hard like you used to do. You always had Clara as your companion until she retired last year, but if you won't live with a housekeeper to help you, you leave me with few other choices.

"If you continually obstruct me when I endeavour to provide a live in companion for you, then you give me no alternative but to arrange for you to stay in a residential hotel, or failing that, a nursing home."

"Is it my fault that since Clara retired all these housekeepers that you've brought to live with me are either antisocial, or steal from me, so that I have to throw them out?"

"Each of those housekeepers you rejected had impeccable references. Not only that, I personally spent hours of my time interviewing every one of them. I can't believe that they were all misfits, or thieves."

"So are you saying your mother's a liar? When you live with any woman, even for a short while, you start to see them as they really are and it's often not a pretty sight, believe me. Every evening I secretly unlocked the wine cupboard and measured the levels of the wine and spirit bottles with a piece of string. I could see with my own eyes when these *schickas* (drunks) and *gunavim* (thieves), had been helping themselves to my sherry, wine and gin."

"Mother, I'd never suggest that you're not telling the truth, but some might consider measuring the contents of every bottle each day a little eccentric."

"It's not true. I only checked the levels at night after they'd gone to bed so they wouldn't see what I was doing. I tell you I'll not have these interlopers eating and drinking me out of house and home. Who knows what else they might be stealing when I'm not watching."

"Mother you don't realise that while you may feel young, you're just not as robust as you used to be. It's simply part of an ageing process."

"That's nonsense! I admit that with the rheumatism in my knees my walking isn't so good anymore, and I need a hearing aid, but I'm fine otherwise."

"Darling, you don't see yourself as others see you. You've become more frail and vulnerable and I'm not prepared to see any woman of eighty living on her own, let alone my own mother, without some reliable help in the home."

"Couldn't we live together as we used to? That's what I 'd like most of all."

"You know I'm a career woman and only have a two bedroom apartment. Vincent and I have to leave before eight every morning and seldom return until six or seven at night. Not only must I consider my husband, but we need a bedroom for Rosa, my housekeeper. There's no way we could afford a larger flat with enough room to accommodate both you and a full time carer, until we've expanded the business."

That left Mark, my eldest son, the one that apart from Steve, none of my children speak to and of course visa-versa. He's lived twenty years with his wife Ann, whom we all call Annie Cohen, which she hates, in a modern four-bedroom semi in Cockfosters and now that their five children are married, could easily make room for me.

"Mark, they want me to go into a prison they all call an old persons' home. I've nowhere to live. Let me come and stay with you and Ann!"

"Of course you can. I'm certain Ann will agree that you can stay for a few days, even a week or two, but, for any longer, that's entirely another matter."

"I'm not asking to stay for just a few days. I've no home to call my own anymore and I don't want to go into some institution. I'm your mother and I'm talking about somewhere I can be happy and stay for the rest of my days."

"We've already explored the possibility that you live with us, many times before, and it simply won't work.

You know we've not exchanged a word with Anne, Essie, or Harry or any of their children in more than seven years, since that unfortunate incident between Harry and me at Ralph and Betty's wedding.

"It's only natural that you'd want to see your other children and that they should want to visit you. Try to look at the logistics for a moment. How would you expect them to call on you in my home? Do you suppose that we'd move out every other evening for them to have access to you? Alternatively should we take you to visit them and wait outside until somebody escorts you out?

"What if you were sick? I'm sorry mother, but, however much it might break your heart, and believe me it hurts me to say this, there's no way that you could live with us for any length of time under those circumstances. If you just stop for a moment and think about it, I'm sure you'll realise that staying with us long term would be totally impractical."

Initially Anne and Vincent attempted to place me in a residential hotel in Westcliff-on-Sea without telling me of their intentions.

"I'm just going out for the day to the seaside. Would you like to come to keep me company on the journey Zoshia? We could have lunch when we arrive and it should make a very pleasant day's outing." Vincent enquired with an inviting smile.

My appointments diary was always empty, so naively I agreed to what had become an increasingly rare opportunity to go out for a ride in the countryside.

He drove me down in his smart limousine, with me reclining in the back on leather upholstered seats by myself like 'Lady Muck', enjoying the outing and listening to classical music from his new tape player. I should have been suspicious. After all, who goes to the seaside in the middle of winter when it's raining and almost blowing a gale? He didn't mention what they'd planned until we arrived at this hotel. He pulled up, turned round inside the car to face me and says,

"We'll have a spot of lunch here, it's strictly *kosher*."(according to dietary law)

We entered the hotel, with me trailing behind, heading for the reception. As we went through the entrance hall, there was no hiding the fact that it was filled with a number of ancient women, all seated in a variety of armchairs, looking like a group of ghosts and old vultures sitting, watching and waiting.

At the reception desk, Vincent announced that he wished to register me as a guest.

"Vincent, surely you don't need to register me for lunch?"

"I've brought a case with your clothes in the car trunk and I thought you might enjoy staying here for a few days after we've had lunch."

His response surprised me and momentarily caught me unawares.

If winter wasn't bad enough then he hadn't looked at the guest list. They were all very old women wearing stained crimplene blouses and creased skirts, topped by cardigans, with food stains and missing buttons. They looked such a pathetic sight as though they'd each borrowed some neighbours' clothes that didn't fit; hardly the ladies who would make the front cover of *Vogue*.

"I can't possibly stay here with all these *alte kakas*! Whatever are you thinking about?"

"Nonsense, you'll love it here. Just fill your lungs. Take a big breath in and smell the ozone. This sea air's so bracing and everyone will want to visit you at the seaside to walk along the front, to buy Ross's ice cream."

"That might be fine for a few days in summer, but not in February and certainly never in this place. You're the pipe smoker, so you breathe in deeply and fill your lungs with the ozone; believe me, you need it more than me. Once you've finished your breathing exercises and cleared the old breathing tubes, I'll treat you to an ice cream, if that's what you really want, after which you can take me straight home."

"Come on, give it a try for a few days. You've nothing to lose." said Vincent with a reassuring smile.

"I'm not staying and that's final!" Adamantly I refused to stay. While I'm in the preliminary stages of what I intend should be a really major tantrum, the like of which I haven't enjoyed in ages, particularly in front of an audience, the coward hoisted the white surrender flag, and spoiled all my fun just as I was getting started.

"All right mother, I hear what you're saying and so does the whole hotel. Don't shout any more, you know how I hate any commotion. You don't have to stay and I'll tell Anne it's all been a terrible mistake, so please let's have no more fuss. We'll order a spot of lunch and then have a drive down by the promenade for a few minutes before we go back home."

We went into the dining room and like a gentleman, he even helped me into my chair and ordered lunch for the two of us from the rather limited menu. It was chicken soup with vermicelli, followed by grilled cod, baked potatoes and tinned peas, with rice pudding for dessert. The alternative to the main course was a lettuce and cheese sandwich. A truly imaginative bill of fare, which they'd obviously heisted right out of a two star Michelin food guide. Was this really where this *schnorrer* (a beggar, somebody mean and penny pinching) was prepared to leave me?

I retired to the ladies room for a few minutes and on my return found he'd gone. The scoundrel had given me the slip, with his old disappearing act, and left me there like a bundle of laundry to be picked up some time later. Of course he left a message with the manager asking him to tell me that he'd been called away unexpectedly and hoped to be back sometime soon.

I might be old, but I'm not an old fool. His 'soon' probably meant next month, or even the following year. I never really trusted that man after the deceptions he'd played on my daughter when he persuaded her to marry him, but I'll tell you about that later. Now I knew my maternal intuition was correct and I could see him for the *meeskait* (a small ugly person) this schnorrer really was.

I had only a few loose coins in my handbag but, thank goodness, long ago I'd developed the habit of concealing a few bank notes in my underclothes in case of an emergency.

I sat at the dining table and asked the manager to call a taxi to take me back to London. The waitress served the chicken soup Vincent had ordered, which finally clinched my distrust of the man. Lukewarm, it wouldn't have mattered if it was kosher or not, because the closest that amber liquid with its short pieces of white vermicelli had been to a chicken was when the bird had strode through the pot on stilts, flapping its wings so as not to get its feet wet.

Before I'd time to finish the cook's deceptive soup offering, my taxi arrived. I didn't care if Vincent had paid a week's money in advance; I simply walked out and into the car, without a backward glance.

I arrived back at my daughter's home in London before Vincent. When he later entered the apartment, I relished the surprised look on his face, like a blowfish that had inadvertently sucked instead of blown, as I greeted him, all innocence.

"Hello Vincent' I thought I'd save you the trouble of going back to pick me up."

The next day it was off to Westcliff, once again, this time my daughter drove me in her car. Our destination was the slightly more up market Glenn Hotel, although I couldn't discern the difference between that and the previous day's offering. I could never quite understand why my children liked Westcliff, with its pier and unromantic mud-flat views of the wide Thames estuary, swept in winter by the biting icy winds blowing in from the North Sea.

"Mother, you're to stay here until I can sort things out and find somewhere for you to live in London!"

I agreed, but later when I searched for my concealed stash of money there was none to be found. Anne had pre-empted me and had removed any hidden funds from my underclothing. My daughter should have felt ashamed at stooping to such an underhand parental trick. I resolved to make myself as intolerably unpleasant and difficult as possible.

After I had been in residence less than four weeks the manager telephoned Anne.

I was close to his office with its open door and gleefully listened to his side of the conversation.

"Mrs Veronique, we've had a number of problems with Mrs Podguszer and must ask you to remove her from the Glenn hotel."……..

"Yes I know that in our agreement we undertake to give you a week's notice, but matters have gone from bad to worse and are completely out of hand." ……..

"No we're not prepared to wait until the end of the week. Were we to do so it's likely that we'd have few staff left in our employ and probably fewer residents. Too many have already threatened to leave." ……..

"I regret that we have to acknowledge that your mother's presence here is causing mayhem amongst staff and clients. We could contend with her moving shoes that had been left outside a residents' bedroom for cleaning, by chalking room numbers on the soles, but last night was the worst. She entered each resident's bedroom while they were asleep, removed every denture that she found on a bedside locker and placed them all in a sink full of water in the kitchen. One of the staff found her leaving the kitchen and when they stopped her, she claimed that she must have been sleepwalking. It's going to take hours, possibly days, to sterilize the dentures and then unite each of our guests with their own set of teeth." ……..

"No. I'm not suggesting and have never implied that she's wicked, but from our viewpoint she's rather difficult and disruptive." ....

"I realise that my request may be coming at an inconvenient time, but I'm appealing that you remove your mother as soon as possible, if only for her own safety, but it must be today." ....

"We'll have her case packed and she'll be ready for you to collect after she's had her lunch, which we'll have to serve in her bedroom." ....

"You ask why? It's because feelings today are running particularly high amongst most of our guests who now have no teeth with which to eat their food and we daren't risk an incident."

Success! I'd achieved my objective and was delighted to leave Westcliff, but my pleasure was short lived and lasted little more than a week. On my return to London I was lodged with Harry and Ginsy, sleeping on what felt like an old army camp bed in the tiniest bedroom I'd ever seen. I was unclear whether it had been designed as a large broom cupboard where the builder had mistakenly installed a window, or a walk-in closet, but it was certainly cramped. I could have contended with the discomfort, but within a few days it was Harry's turn to reject his mother. Without my consent, he and Ginsy placed me in a nursing home in Finchley.

I don't recall the name of that Dickensian establishment. It was probably Heartbreak House, but after two days I'd had enough. Without giving notice and leaving my luggage behind, I fled.

Clinging for dear life to the polished brass handrail with one hand and almost falling down the outside steps, I shuffled into the street on my two walking sticks with all the dignity that I could muster. Within moments I managed to hail a passing taxi and, giving the driver my son's address in Cockfosters, I was speeding on my way to Heddon Court Avenue. I couldn't remember the number, but I could identify it as the first white stucco house with a green ceramic tile roof.

It was early evening and fortunately Mark and Ann were home. I stayed a little under two weeks and it became increasingly obvious that my daughter in law was not enamoured with my company and wanted me gone from her home.

We'd never hit it off, even from that very first time we'd met way back in 1915 when she'd arrived to work for me and later that same day complained to my husband that I must be a '*bissle meshuga*' (a bit mad).

Here we were forty-five years later and she still couldn't acknowledge the reality that, in spite of my age, I was still the better woman. Perhaps she couldn't accept the fact that I was a superior card player. Whether we played kalookie, gin rummy, or casino, I invariably won and I insisted that we always played for money.

I confess that over the years I'd acquired the habit of cheating a little at cards. Modestly I admit that I'd become quite skilful at it, which considerably improved my ability to win. When anybody found me out I always owned up to an unintentional mistake with a host of rehearsed excuses and profuse apologies blaming some error in my vision and the need to change my glasses.

In mitigation, whenever I played with my young grandchildren, and I taught them all to play from an early age, we always played for money and I always returned my winnings. It certainly made me a popular grandmother particularly when I added a sixpence or a shilling bonus for good measure.

One evening when in bed I hadn't yet removed my hearing aid when I heard raised voices as Mark and my daughter in law argued in the bedroom next door.

"I've had enough of her nonsense. I know she's your mother, but from the very first time we met she's been deliberately wicked and hurtful towards me and throughout all these years her attitude hasn't changed a bit. She may be old but she's still up to all her usual spiteful tricks.

"No matter how busy I might be she's forever wasting my time and treats me like a scullery maid. 'Ann bring me this.' 'Ann carry and do that.' and sends me rushing up and down the stairs at her every whim every five minutes. To crown it all she constantly wants me to play cards for money and then deliberately cheats to win. I simply can't take any more of it. I want my home and my life back and I need her out of this house." I heard him protesting, but on this occasion he came off second best.

As they packed my luggage the following day I realised that once again I had nowhere to live. I never dreamt that my daughter in law would bear a grudge for all those years, but she did. That evening after dinner I got into their Rover saloon with my single remaining suitcase in the trunk. It's quite remarkable how few personal possessions I now had to call my own after all my moves.

Mark and Ann sat in the front while I sat in the rear with my grandson Michael, Mark's youngest son, a smart young man in advertising in his 20s. As the car drove away, I thought of the time that Michael had been so close to death in 1939 when he had an operation for a mastoid bone infection at Great Ormond Street Children's Hospital. He was only four at the time and he survived, although there was no penicillin, but it left him permanently deaf in one ear.

When he was sixteen years old, in the spring of 1950, he'd left school but couldn't find employment. His father didn't seem to be of much help, so I took it upon myself to get involved.

"*Tuttelah* (little father, a term of endearment), I hear from your father that you left school more than three months ago and you can't find work. He say's that you're too idle to look for a job. Be truthful and tell grandma what's wrong?"

"Grandma, it's very simple and laziness has nothing to do with it."

"Then why does your father say you're lazy?"

"He just doesn't seem to understand. The problem is that at 18, every young man has to do two years National Service in the military, unless he's exempt on grounds of ill health or it's postponed while he's on a course of higher education. No employer wants to accept me as an apprentice once they know my age and with the likelihood of National Service just round the corner."

"But, Michael, surely with your ear trouble you would never be accepted into the forces, even with the war in Korea."

"Of course, you're absolutely right grandma, but I can't convince any potential employer of that fact, without a certificate of exemption."

"Well darling, all that you have to do is obtain the certificate."

"But that's the stumbling block. The certificate is only available once I've had and then failed my medical. I'm not eligible for a medical until I'm seventeen and a half when I can volunteer for military service. That means a year and a half wait."

"Isn't there any way round this?"

"None that I know of."

"Michael, just leave this to Grandma. I'll find some way to solve your problem. Phone me after supper and I'll tell you what we can do."

That evening I explained to Michael that I'd made an appointment the following morning for him to be seen at the Royal National Ear Nose and Throat Hospital in Grays Inn Road and that I'd accompany him on the appointment.

"Just meet me at Paddington Station in the main booking hall at 10 a.m."

The next morning Michael met me as we'd arranged.

"Grandma, I've never known anybody obtain a National Health appointment in less than three months, however did you manage it?"

"I'll tell you later, but where there's a will there has to be a way."

We took a bus to the hospital. When we alighted I insisted that we go in through the back door. The reason that we squeezed through the hospital's way-out turnpike grille was that in reality we didn't have an appointment. New patients without an appointment could only be seen by a lengthy queuing procedure, which I was determined to avoid.

When we found a nurse I explained that I'd been waiting for more than two hours and had unfortunately lost my ticket for my turn to see the consultant, when I'd visited the toilet. She asked which consultant I was due to see. I'd noticed a Polish name on one of the doors and gave that name. She asked me to wait and she'd see that we were the next patients to be seen.

Within a few minutes we entered the consulting room and I immediately said in Polish.

"*Dzien dobry* Doctor." (good morning).

"*Dzien dobry Babcia.*" (good morning Grandmother) he replied, after which we had a brief social chat. We laughed as we discovered we were two kindred Polish spirits, exiled from Warsaw. He told me that he could never return to Poland, fearing what the communist authorities would do to him. Then suddenly he leaned over and kissed my cheek as, almost in tears, he called me his 'Babcia', likening me to his grandmother who he would never see again. Having a mop of well-groomed grey hair at times had its advantages!

We got on famously as I explained in Polish my grandson's problem. Having taken a brief medical history he examined Michael, and confirmed that in no way could he ever be considered fit for any active military service and he would be delighted to provide a written medical report to that effect. I asked if he would be generous enough to provide his report today, so that I might take it with me, to which he agreed, provided I could wait until after lunchtime when he signed the letters that he'd earlier dictated to his secretary.

"Doctor, I wonder if you could perhaps sign it before lunch, because I have a 2 o'clock train to catch from Paddington and the next one after that would mean waiting for three hours?"

"Certainly Babcia. No trouble at all, it will be an honour. I'll have it ready for you in twenty minutes." He gave a little bow to me as we left the consulting room, after which we went to a nearby café for a coffee. As we waited Michael asked me,

"Grandma, why did we have to go into the hospital through the back door?"

"We'd have had to wait months for an appointment. Because we didn't have one, I decided that with a couple of fibs we could bluff our way in and it succeeded. It was pure coincidence that I found a Polish doctor, but it worked."

Once we had the consultant's report, Michael was able to attend for his National Service medical. He received a 4 F grade, and was officially rejected.

With the appropriate documentation he was able to attend for his apprentice job interviews and was soon employed as a trainee in advertising with C. F. Hiams, a prominent advertising agency. When Michael phoned to thank me and tell me of his new job, I explained that all it had taken to achieve this successful outcome was a mixture of common sense and *chutzpah* (impudence, or cheek). I told him.

"In life, with a little touch of chutzpah, you can make your own good luck."

After we'd been driving about half an hour I recognised Marble Arch, shortly after which the car pulled up outside 55 Park Lane, Anne's home. There Mark instructed Michael to escort me into the vestibule with my suitcase and request the hall porter to take me to Mrs. Veronique's flat on the fourth floor. Mark and Ann said goodbye and remained in the car waiting, as Michael helped me struggle out of the vehicle, and escorted me into the apartment block, where he gave me a kiss on my cheek.

"Good-bye Grandma."

"Michael, listen to me for a minute. Before you go I want you to think about something. In the old days, back in Poland we were poor people but we always made time for our grandparents and looked after them, no matter how little room we had in our homes. Now nobody's really poor any more. Some may claim they are, but they have shoes on their feet and never go to bed night after night with an empty belly in winter, as my parents and grandparents often had to do.

I'd have done anything for my children, even gladly given my life for any one of them; so is this any way to treat a mother? Tell me; if you can't look after your own family better than this, when they're old, is that what all you clever young people call progress?"

His response was to shrug his shoulders.

"You're right. I promise we'll talk about it later when there's a little more time, but I can't answer you at the moment Grandma, because mum and dad are waiting outside in the car." He kissed me good-bye once again and then left me standing with my case and walking stick with the concierge as he hurriedly walked away. Anne greeted me with a hug when I entered, although Vincent with his fixed smile of welcome seemed a little put out. I sensed that distraught might have been a better description of his frosty demeanour.

I was given their Italian housekeeper's bedroom and Rosa slept on a couch in the sumptuously furnished lounge, with its deep piled Persian carpet, baroque art and antique 18th century church candelabra covered in gold leaf. It's truly amazing how people cherish and value very old objects! The more ancient the antique, with its patina of age, the more highly prized, in contrast to elderly parents. Perhaps it's because antiques are rare, while living elderly relatives become embarrassing nuisances who ultimately produce noxious odours and provide constant feelings of guilt.

That night, safe in my daughter's home, I slept well once more. Why couldn't I remain contentedly living with one of my children as I wished? Surely any temporary inconvenience would be far outweighed by the pleasure derived from seeing a contented elderly widowed mother. I sensed that my children valued their antiques rather more than an elderly mother and told them so. I think I touched a raw nerve judging by the chorus of protests to the contrary.

Early next morning, Rosa knocked on my door and entered with her cheerful,

"*Bon-giorno* (good morning) Signora Maurice." With her beaming Italian smile she brought me in an early morning cup of tea with two digestive biscuits neatly arranged on a matching small, delicate, gold-rimmed porcelain plate. We'd come a long way in the fifty five years since we'd arrived as penniless refugees and lived in that cockroach-infested, East-End tenement building, with seven of us living, and working in two minuscule rooms.

A little later I went into the dining room and sat at the table for breakfast. Anne had finished and was nowhere to be seen. I sat opposite a glacially cool son-in-law whose head was buried in the morning newspaper. Although I couldn't see her, I could hear Anne in the next room having one of her urgently intense phone conversations. Without being able to hear precisely what was being said, I felt certain that it concerned me.

Two mornings later I thanked dear, sweet Rosa, for giving me the use of her bedroom. As I said goodbye we embraced. There were tears in her eyes, for we'd known each other many years, since she arrived in England to work for Anne just after the war. Unknown to either of us, this was to be our final parting as my solitary case and I were escorted by the uniformed porter along the corridor to the lift and out of the front door. Outside Anne was waiting, seated in the driver's seat of her cherished black Rover limousine with its leather-upholstered seats.

With my case installed in the trunk, and me in the back seat, Anne drove. We crossed Westminster Bridge with the signs pointing to Elephant and Castle and South London. She barely said a word throughout the journey other than to tell me that staying in the Nightingale Nursing Home was for my own good.

On arrival I found myself admitted, with the minimum of fuss, without money, or any avenue of escape. As Anne turned to go I cried out, shedding real tears.

"Don't leave me here, I'm begging you!" I'd have even gone down on my bended knees, except they didn't bend so well and I'd have looked a laughing stock struggling to regain my feet. But while silently debating this option, Anne was no longer looking, as she hurriedly exited through the front door.

My children had passed me round like an unwanted package, and the feeling of rejection hurt deep down inside, worse than any knife thrust. They had behaved shoddily and I'm convinced they'd have treated a total stranger better than this.

Grief stricken, I felt totally alone and it was more than I could bear.

Only one thing kept going round incessantly in my head, as I kept repeating;

"*Ich bin in drerd.* (I'm in hell). Thank God my Moisheka, ova sholom, never lived to see the way our children have discarded their mother! "

I was so upset that for weeks I couldn't stop weeping. I even contemplated ending it all. I decided I would climb on a chair and throw myself out of my second floor bedroom window. My children would then be full of remorse and guilt for the rest of their days and it would serve them right for abandoning me and causing me such unhappiness.

With my arthritis I couldn't climb onto the chair without assistance, no matter how hard I tried and asking one of the staff was out of the question. Had I succeeded in standing on it without my walking stick or a Zimmer frame for support, it was just as likely that I'd have overbalanced and fallen onto the floor where I couldn't pick myself up, or heaven forbid, might even have broken some major bone. Having witnessed the staff response time when summonsed, I'd have had to lie there for hours calling for help before one of the staff might have found me. I might possibly die of shock, or even thirst, before anyone finally turned up so I decided to call the whole thing off.

After a few minutes, my breakfast arrived. Nobody ever remembered the simple courtesy of knocking on the door before entering. The breakfast tray was placed on my over bed table with a smile from Angel, the Caribbean kitchen maid. The others in my room, thank goodness, were still sleeping.

"Good morning Sophie. Would you like marmalade, or jam on your toast today?"

"I'll have marmalade and how often do I need to tell you its Mrs. Maurice to you, not Sophie."

"Have it your own way - Mrs. Maurice." The name was spoken with an exaggerated emphasis bordering on the insolent. "I hear you escaped downstairs this morning in your nightie, like some sort of crazy woman. What did you want to do that for? You got us all into trouble. "

"Because I'm crazy like you say. I have to be crazy to put up with your nonsense and to live where all these old women have lost their dignity along with their hair and teeth, and fart all night."

"Once you get a little food in your tummy I'm sure you'll feel better. They say a low blood sugar makes folk behave in strange ways, like they've had too much to drink."

"There's nothing odd about my behaviour. I simply want to get out of this place, to go home and do my own thing."

"I've heard that story lots of times before. All you old folk ever says is like young children. "I wanna go home!", an' "Lemmie go home!". But you ain't got no home but here, so where you fixin to stay and how are you gonna do your own thing when you can barely walk?"

"Don't you worry, I'll manage. I always have."

"Even with a frame? You claims you's a smart woman but it's all wishful thinkin'. Your kids don't have no place for you no matter what they says, so just eat some food like a good girl and you'll feel much better."

"Don't patronise me. I'm not your good girl. See how they've roughed me up, my arms are black and blue."

"But you've had those bruises a long time. Now you put some food inside that belly and see how much better you'll feel."

Following this encouraging advice I tucked into my breakfast with pretended gusto. I'm supposed to relish the regular morning's cold soggy toast and the day's roughage of lumpy porridge, washed down by tepid lemon tea, which I sip with a lump of sugar clenched between my teeth. As I savour these culinary delights, I reflect on my conversation with Angel. I have to admit that she's truthful and smart. Were I her employer, I'd single her out for some future promotion to something better than a scullery maid.

Can I ever live independently, even if I can break out of this detention centre? With arthritic knees and hips I can barely walk, let alone race carrying my Zimmer frame, which is no way to outpace these young carers. I realise that from now on, if there's to be any escape, it can only be in my mind, where I can reminisce about better times and explore thoughts of what might have been. Had my daughter employed Angel, or somebody like her to be my companion-housekeeper when Clara retired then I'm certain that things would have worked out differently and I wouldn't be in this place.

Perhaps it's my sleeping companions, with their dementias and memory loss that are really the lucky ones. They don't understand the fix they're in and won't ever be disappointed in their children's attitudes towards them as they grow older and fade into aged parental oblivion.

Confined in here I've had ample time to ask myself where and why has everything gone so wrong in my life? I never spent my hard earned money on myself, or owned expensive clothes, furs, or jewellery. Unstintingly, I always gave everything to my children and grandchildren. Many of my contemporaries considered that I was ambitious and industrious, even shrewd, so what happened?

It's strange how the mistakes that we made when we were young, come back to haunt us when there's little that we can do but wallow in regret and self-pity. What was done then can never be undone, no matter how many prayers are offered, or tears are spilled. Believe me I know. I've made some generous contributions over the years. I've been over it in my mind time and time again until I feel certain that I can identify the precise time, not that it's of any use now.

It all started to unravel in September 1932.

Chapter 2

London 1932

My problem started thirty years ago although I didn't recognise it at that time. It was the Friday after my youngest son Solly's marriage to Elsie Gershon.

They were married in the Mile End *shule* (synagogue) on Wednesday September the 21st, and following the ceremony there was a fine reception and dinner. The party was modest compared to some wedding celebrations I'd been to. Elsie had lost her father the previous year and I ended up having to pay for everything.

I hired the small *shule* hall and engaged a quartet to play for the occasion. The caterer did a marvellous job serving a fabulous roast chicken dinner with all the trimmings for almost a hundred guests.

The bride looked stunning in her bridal gown, for which I'd also had to pay and Solly looked so slim and handsome dressed in his hired black top hat and dinner suit. They made a handsome couple. Tears kept blurring my vision and how I wished my Moisheka, ova sholom, could have stood with me under their *chupah* (marriage canopy); he'd have been so proud of his youngest son.

At the conclusion of the meal there was dancing and Essie, the darling girl, prompted more tears of happiness, when she sat on my lap and sang 'My Yiddisha Mumma' in that lovely soprano voice. Every one enjoyed the '*simcha*' (festivity) and at the evening's end as our guests departed they all said they'd had a wonderful time.

As days go, it should have been a deliriously happy occasion with my youngest boy married, but somehow it wasn't for me.

I could see that those tongues never stopped wagging. I couldn't hear them, but I sensed it and could see from the concealed glances, sniggers and whispers. Within, I felt deeply humiliated, yet I had nobody in whom I could confide my distress.

My problem was that I had two unmarried daughters older than Solly. It was a predicament that I could no longer hide. With this wedding, my embarrassment was laid bare for all my family and friends to see and how I missed being able to talk these things over with Morris.

When Solly decided to marry, I felt the humiliation of two unmarried but eligible single daughters in their late twenties. My daughters were fair, pretty and slim, with alluring blue grey eyes, just like their father's and would have made a good catch for any man. Even though I'd been a widow for almost six years, business had been good and I'd managed to accumulate a substantial dowry for each. I discretely let these facts be known amongst my family and as wide a circle as possible where it might encourage an eligible young man to come calling, yet somehow none who was suitable ever did.

To make matters worse, Solly wouldn't wait until one of his older sisters was at least engaged, or had a serious boy friend, no matter how much I pleaded with him. Furthermore I was greatly disappointed in the partner he'd chosen and I told him so in no uncertain terms.

Solly at 24 was old enough to marry, yet he hadn't acquired any particular work skill or trade. He never seemed able to hold down a job for more than a few months, which in his estimation was a considerable time. He worked for me for a few weeks as a sales representative, and then with a little money in his pocket he'd be off on some madcap scheme until he was compelled to come crawling back asking for his old job back. This happened time and again and, without a father's firm parental guidance, he'd become too much of a playboy for my liking. Even worse he'd been in trouble with the police on a couple of occasions.

Like my other boys he was a kind, good-natured fellow who was very generous and outward going. Like them, he had blue-eyes, was handsome and presentable with sturdy rugged features, a cleft-like dimple in the middle of a strong well-structured chin, like his father.

Unfortunately, he tended to be a little headstrong at times and preferred not to listen to his mother's advice. Somehow none of my boys would accept my counsel when it came to choosing a bride. He could have had his pick of any one of a clutch of eligible young women whose fathers could have taken him into an existing business, or even set him up to earn a comfortable living. But no, he always knew best and wouldn't pay attention to me, and even told me I was old fashioned.

Naturally he had to fall for the stunning good looks and flighty ways of a blonde, millinery salesgirl he'd met while selling goods for me. I'll grant him that Elsie was pretty, but she was as thin as a rake, and came without even a penny piece for a dowry. When her father, Gershon Chandler, had died, he'd left an impoverished wife and daughter, so there was no financial help from that family.

I explained that I'd pay for the wedding, but that was all. With two unmarried daughters I had to conserve my resources to make weddings and provide dowries for my girls. I told him that he'd made his choice and sooner or later would need to face the consequences of making his way in the world, since I couldn't provide any funds to give him a start.

He and his new bride were away for a week's holiday in Margate, which they could ill afford, since Solly was again out of work and there was so much unemployment. Heaven only knew how they would manage once they returned, although I was confident that Solly would soon be back once more asking me to employ him as a cutter, or preferably a salesman on commission. How could I possibly refuse him, the baby of my family, no matter how often he'd thrown in his job previously, or how inadequately he'd chosen his bride?

Two days later, Anne, Becky and I were sitting down to Friday evening dinner in the kitchen, the candles burning brightly on the table. We chatted about the wedding, what the ladies had worn and the gifts Solly and Elsie had received, when Anne quite casually delivered her bombshell. Smiling coyly, as was always her way, she announced.

"I've decided to take an apartment in the West End."

"Are you out of your mind? You can't leave home and live on your own. It's tradition that an unmarried girl has to live at home with her parents until she gets married. It would break my heart if you left home that way. Even if that doesn't bother you, what would the family say? Think of all the gossipmongers; I'd never be able to show my face in public again for the shame of it."

"Mother, times have changed. We've entered a new era of emancipation for women. Amelia Earhart has just flown solo across the Atlantic, just like Lindbergh. A woman is capable of doing anything as well as any man."

"You're not leaving home until you're married and that's final."

"I'm nearly thirty and I'm eligible to vote at the next elections. I've just been promoted to company secretary in a furniture company, earning as much as any man I know and I need to be independent. I can't live at home tied to your apron strings any longer. Anyway it'll cut down on my travelling time, when I have to attend meetings in the City."

"It's Hymie Lazarus isn't it? He's put you up to this idea of leaving home to live on your own."

"He's just my employer and moving into my own flat has nothing to do with him. He's given me this marvellous opportunity to prove my worth in an industry that's always been the preserve of men and I'm determined to succeed."

"You can pull the wool over everybody else's eyes, but not over mine. How is it that an attractive young woman like you never has any men friends? The only man you ever talk about, or have dinner with when you're not at home, is your employer. Your whole conversation revolves around your work. 'Mummy, I negotiated this for Hymie.' 'Mummy, I did that for him and Hymie took me out to dinner to celebrate'. It's always Hyman Lazarus."

"I enjoy my work, I find it exhilarating to challenge and beat men who've been in the furniture trade for decades. I admit I find Hymie Lazarus intelligent and attractive, but he's a business colleague and nothing more. Anyway it's entirely my concern who I care to dine with and choose as my friends."

"I bet she's in love with him!" interrupted Becky.

"Don't talk such utter rubbish and don't poke your nose into my affairs where it's not wanted."

"You see, Mummy, I told you so."

"I'm trying to have a serious conversation and you keep chiming in with these irrelevant remarks, so please mind your own business, when you've nothing sensible to contribute, which is most of the time!"

"Girls, stop this squabbling. He's a married man and you shouldn't dine with him alone. Nothing good can ever come of such a relationship. Don't let the infatuation you might have for a successful and wealthy businessman blind you to the realities of life. You can never find happiness at the expense of another woman and her children.."

"Mother's right." chimed in Becky who'd always been envious of her more dynamic elder sister.

"Becky, I've told you before, and I'm warning you for the last time. Keep out of matters that don't concern you! I take exception to what's being implied here, but I'm determined to live my life as I want, without worrying about the convention that a woman has to live at home until she's married.

"This is the twentieth century and I've now achieved an income that will enable me to live any way I damned well please. So I think this no longer has anything to do with you, Becky, or anyone else in this family. I'm a mature adult and I shall do whatever I choose, and live as I wish."

"I positively forbid any more of this talk. You'll live in this house with me, whether you like it or not, until you're married."

"And I tell you I'm moving into my own flat. You can live in your own time warp of arranged marriages and such like, to your heart's content, but I don't have to be a part of your old fashioned ideas. Attitudes are changing and I'm part of a new emancipated generation. Whatever happens, I'm going to live life to the full. I'm going to prove that I'm not only the equal of any man, but I can be a hell of a lot better than most of them."

"You're far too headstrong. I think that you've been seeing too many Hollywood films for your own good. Find yourself an eligible bachelor with whom you can settle down and have a family!"

"I'm financially independent. I don't need a man to provide for my security, or to keep me."

"That's enough of this talk Anne. You're upsetting me."

"I don't care that you disapprove, I'm moving into my own flat. I intend to lead my life without advice or interference from you or anybody else. Surely you interfered enough in my brothers' choice of partners and see where that got you! If you still want to arrange a marriage, then do something for my pest of a sister. Becky's a 25-year-old nuisance and it's long overdue that you found a husband for her. I've other priorities and having children isn't one of them, so leave me alone."

"She's just like Greta Garbo. She wants to be alone." interrupted Becky.

"Becky if you make another remark like that, take any more of my outfits, or use my cosmetics just once more without my permission, I swear I'll not be responsible for my actions!

"Mother, I no longer need to be lectured to by you, Becky, or any other member of this family. It's my business if I wish to live alone, or whom I choose as my friends. Now the matter's closed; finished."

I was terribly upset as you can imagine, but September 1932 was only the start. There was far more to come. Within days, Anne announced that she'd located a bachelor flat in Park Lane and was signing a lease and moving in on November first. I'm certain that she couldn't have found a flat, then decorated and furnished it that quickly. She must have been planning this for some time. I just had to accept it and worst of all, to face the reality of the loss of my parental authority. I'm certain that had Morris been at my side, Anne would never have challenged me like this.

That was just the beginning. Slowly and stealthily she started to control my activities, no matter how innocent her intentions may have been. I'm certain that she never intended the role reversal in our relationship that she soon achieved, but within less than a year I realised, all too late, that it had happened and there was no going back.

It continued innocently enough that first Friday evening in November when Anne returned for dinner. Both her sisters were there, although Essie's husband, Titch, was working late as usual in his pub, since Friday was one of the busiest times, when office and factory workers were paid.

"Mummy, why do you need to continue renting this factory and a huge house with only you and Becky living here?"

"What a ridiculous question. It's my home that's why!"

"Ever since you leased this old place you've known it's been cold and draughty. It lets the wind in like a sieve round every window and door. It's infested with vermin and even two cats aren't able to keep the rising mouse population at bay. The kitchen's terrible and there's no internal toilet. The damp's rising up from the basement and coming down from under the eaves, even though the landlord claims it's just the humidity and you believe him.

"I've just seen a lovely modern 3 bedroom end of terrace house in Stamford Hill that's recently been built which I can buy with a mortgage for half the money that you pay here in rent."

"I tell you I'm not interested. This is my home."

"At least have a look. It has a beautiful garden and it's just a short walk from all the shops."

Both my other girls chimed in that I had nothing to lose by having a look. It was only later that I realised that Anne must have briefed them to persuade me to view the property. I never considered until much later that this was a conspiracy and that I was unwittingly being manipulated and outmanoeuvered by my daughters.

"Alright. I'll have a look, just to please you, but I tell you I'm not moving."

Within the week Anne took me in her new car to see this house at the top of a small incline in Overlea Road.

We stopped outside number 25, where the estate agent was waiting with the keys. It was all that Anne had told me. There was a bright modern kitchen, with its new gas cooker and pride of place, a wonderful cream coloured refrigerator. A door led out to a rear garden with shrubs and bushes enclosing a central well-tended lawn, which could also be viewed from the dining room. In the front was a comfortable lounge; while upstairs were 3 bedrooms and a bathroom. There would be no more trudging outside to use the toilet, no matter how cold and with an ascot gas heater, there could be as many baths whenever anyone wanted, without having to journey to the public baths each week.

"I agree it would be very tempting to live there, but what about the factory?"

"Mother you're 54 and you've been a widow for six years. When daddy, ova sholom, passed away, I told you it was time for you to retire and that I wanted to look after you. I'm a dedicated career woman and I never intend to have children; there are enough of them in this world without my adding to the number. You're my family and, now that I'm financially secure, I'm determined that you should retire and give me the privilege of caring for you. After all, you used to look after your parents in Poland, sending them money regularly when I know you couldn't afford it. Let me look after you for a change."

"I'm very touched by your sentiments, believe me, but I've grown used to working without your father and work has become a way of life that I really enjoy."

"Please Mummy, it's been a lifelong dream of mine, since I was a little girl, that when old enough I would be able to care for you. By agreeing, you'll help fulfill something I've yearned to do for years. You're no longer a young woman. You've worked hard all your life caring for us and it's about time you had the opportunity to sit back to enjoy some of life's luxuries and see a little more of your grandchildren. I want you to learn to relax. Let me take care of you as you cared for us."

"I still need to earn a living. While I've a little saved up there's no pension and I don't have sufficient to last very long."

"You could give the business to Solly. He's still without a job. Becky could help him and then you could retire."

"That still leaves me with the problem of an income."

"Mother, I would own the new house, which would give me a wonderful investment, so there's no rent to pay. I'd pay the rates and utility bills, and besides that I'd give you a more than adequate monthly allowance that you can use to your heart's content, without ever needing to ask for a penny from me or anyone else, for the rest of your life."

"That's so generous that I'm simply lost for words. I just don't know how to say thank you, but I'd be mad to put myself in a position to have to ask my own daughter for money every week, as though I were a child."

"I love you Mother, you don't need to say thank you. I'm just trying to make life easier for you. I'll arrange for an allowance to be paid into your bank account like clockwork, every month, so you'll never feel demeaned by needing to ask me, or any-one else for money ever again. Not only that, I intend to pay for you to have a housekeeper. There's a young woman I know at work; her name's Clara and she'd jump at the opportunity to work for you. She's honest and industrious and I think she'd make a splendid companion."

"That sounds too good to be true. But what would I do if anything, heaven forbid, happened to you?"

"That's easily solved. It's something that I've already considered. I'll buy an annuity for you and, if for any reason I'm sick, I'll also have a sickness policy."

"It sounds very tempting, but I need a few days to think about it."

Anne had a contract with this furniture manufacturing company 'H. Lazarus Furniture' and was earning an enormous salary, which is why, bless her, she wanted to take care of me.

Well, I thought long and hard about her offer. I spoke to my brother, an experienced businessman, and all my children to sound them out. The only dissenting voice came from my eldest boy, Mark.

"Mother, if you give up your home, then for heavens' sake don't give up your business. If you're determined to retire, then at least keep your own home, where you pay the rent."

"Mark, if I retire, then how can I ever afford to maintain my own home?"

"That's easy enough. Either give the business to me with the understanding that I pay you a salary out of its profits, or sell the business which will give you a capital sum and each of your children will help contribute to your upkeep."

"Anne says that she wants to give me an allowance so that I'm independent and won't need money from my other children."

"That's very magnanimous, but what if something unforeseen happens? She might lose her job, or perhaps when she's married her husband objects to her supporting you?"

"Heaven forbid; but then I'd need to ask all my children to contribute to supporting me, in which case I'd be no worse off."

"Surely the best solution is to let me have your business. A solicitor can draw up all the necessary documents to protect you and you can continue to enjoy the income that it generates."

"That's very tempting Mark, but I must consider Becky and Solly and let them have it."

"Mother, you can't be serious. To give it to either of them would be idiotic. They're simply not ready for it and I can guarantee it wouldn't last three months. I know Solly's my brother, but he's feckless and immature and Becky's tarred with the same brush. They've never shown any ability to economise or save money. With the recession, trade has been difficult and coupled with that neither of them has any real experience. They're too unreliable and I certainly wouldn't employ either of them. If you're not prepared to let me have your business, then realise some capital for yourself and sell it."

All my children, apart from Mark, were delighted with the idea that Anne should accept the financial responsibility for my care. Solly and Becky were excited with the prospect that they would not only run my business but with innovative new ideas they could expand it. I was enamoured with the thought of a new home with the modern amenities of a bath whenever I chose and a toilet that no longer required a journey outdoors into the cold. The clincher was the kitchen with its new gas cooker, oven and refrigerator so that I didn't need to go shopping every day. Then there was the additional pleasure of windows and doors that fitted properly to exclude the winter's chills and draughts.

I just couldn't resist the choice of such a fine new home. I accepted Anne's offer. I considered myself a shrewd woman, but somehow I didn't think of all the possible pitfalls that might lie ahead. It was a verbal contract and there was no small print to read.

I gave up the lease to the factory and my draughty old home in Kingsland Road and moved into my new home. Clara, my new companion/ housekeeper, moved in and we immediately hit it off. It was unbelievable and one of the happiest days I'd experienced in many years. It was like the sweet breath of heaven.

Solly and Becky acquired a lease on the third floor of a factory building in Golden Lane, where they transferred my business. I became a retired lady of leisure. I felt rejuvenated and free, living in the lap of luxury, without a care in the world,.

Within days, Solly, had his name in the evening papers, except he was called Steve, and initially I had no idea they were writing about my youngest son.

The gas company had announced that it was going to present him with an award for bravery. The previous afternoon two workmen had been digging in the street close to his factory, to investigate a gas leak. They had dug a deep hole, which had filled with gas causing them to collapse losing consciousness in it. Without consideration for his own safety, Steve had gone to their aid and helped rescue them. His prompt action not only exposed himself to danger, but undoubtedly also saved the lives of both men. I was a very proud mother.

Everything went well for the next few months and then I had the first tiny inkling of the foolishness in my decision to retire. Imperceptibly I began to realise the terrible price to be exacted for accepting my daughter's generosity and the security it promised.

The first thing to go wrong was as Mark had predicted. Steve, as he now wished to be called had no idea about running a business and Becky, who now called herself Betty, was no better. They should have given more time to work than renaming themselves. Merchandise was being sold and neither of them chased the outstanding accounts. Within six months, there were financial problems of such magnitude that liquidators were brought in and the business that I had struggled so hard to establish and maintain for more than 25 years was closed. I was heartbroken, and both my children were out of work and penniless.

To make matters worse, I no longer had my own independent means to give them any financial help. I appealed to Anne.

"With the liquidators closing the factory I need a little more money to help Becky and Steve."

"Absolutely not! I undertook to support you, but nowhere did I envisage that I would have to prop up my brothers and sisters. If they weren't able to manage what you generously gave them on a plate, then they must find jobs, no matter how menial, or starve." was Anne's terse response.

I couldn't believe my ears. Had I retained my financial independence, as Mark had recommended, then I could have been of some assistance, but now this was absolutely beyond my means. It's impossible to imagine how frustrated I felt that I was unable to help them. Fortunately, Anne realised how this upset me and was instrumental in helping Steve obtain a job, while Betty was encouraged to go on a manicurists' training course for which I persuaded Anne to pay.

The next problem I experienced, and hadn't foreseen was boredom. Never in my wildest dreams would I have considered that I would long to return to work. I had worked every day of my life from the age of 13 and spent most of those years in the millinery trade. I never realised that my very being depended on the stimulus and challenge of work.

Without wishing to sound my own trumpet, I was one of the best, a real *bulabusta* (capable woman). I could design and create a new range of hats and accessories with my eyes closed. I was blessed with a manual dexterity that was the envy of others in my trade. My fingers were nimble and quick, in spite of my age and my work exquisitely neat. Above all I knew how to delegate. I could achieve production targets with others working under my supervision to faithfully copy my designs and accurately manufacture them. I knew how to buy and to budget and where my markets lay. Experience had taught me how to keep my customers paying their debts on time and sweetly encouraging them to purchase more goods from me rather than my competitors. In addition, I dealt with the bank manager when finance was needed and advantageously handled my creditors while somehow juggling all these with the time required raising my six children.

When I'd been that busy for years on end and enjoyed the hustle and bustle that was my daily life, how could I just bring so much activity to an abrupt stop in one day? Life isn't like that unless there's some misfortune like a major illness.

Now I was relegated to the minor role of housekeeping, which meant supervising a daily woman and housekeeper, whereas previously I'd employed up to a dozen women in my factory and more than three times that number of outdoor workers.

My culinary skills were very poor. As my marriage and partnership with my husband evolved, it rapidly became apparent that he understood far more about meat, poultry, fish and food generally and enjoyed cooking, whereas my expertise was in manufacturing. This meant that he was more skilled in domestic matters and preparing meals. He also enjoyed teaching all our children to cook, where I had little interest in such affairs. In fact every one of my children was an excellent cook, particularly the boys and I never contributed anything but the most minor part in those activities that took place in the kitchen. The only dish that I could really prepare well was a bean and barley soup, made with a meat stock that was a complete meal in itself, while I was also very adept at pickling cucumbers and vegetables.

I could read Polish and Yiddish and was numerate, but I always counted in Yiddish and never had, or made time to improve my skills of reading and writing in English beyond those of a six year old. This meant that I never read a book and could barely deal with a newspaper beyond its headlines. I had loads of acquaintances, but apart from regularly seeing my brother, sister and their children, I never had time to establish friendships with more than a couple of people.

Chapter 3

Summer 1905

Morris Podguszer had joined the Bund, the Polish Jewish labour movement, when in his mid teens, as a means of non-violent protest. Completely uninterested in politics and far from being a political activist, he wished to complain, to protest that as a Jew he was not allowed to vote in an election and yet would soon be eligible for military service, where he could be called upon to fight and if necessary die for his homeland. Furthermore while in the Russian military, no matter what his capabilities, he would not be permitted, as a Jew, to rise above the rank of private, a regulation that was not rescinded until 1915.

He had no love for the Romanov dynasty to which he felt indifferent, but neither was he a revolutionary like some of the younger hotheads amongst whose ranks were many young Jewish men.

Morris's father, Marcus, was a butcher and his business had been declining as his customer base dwindled due to economic stringency and the numbers who had emigrated to America. At the turn of the century when he died, his family continued to struggle and as the poor had always done, managed somehow to survive on very little.

In 1905 there were reports in the newspapers and rumours, which spread like a brush fire, telling of increasing unrest throughout the country. Unexpectedly, Morris received a call from members of the Bund requesting his assistance. Since he had completed his military service and had handled firearms, he was asked whether he would he be prepared to join the 'Samooborana', the Jewish self-defence unit to protect Jewish communities, in case of any serious disturbance, which threatened them? Morris declined stating that, with a wife and three small children to support, he could not be a part of any organisation using unofficial firearms to maintain order should trouble arise in any of the outlying communities.

Morris Podguszer, like the majority of Russian Poland's Jewish citizens, was law-abiding. Although poor they endeavoured to live quiet, sober lives, maintaining as low a profile as possible. In spite of this, violence suddenly and unexpectedly erupted from amongst their Catholic Polish neighbours, the poor victims never knowing the cause or reason why. For the Jewish populace it was like constantly walking on eggshells while attempting neither to break any, nor to make any noise. Fraught with uncertainty and danger, it was an appalling way to live.

Sometimes the pretext for violence might be a newspaper article published in Vienna, or some other publication. Perhaps the report of a papal speech in Rome, or the Sunday sermon of a local priest might spark a riot. Often nothing apart from a little too much vodka, which was often the case, might be the starting point for aggression coming to the doors of Jewish citizens.

Jewish shops and homes were periodically ransacked and firebombed for the greater good of the mob to enjoy the spectacle of the anguished owner's frantic attempts to save his family and himself. The police and upholders of the law who should, and could have prevented these atrocities, were totally indifferent and were content to stand by and watch. Later they were strangely unable to identify or apprehend the perpetrators. This was a stain on what was deemed a civilised society. The fear these attacks and insults engendered was made worse by the unconcern of all but a few outside the Jewish community to know, or even care.

Late one sweltering evening in July 1905, there was a knock at the door of our fourth floor apartment. It had been one of those typical mid summer days with a blazing sun radiating unmercifully out of a cloudless, azure blue sky, with so little breeze that, even with the windows fully open, the apartment felt more akin to a sauna. Fearing the noise might awaken any of the three children Morris hastened forward. The children had been fretful and had only just gone to sleep.

Reaching the door, and to avoid any more knocking, he hurriedly called out.

"Who's there?"

"It's me; your old friend Shloima." came the hoarse response. Morris quickly released the bolt, and keeping the security chain in place, opened the door just wide enough to see whom his unexpected visitor might be. There in the dimly illumined stairwell stood a pale, bearded, young man whom Morris instantly recognised. The visitor smiled somewhat apprehensively as the flickering yellow light from the oil lamp in the apartment shone onto his face.

"Hello Moisheka. How are you?"

Hastily he released the restraining chain and threw the door open.

"Shloima, come in, come in! Haven't seen you in ages. How long has it been? Five, maybe six years? Anyway far too long." They shook hands warmly.

" You look as though you could do with a little refreshment." Almost pulling him through the doorway into his modest kitchen he exclaimed;

"Come in and pull up a chair!" Then he turned to me. "Zlata, this is my old comrade Shloima. We were in the army together. Would you please make us both a glass of tea."

"Thank you, that would be most welcome." Shloima nodded.

As they sat at the kitchen table, Morris enquired,

"Nu (well) what brings you out this evening? You look exhausted, or maybe you've seen a ghost. Is anything wrong or are you just out of training? "

"Moisheka, you'll never guess what's happened."

"Muzzletov. Zelda's having another baby!"

"No. I wish to God that was the case. In your wildest dream you'll never guess, so I'll tell you. Two days ago I received my call up papers. And not just me, Yossle, also."

"You've got to be joking. Zlata, did you hear that? After all these years Shloima's just come here to pull my leg!"

"I hoped to heaven it weren't true, but in another five days I have to report for duty. I don't have a vote, I have no say in the affairs of this country but I'm given the privilege to see my wife and children cast destitute into the streets, while I die for my Tzar in an infantryman's uniform thousands of kilometres from home. I completed my military service ten years ago and now they want me back again."

"Then you must appeal the decision. Tell them you're a married man with children and responsibilities."

"I went to the recruiting centre. They told me I've got two legs, two arms and I can see to fire a gun. There's a national emergency. The motherland needs troops urgently in the Far East to contain the Japanese invasion. There's no time to train new recruits so those with military experience are being re-enlisted."

"That's crazy! Russia has a huge armed force. They don't need you."

"Moisheka, have you been hiding somewhere, or just asleep? There are riots and threats of revolt in every municipality. There's revolution in the air, and in every town there are posters and leaflets calling for the overthrow of the Romanovs. The government is using every available soldier to maintain law and order and to keep an eye on all the revolutionary firebrands.

There are defeats in the Far East. The Japanese yellow hordes fight like demons and there's no holding them back. I tell you the Tzar is desperate. There's revolution afoot and that's why we're seeing all these pogroms. The Tzar is trying his old tricks again to persuade the ignorant peasants that it's all the fault of us Jews. I hear he's even had a book published, 'The protocol of the elders of Zion', claiming that this war was fomented, as are all wars, by the Jews who want to dominate and control the world. It's full of lies and rubbish but there's always a group somewhere who'll believe anything once it's in print."

"The Russian people should only know how rich and powerful we are and how we love war!"

"Moisheka, that's not the point. When you throw enough mud, like these lies, some of it's always bound to stick. All the young men are talking of revolution as the only way to give the workers freedom, and lots of our people are supporting these plans. That's another reason why the authorities are conscripting so many Jews into the army. It's where they can keep a better eye on them. Should they step out of line, then there's a drumhead court martial, followed by a firing squad, and no questions asked. That's their way of dealing with troublemakers who want a vote, or simply breathe the word freedom too loudly. A little acute indigestion from a couple of lead bullets in the gullet at sunrise."

"You're exaggerating! The Polish people won't support those ideas and we're Poles.

"Don't you believe it Moisheka. The Poles are not only ignorant peasants, they're prejudiced to a man against us."

"You mean we're not intolerant and bigoted like them?"

"That's another matter. The difference between them and us is that we know we're ignoramuses, but we stay sober and study to improve ourselves. They're unaware that they're ignorant, and squander the little money they have on vodka and then believe the authorities who tell them we're the trouble makers."

"Well what are you going to do?"

"Believe me I've thought long and hard these past two days. There are three options. I can break an arm or leg, run and hide somewhere, or go quietly and possibly never see my family again."

"Are those really the choices?"

"Well there is one other. I could ask you to poke out one of my eyes."

"Heaven forbid!"

"Then I must run away; if I could somehow get out of the country I'd escape to France, or England, to start a new life and then later send for my family. But to do that I need money and Moisheka, old friend, that's why I'm here. Could you please lend your old comrade the fare money for my journey?"

"Right now things are a bit difficult. I think you remember my father, Marcus, ova sholom; well he'd been sick for a long time and, when he passed away five years ago, he left a lot of debts and a butcher's shop that I wasn't able to keep going."

"Moisheka, I tell you I'm beside myself with worry. If I don't get away it'll be all up for Zelda, and the kids as well as me. I swear I'll pay you back every last Zloty once I find work."

"Look I don't have any money here and I don't have much anyway but you're welcome to the little I can raise by scrounging from my family tomorrow."

The conversation went on late into the evening, discussing alternatives and possible methods by which Shloima could escape to the West. The insecurity and increased worry was the only thing they could agree upon with any certainty as they arranged to meet the following evening.

Some like Morris Podguszer remained undecided. Many like him still waited, fearful of altering the status quo and always hoping that better times would shortly return, except that it had become increasingly difficult for anybody to even recall the so called better times.

The majority denied the evidence that faced them each day. Insults of every conceivable kind and assaults had become the frequent daily reality.

The rock hurled to break a window and terrify those within. The daily beatings, should a Jew stray out of his own imposed ungated ghetto living area. Deliberately being bumped into and jostled off the pavement into the roadway, or to stand and wait in a queue for some food item only to be told when arriving at the counter:

"Go away! We don't serve Yids!"

All these and even more serious assaults were regular occurrences. They denied their own senses that indicated imminent danger, until too late, when the reality of a pogrom was upon them.

With the morning post there was a sudden numbing surprise. A formal letter arrived from the military authorities commanding:

'That the Jew, Morris Podguszer, present himself in seven days at the local barracks for additional military service, with severe penalties should he fail to report on time, as ordered.'

"I'm a married man with children to support. How can they do this to me?" he cried out in dismay to Zlata.

"You must go immediately to the recruiting office and explain that there's been a terrible mistake and that you've already completed your military service. Tell them that you've a wife and three children, with a fourth on the way and a widowed mother with four young unmarried sisters who all count on you." I said.

Taking his old discharge papers with him, Morris rushed out to plead his case. At the recruitment office there was a sense of bewildered confusion. Everywhere there were young men milling about with identical problems, most of whom were Jews.

"But I'm 34, a middle aged married man with responsibilities and a wife and children to support."

"It doesn't matter. Your Tzar needs you now and you have an obligation to fight for him and your country."

"I never did any fighting, I was a chorister and always sang in the choir."

"Then at last you'll have an opportunity to learn how to fight. Just make sure you report for duty or you'll find yourself singing from a different songbook if we have to bring you in. I guarantee you won't find being chained up so funny."

"I'm not fit. I can hardly run, I'm out of condition."

"You Yids are all the same. Always willing to live off the fat of the land, lording it over the rest of us, but unwilling to risk a little discomfort for the Tzar. When those little yellow bastards get their sights on you, you'll learn pretty damn quick how to fight, or to run like the others.

"A few pork sausages will soon knock your kind into shape. Just report in seven days like the notice says or we'll come and get you with a military escort, which I guarantee you won't find anything to sing about!"

Despondently Morris returned home, mind-numbingly aware that if he was sent to the Far East it would be years before he could return home, that is if he were to survive, and there would be nobody to support his wife and children while he was away other than his own family who were barely able to cope and make a living for themselves.

At home Morris and I talked urgently, aware that time was now swiftly running out.

"Morris, there's my brother Isaac in America, and Abraham in London. You've no choice but to get out of Warsaw right now and join one of them."

"I know, but how can we abscond without travel documents, and anyway I don't have sufficient money to journey to New York."

"Morris, we've enough money for you to travel to Berlin and if we borrow, maybe it will get you as far as London. We'll write to Abraham today to expect you. I can follow on later with the children once you're able to send me the fare money."

"Zlata, you've three children and another due before the end of the year, how will you manage without me?"

"If you don't leave now, then you might never see the baby I'm carrying and I'll have to manage without you forever. It's the army or London, so for heaven's sake make up your mind and go. When Shloima arrives, see if you can persuade him that the two of you journey together."

"I can't leave just like that without saying goodbye to my family and friends."

"The sooner you go and the fewer people you see and tell of your plans, the greater your chance of being able to escape into Germany without being stopped by Polish border guards and turned back."

"You're right. I'll have to find a way of crossing the frontier and once I'm in London, I'll find work and send you money. I've been thinking and I've the germ of an idea of how Shloima and I can find a way to ride out of Russia and then to hell with the Tzar and the Romanovs.

"I'm going out to see an old business acquaintance who may provide an answer to our problem of escaping from Poland. Meanwhile, we'll write to your brother and tell him to expect me."

Later that evening when Shloima arrived, Morris filled him in with all that had happened at the recruitment office.

"Shloima, old chap, I've thought of a plan that will enable us to travel safely and at no cost from Warsaw, to Berlin, after which we'll need to pay for our tickets to London."

"How's that possible? Are you borrowing a hot air balloon and hoping the wind will carry us in the right direction or have you acquired a magic carpet?"

"Shloima, you're closer than you think with your suggestion, but don't tell anybody apart from your wife that you're leaving. All you need do is meet me here early tomorrow morning. Bring as much money as you have, food for a couple of days, a topcoat, hat, gloves and your warmest clothes and be prepared to be a little uncomfortable for a few hours."

"Are you crazy? This is the middle of one of the hottest summers we've ever known and you want me to wear an overcoat and warm clothes. What a fantastic idea. You want me to die from heat exhaustion to avoid conscription? That's one scheme I'd never thought of and I bet even the Tsar's advisors would never have dreamed that one up. Have you turned a *bissle meshuga* (light in the head)?

Zlata, that's it. Your husband, poor fellow, has flipped. The news today has turned his mind. You try to humour him while I go out to fetch a doctor!"

"Don't be an idiot. I know that what I'm telling you sounds strange, but have a little faith in me."

"Moisheka, old friend, why on earth do I need a coat and warm clothes in the middle of summer?"

"Just do as I say, or I can't take you with me. Have a little trust and confidence in your old comrade here and I'll explain everything tomorrow."

With a shrug of his shoulders, indicating that he had little to lose, Shloima agreed to meet Moisheka at sun-rise the following morning.

Early next day, with Shloima's arrival, Morris bade farewell. I was in tears, but Moisheka promised me that he'd write as soon as he arrived in Berlin.

"I promise you that, whether I have to beg, borrow, or steal, I'll send you money to join me before the baby arrives."

As they quietly left the apartment, Morris carried two large tough linen shopping bags, one inside the other.

Shloima enquired. "Moisheka, *nu*? (well?) When are you going to tell me your plan?"

"Be patient! We've got no time to waste and I'll tell you as we walk."

"Where are we walking to? Do you propose we walk across the border like a couple of tourist hitchhikers? If so I'd have brought my old army boots and a rucksack."

"It's very simple. We're heading for the meat market and then to Warsaw West station."

"Moisheka, Zelda already packed some bread, cheese and boiled eggs for me this morning and I've more than enough for both of us. In fact she made enough for a small army on manoeuvres, so we don't need any meat."

"If you can stop talking for a moment I'll explain what's what, but keep walking, or we'll be late.

Felix, an acquaintance of mine, ships a railroad car full of freshly slaughtered beef and pork from Warsaw West station to market in

Berlin once a week. We'll help load the carcasses onto the wagon and then hitch a ride."

"That's ridiculous! In this summer heat they'll start rotting and stink to high heaven within a few hours. We'd stand a better chance of escape by going north to Danzig and finding work as seamen on a boat to America."

"That's a real possibility, I agree, but we might have to wait ages for a boat and then think of how much more fare money we'd have to find for our families to join us. Let's take advantage of my contact in the meat trade and take our chances on the train.

Ordinarily the only way to send meat like this would be in winter, but thanks to a wonderful American invention all that's changed. Now they have special insulated railroad cars with ice packed in at either end. Air is blown over the ice into the main compartment where the meat hangs, which lowers the temperature as though you're in the arctic, so you can transport fresh food of any kind hundreds of miles by train in summer, without anything rotting, or going bad."

"That's fine, but how do you think this is going to work for us."

"I've told Felix that we desperately need money and are prepared to help load the animal carcasses for half the normal pay. Being a shrewd fellow and a *goy* (a gentile), he saw the humour in having a couple of Jews load his pork for half the normal rate and he's agreed.

"Morris, I can't do it. I just can't handle pigs, whether alive or dead. They're *treife* (not kosher)."

"Shloima, are you stupid? We're not eating the stuff. There's nothing in the *din* (law) to say we can't handle it. Nobody would suspect that a couple of Jews would be hitching a ride in a container truck full of pork. Once the meat is loaded, the train leaves Warsaw and heads straight to Berlin as rapidly as possible. All we have to do is make certain that nobody sees us hide inside the insulated railcar. The customs never open or disturb the refrigerated carriage so we just do our best to keep warm for five or six hours until we arrive in Berlin. After that we wash our clothes and ourselves and head for London. It's simple and saves on fare money."

"I still don't like it."

"If you've got a better idea tell me, or just shut up about not liking pork. I think the idea's a bit of inspiration and that's what I'm going to do whether you're with me or not."

"Alright I'll give it a try. What've we got to lose? After all if we're discovered, they can only arrest us and throw us into jail, before shipping us out to Siberia for a long vacation as the Tzar's guests. The accommodation's very basic, but I hear the water's particularly cool and clear, though the bread's not up to much."

"That's the spirit; optimistic as always! Think of what tales you'll be able to tell the kids when they're older."

"If the border guards catch us we'll never live long enough to see the children when they're older, to tell them any stories."

Arriving at the rail depot, where cartloads of meat were arriving from the meat market, Moisheka left his top clothing in the carrier bag with Shloima, with instructions to wait for his return. He then went in search of his acquaintance and reported for work.

"Thought there were two of you yids, where's the other one? Trying to pull a fast one are you?" enquired Felix.

"Nothing of the kind. He'll be along in a couple of minutes. Just tell me which carriage to load and we'll get on with it, and by the way where do we collect our pay when we're finished?"

"You've five hours to load the wagon and there's a crew of four of you doing the loading. The train leaves at noon, so you'd best get on with it, there's a lot of meat that'll spoil if we don't get it cooled real quick. When you're done see me here and I'll settle up with you."

Moisheka then returned to his friend and explained the plan of action. "I'll put our clothes in the corner of the compartment and we'll see to it that, as we load, one of us is always in the coach to keep an eye open so that none of our porter friends walks off with anything. When we're finished you remain behind and 'I'll collect our wages before joining you. Now while I take the clothes you report to my colleague, Felix, so that he knows there are two of us working. Just tell him you're with me."

Everything went according to plan. As the shipment was all but fully loaded, Shloima hid in the back of the carriage, having donned his winter clothes, while Moisheka went to collect their wages. On his return he slipped into the compartment, joining his friend and speedily dressed in his warm outer garments. Within minutes the sliding door was slammed and bolted, leaving them in total darkness, shortly after which, the train moved off.

"I can't see in here. It's freezing and I'm hungry."

"Shloima, there's no need to whisper, the carcasses can't hear us. Now let's eat some food and get some sleep. I checked the time of arrival and we'll be in Berlin before five o'clock."

"How can I eat kosher food and sandwiches when I've been handling pork all morning and haven't washed my hands? You should have told me to bring something so I could wash."

"I'm really so sorry Shloima. You know how these things are. I intended to reserve you a seat on the Orient Express as a surprise, but my wife messed up the reservation. Just eat some food like a good fellow and I'll say a special blessing to the Almighty so he'll forgive us this once."

After a brief sleep, Shloima enquired. "Are you awake Moisheka? Shouldn't we be there by now?"

"If we'd remembered to bring a match, or flint, I could have told you the time, but it's too dark in here to see my pocket watch. We seem to have been travelling a good while and I'm certain from the sounds of the wheels that we're making fairly good speed. Be patient and I'm certain we'll be there soon."

The train slowed and then stopped. Noises followed, indicating the carriage was being uncoupled. Outside they heard voices.

"They're speaking in German and saying that this one isn't for Berlin."

"Well Moisheka, what do we do now?"

"Just sit tight and when they open the door we'll jump down."

"We're trapped. What happens if they don't open the doors until next week or next month?" whispered Shloima.

"I guarantee they'll open the sliding door the moment we arrive in Berlin, because, if they don't, the meat will start to spoil once the ice keeping everything cold has melted. Stop worrying all the time! I tell you we're not trapped. Believe me! "

Suddenly there was the noise of the carriage being recoupled and with a judder the coach started moving and rapidly picked up speed again.

"I'm certain that was Berlin. Where are they taking us?" Asked Shloima, the hint of a sob in his voice.

"Oh I'm sorry. I knew I'd forgotten something. Didn't I mention that we have reservations at the Paris Opera?"

"No. You're joking with me."

"Of course not. We've got seats at the opera to see Rigoletto, and before the performance we're dining at Maxims. We've a table for two booked at seven o'clock. I sent a message to the train driver before we started that he wasn't to stop in Berlin, but to put on a little extra speed because the maitre d'hotel becomes a little agitated when clients are late. I thought I'd keep the reservation a special secret because I knew that if I told you any sooner you'd ask me a lot more fool questions like you're doing right now.

"How the hell do I know where they're taking us? For all I know the train's headed East towards Moscow. Felix assured me the shipment was for Berlin and that's it!"

"Moisheka, there's no need for rudeness and shouting. Let's try to be civilised. Admit you should have checked to confirm the destination. There's always a card or document on the outside of the carriage. "

"So all right. If it makes you feel any better I confess I made a mistake. Next time we travel like this I'll check the destination label."

"Moisheka, you also forgot the matches."

"Yes that too. I can't deny I forgot the matches, so it's lucky we don't smoke. Anything else?" he replied with some irritation.

"Well we should have brought something to drink and to at least wash our hands. If you hadn't been so secretive about your plan, I could have reminded you what we should bring. Certainly some matches and maybe a compass would've been very useful."

"*Kvetch! kvetch! kvetch*! that's enough complaining! Shloima, you're like an old housewife driving me *meshugga* (mad) with this nonsense. If you want to remain my friend stop this kvetching. Don't mention matches, destination labels, compasses, washing hands, or even Berlin, again on this journey. The moment we get out of here I'll tell you exactly where we are, but until then I've no idea. So you'd better get some rest because we'll need all our energy once we arrive."

"I'm beginning to have my doubts about whether this was such a good idea of yours."

Rather than escalate a misunderstanding into something more serious, Moisheka chose not to respond and after what appeared an interminable time the train slowed and then ground to a halt. A few minutes later the door suddenly slid open. Outside there was a full moon; otherwise all remained dark within the wagon as the warm air flooded in.

"Shloima. Don't ask questions. Take off all your warm clothes and place your belongings in the spare carrier bag as quickly as possible. Then you hold both the bags and just follow me. Above all don't talk to anyone, no matter what happens."

Rapidly they groped their way towards the moonlight, which illumined the exit and then jumped down.

Their sudden and unexpected arrival startled the porter who had just opened the door and was now in the process of lighting a cigarette. Moisheka immediately took the initiative, grabbed Shloima's arm and in his best German addressed the porter.

"*Du kennst die regeln!* (You know the regulations). *Machen sie die zigarette aus!*" (put that cigarette out). The porter instantly dropped his cigarette as though it were a poisonous snake, and vigorously stamped on it twice, as he extinguished the red tip.

"Don't stand there staring like an imbecile. I'm special security. Just found this scoundrel trying to steal from this wagon. Point me in the direction of the station-master's office so that he can be handed over to the police."

The porter looked startled but pointed in the direction up the line ahead and indicated he would show them the way.

"No! You don't need to go with me. It's essential that you remain here and guard this consignment until you're relieved. Don't let anybody tamper with or remove any of the contents pending my return, or you could also find yourself in trouble with the police. In fact, you'd best lock the door again until I get back."

The porter saluted and started to slide the heavy carriage door closed as he'd been instructed.

"*Auf los!* (Quick march.) Go in front of me!" Moisheka ordered Shloima.

The pair marched away into the dark and after they'd covered a hundred metres and were out of the porter's sight, they simultaneously started giggling like young schoolboys, then laughing fit to burst, they broke into a run.

"How did you ever have the *chutzpah* (impudence, or cheek) to do that?" gasped Shloima, still chuckling as they ran.

"Simple enough! These Germans are so strictly disciplined that if an order is issued and you can convince them that it's genuine, they'll obey it to the letter. And did you see how he saluted me?" hooted Morris, as they collapsed into further fits of laughter.

They continued walking alongside the rail track until they came upon a station sign that clearly read: Bremen Port Authority. They couldn't believe their good fortune. They'd travelled more than half way across Germany and were in a North Sea port, where they could easily obtain passage to England. Fate had dealt kindly with them and they would soon be in London, with money to spare.

Chapter 4

October 1905

*I*t was almost three months after Morris's departure, before I received my rail and boat tickets for London. Morris had written a few days earlier saying that he was sending them and that we should be ready to leave straight away. My hands trembled with excitement as I opened the small package when it arrived. I dressed the children immediately and rushed round with them to my mother to tell her the news.

With three young children to look after, there was little that I could possibly take with me, apart from what we needed on our journey. While I looked after Annie, who I was still breast feeding, even though she was two, it was essential that somebody should accompany me to help with, Mark, and Harry, who were mischievous little boys, and quite a handful. Morris's youngest sister, Hilda, a slip of an 18 year old volunteered and the arrangement, agreed with her mother, was that once in London, she would stay on to live with us.

Loaded down with kosher food for the two-day journey, there was no way in which I could carry anything more than dry clothes for the children, some blankets, and my precious candlesticks, which were a wedding gift from my parents.

Following our tearful farewells at Warsaw's Central Station we travelled to Berlin where we had to change trains. Hilda had never been given the responsibility to care for youngsters and was proving next to useless. Constantly in awe of her new surroundings, she invariably lagged behind while holding her two impish nephews by the hand, and was often in danger of becoming separated from me.

Holding Annie, I struggled with a pair of large, long handled, heavy shopping bags, hooked, one over each shoulder, containing food and the necessities for our journey and had to keep looking back, calling to Hilda to keep up.

In Berlin we had to wait four hours for our connection, but once aboard we remained on the same train as it travelled westwards to reach the North Sea coast a little more than twenty-four hours after our departure from Warsaw. On arrival at the Hook of Holland we left the train. Following a few minor formalities we passed through customs and immigration and then boarded the cross-channel craft that was to convey us to England.

Never before had we smelt the salt laden sea breeze or seen a boat of such a gigantic size as the steamer moored at the quayside, although years later I realised how tiny it really was compared with the liner in which I crossed the Atlantic in 1947,

Seated on the uncomfortable slatted third class wooden seats, on our train journey across Europe, the journey had exhausted us but once aboard the ship and with the fierce wind that was blowing in across the harbour I now more fully realised that we faced the unknown perils of the North Sea. As we moved away from the quayside Hilda and I were amazed at the vast expanse of water, since we'd never seen a stretch of water larger than the Vistula, or the punier river tributaries along whose banks we'd picnicked from time to time on a warm summer's day.

As the ship began its journey and moved within the sheltering harbour wall we became increasingly aware of the autumnal gale that was blowing. No sooner had the ship cleared the breakwater than the full impact of a force 8 gale struck. Thunderous leaden clouds, which scudded across the sky, were constantly in collision with the monstrous seas boiling in turmoil about the ship. The vessel, in response, bucked and swayed as it moved slowly westwards through elements that ferociously tore against the boat's side. All who sailed that day remembered the autumn channel crossing as a nightmare. The freezing wind howled through the ship's rigging like demons in noisy pursuit of their prey. The ship crested each huge wave, and as the bow crashed down after overcoming every fresh new foaming adversary, it jettisoned fuming spray, which mercilessly lashed the deck and superstructure drenching, in retribution, any seaman foolhardy enough to stand in its way.

The children cried in inconsolable chorus, and threw up time and again until nothing more remained, while few of the other passengers sheltering in the ship's saloon fared any better. This added to the overwhelming stench and communal misery, where most felt certain that an immediate afterlife might prove a more acceptable option than continued existence in such a perilous storm.

I confess I felt closer to death than at any time previously, and in spite of my own terror and seasickness I somehow roused myself through some superhuman effort to comfort and nurse my children, as we huddled together. I noticed that my poor sister in law was almost comatose. She lay huddled in a foetal position, with closed eyes. Only the movement of her pale lips in prayer, framed by her deathly white skin, indicated any sign of life. From time to time she moaned and wretched for the duration of the four-hour crossing as she desperately clutched her red flannel cloth patch. This had been pinned to her bodice by her mother, in one last maternal gesture to ward off the evil eye, just before we left the Warsaw Railway terminus.

Once docked in the calm water at the Harwich quayside, we wearily straggled down the gangway, thankfully relieved to be on firm land again. We were totally exhausted and to make matters worse, while walking those first few steps on solid ground, we staggered like drunkards for the first few minutes in anticipation of further heaving motion, although blissfully, the land remained reassuringly stationary.

Feeling weak and unwell I encouraged Hilda with the boys to hurry forward as best they could towards the waiting uniformed immigration officers, fearing that any delay might result in our missing the train scheduled to convey us to London.

Completing the brief but incomprehensible immigration formalities and frustrated at the lack of language communication, I hustled onwards with the children.

We shuffled and hurried forward as best as we were able onto the cold cheerless, platform fearful that the train might depart at any moment without us onboard. There, the dimly illuminating gas lamps revealed our train. It stood alongside the platform with its soot-encrusted, grimy, green engine, panting in anticipation of the guard's signal to leave

Harwich to charge onward to London. Periodically the engine belched and hissed its mixture of soot and steam, terrifying the children as we walked past.

As I drove my young charges forward, my heavy coat billowed open to reveal my protruding belly. One of the porters noticing my advanced pregnancy kindly came forward to help us board the train. I sensed that we really had arrived in a free society, for a porter helping a Jewish family in Warsaw would have been something of a rarity.

This was my fifth pregnancy in as many years, but unfortunately, my fourth had ended in a miscarriage. Before marriage, just six years earlier, Moisheka and I had romantically planned to have a family, but never in my wildest imagination had I thought there would be one child every year. My mother had counselled breastfeeding each child for as long as possible to help avoid conception, and yet in spite of adhering religiously to this instruction, I kept becoming pregnant. There seemed no help from anyone I knew who could advise me how to avoid this situation.

Once aboard the train, I gave each child a small drink of milk from a flask that I carried in my shoulder bag, following which they immediately closed their eyes and slept in exhausted repose.

Pleased to be safe on land, I silently resolved that I would never board a ship or venture across the sea again. I was thankful to rest and as I relaxed I was amazed at the comfort and opulence of the compartment and the seating. I was convinced that the porter must have shown us to the wrong carriage. Third class on the continent was slatted wooden benches, and this heavy velour covered upholstered seating in which our exhausted bodies now thankfully sprawled was certainly second class, or better, but I wasn't complaining and had no intention of moving if it could be avoided.

Within minutes the guard's shrill whistle sounded followed by a sudden commotion, with shouted unfathomable English instructions. Doors slammed as the guard waved his flag, and then the train glided slowly from the station with its engine noisily puffing and coughing like some elderly bronchitic. Leaving Harwich, it ground slowly through the Suffolk countryside. Hilda and the children were totally worn out and sleeping and I was too weary to admire the passing scenery.

As we journeyed my fingers unconsciously caressed the upholstery and I found myself mentally calculating the cost of the fabric on which we rested and the enormous wealth that must exist in England to provide such unaccustomed luxury for passengers like me, travelling third class. I endeavoured to keep my eyes open to maintain a watch on the children, but with the repetitive clickety-clack, clickety-clack of steel wheels regularly passing over steel railway line abutting on railway line, my head sank onto my chest. No matter how hard I fought against closing my eyelids I nodded into a fitful sleep, like my exhausted little ones, although I kept waking with a multitude of thoughts whirling round inside my mind and then nodded off again.

Since our decision to leave Warsaw, I was assailed by conflicting emotions. I loathed the frightening challenge of anti-Semitism that had erupted anew since the beginning of the year and hated the Poles for the pogroms directed against us. I also despised them for making us leave our homeland, and in-spite of our poverty, all that we loved.

Never again would I see my parents, family and friends who, unless they emigrated to London, would become mere cherished memories. No longer could I enjoy once favourite walks in gardens and parks, and nor could I ever visit familiar homes and apartments and see and touch familiar furnishings, however scant and threadbare. All would be lost forever. Sanctuary came with a high, price, and it was almost too much to bear.

My thoughts also flitted back to happier days, when before marriage and the responsibility of children, I'd registered at school as Zlata Chisick, when seven years old. I was the middle child of five surviving children, with two older brothers and two younger sisters. Within days of starting school my elder brothers had left home to emigrate to New York, but somehow Abraham, the eldest, and my favourite, ended up in London.

Shortly after my 13th birthday, my formal education had ended. It was June 1892, and as I reflected it now seemed so long ago, that it could have been in another life and yet only thirteen years had elapsed.

Leaving school I was expected to stay home to help mother. My preference had been to be a nurse, like some of the other girls, but my parents were not prepared, under any circumstances, to consider that degree of freedom. As a nurse I would have needed to submit to rigorous training and the many nursing regulations, which forbade marriage and required that I live in the hospital. Ever since I could remember mother had repeatedly announced, at every family wedding that she would arrange for each of her three daughters to marry some eligible bachelor before they reached the spinsterhood age of twenty.

I was determined, however, not to remain at home as a drudge to mother with her touchy temperament. I liked the glamour provided by a uniform and since I couldn't be a nurse I chose the next best thing, which was to work as a children's auxiliary.

Without any help from my parents I inquired about a possible vacancy at the local Jewish dispensary. I was thrilled to discover that there was an opening for the right young woman and learned that I would first have to make a formal application, supported by a letter of recommendation from my school principal and written parental authorisation.

I was determined that nothing should stop me from my chosen career. There were a number of obstacles to overcome, the first of which was to obtain father's permission. Mother, I knew, would never agree, but if father said yes, then I could continue with my job application. To persuade father was quite a problem. Mother's method would have been to brow beat him into submission, but that choice was not open to me, although later in life I discovered that when it came to dealing with a difficult husband, this was as effective a means of persuasion as any.

I decided to become a *nudgnik* (some one who nags). What with mother brow beating him on one side, and me with constantly pleading, or alternatively nagging on the other, it was a forgone conclusion that he would have to give in. Exposed to almost a week of intense feminine-guile, father capitulated, and I managed to prise his reluctant consent from him.

In spite of mother's continued opposition, I made father give me his written authorisation and sign it Pesach Chisick, parent.

Promptly I delivered it to the dispensary with a letter from my school head teacher requesting that I be employed in any post that would enable me to work amongst young children.

Days later a letter arrived requesting that I attend for interview.

On the appointed day mother insisted on accompanying me. When I entered the boardroom, I sat in front of two board members, who proceeded to question me. I was so nervous that afterwards I couldn't remember a thing they'd asked me. After a few minutes, they requested that I wait outside for their decision. Less than five minutes later I was outside in the street, deliriously happy, knowing that my application had been successful. The next day I attended the dispensary to receive my two uniforms prior to starting work the following week. Rushing home I couldn't wait to try one on.

As I stood in front of the mirror admiring my reflection, my joy knew no bounds. With its white apron tied round my waist across a long-sleeved white high-collared blouse, and a covering short, navy-blue cape, it accentuated my youthfully slim figure. A small white cap perched precariously on the crown of my head made me look even taller and helped emphasise my face, with its Slavic high cheekbones framed by dark brown hair.

Even my parents had to admit that the clothing supplied by the dispensary made me look more elegant and mature. Later I discovered that they had privately acknowledged that I would never experience any difficulties when the time came for them to find a suitable *shiddach* (marriage partner) for me.

I worked happily and contentedly at the dispensary until shortly before my marriage, seven years later. I was repeatedly told how my clear blue grey eyes and shy smile enchanted the children, but that wasn't for me to judge. I do know that I revelled in the love and affection I received each day from my young charges and that entire period was one of contentment and happiness.

Once turned nineteen, with mother constantly badgering that it was high time to think of marriage, I was to be introduced to the man my parents had chosen for me. This was to be the customary arranged marriage.

In the late summer of 1898 the man selected for me had been invited to our home. Before his arrival, I questioned and nagged mother. I knew he was eight years older than me. He was a man of 27 and had completed his military service. Both he and his father were butchers and, as my mother cynically commented,

"Well at least you and your children will never go hungry with this man as your husband." Had he been a hunchback and a widower of fifty with ten children, I knew perfectly well that I would be given little choice in the matter.

That Sunday afternoon there was a hesitant knocking at the door, which my father promptly opened. With an encouraging smile Pesach Chisick invited the young man in. Shyly he stood there in the kitchen, clean-shaven, with a little dimple in his chin. But heavens, even without shoes on, I was taller than him.

He would have remained standing there had mother not almost pushed him into a chair and announced.

"You must be hot and tired. Sit down and take the weight off your feet. Zlate was just making a glass of tea. The way she makes it is so refreshing, I'm sure you'd like to stay and join us."

By the time I'd sliced a lemon and poured the hot water from the samovar into the glass and turned round, I found that my parents had quietly disappeared into an inner room, leaving me with our tongue-tied visitor to get acquainted.

Bashfully we chatted. He told me that everyone called him Moisheka although his real name was Morris Podguszer, and that while he had been born in Warsaw his family had originated from the small village of Podgura just to the east of Krakow. He was the eldest of six children, with one brother, Lev, two years younger and four younger sisters. As he spoke, he had a pleasing voice, although I noted that although a young man he had put on sufficient weight that he could no longer be termed slim. He was fair complexioned, with short stubby hair, and with his adorable iridescent blue eyes he could certainly be described as handsome.

As he talked he lost some of his timidity, telling me how he'd won a singing contest in his teens, after which he'd taken voice lessons, which had been interrupted when he was conscripted into the army. I learned that he'd been discharged from the army almost four years earlier following more than four years compulsory service as a private infantryman.

He explained that he'd never seen active military service and had led an uneventful martial career. During his initial weeks of military training his commanding officer had discovered his fine tenor voice, and considered that he would be more useful on the home front singing and entertaining in a choir than as an inadequate soldier in some outpost of the Imperial Russian Empire. As a consequence his voice had secured him a permanent place in the military choir. At the conclusion of his army career he'd returned to civilian life where he again assisted his father in their butcher's shop.

He asked if I'd like to attend a choral concert on the next Sunday, where he was one of the choristers and I agreed to go if my parents gave their permission.

I attended the concert with aunt Ryfka, mother's younger sister, as escort. I spotted Morris who was standing in the second row of the choir, almost hidden. He stood a little shorter amongst all the others, where I would never have otherwise spotted him until he stepped forward to sing a solo tenor role.

His voice carried clearly over the piano accompaniment and the sweet lyrical tones emanating from this handsome fair-haired man entranced me. At the conclusion of the concert I rushed brazenly forward, defying protocol, to offer my congratulations to the singer who possessed a voice and sparkling blue eyes I had now fallen madly in love with.

As we spoke, he asked if I'd care to meet him the following weekend when we could walk together in Lazienki Park and perhaps attend a concert in the Summer Palace. At home that evening, I confessed to mother that I'd fallen head over heels in love with the man that they'd arranged for me to marry.

Over the following weeks a brief chaperoned courtship ensued, when Morris and I walked in Praga Park along the Vistula and strolled in Warsaw's many other fine parks. Whenever we met there was always an older female relative in attendance discreetly following a few paces behind, preventing any intimacy more daring than holding hands as we happily sauntered and chatted.

Some weeks later our parents met each other formally and our betrothal was announced. Arrangements were made for our marriage, and we secured living accommodation on the fourth floor of a five-story apartment block, built round a paved square courtyard close to where my parents lived. The heavy dark pine front door opened directly from the staircase landing into a simple living room /kitchen, in which was a stoneware sink, beyond which was a short corridor, off of which were two small bedrooms. There was no internal bathroom and the four communal toilets nestled in the far corner of the central courtyard.

Shortly after our wedding, Morris's father Marcus, who was short and very overweight, died. He was just 49, and left five unmarried children to be cared for by his widow, Anna, to whom he bequeathed a quantity of debts. To satisfy a small pressing group of unsympathetic creditors, the butcher's shop was sold. Without a job, Morris was compelled to accept a more menial situation as a butcher's assistant, with a commensurate reduction in pay.

Naturally, Anna Podguszer turned to her Wladov family for help in her financial predicament. They were unable to assist in any way and justified their inability by taking the self-righteous attitude that there were two adult sons, Morris and Lev, who could work to support Anna and her four young daughters.

I was pregnant at the time and unable to resume my dispensary work to help out in the family's dire financial needs. I had a friend however, who made artificial flowers, hats and feather hat accessories, who offered to help me learn the millinery trade. I learnt quickly and obtained work as an outdoor worker, which enabled me to remain at home, to earn those extra few zlotys to keep our heads above water.

As time went by, the first of our children arrived. Mark, who was named after my late father in law, Marcus, was born at home on October 23rd, 1900, of the old Julian calendar and Morris registered his birth at Warsaw's municipal office of the Non Christians. This segregated office provided an additional reminder of the anti-Semitic discrimination exercised against Russian-Polish Jewish citizens, no matter how many generations their ancestors had lived and worked in Poland.

I continued working at home and became dexterously adept at making artificial flowers. Although the work was badly paid, we desperately needed the little money that I could earn, while working at home.

By the time our second son, Harry, arrived in 1902, my skill and manual adroitness enabled me to experiment. I designed and made floral and feather hat accessories for the felt and straw hats that I bought and molded to my designs from materials that I purchased independently and which Morris could sell in any-one of a number of local street markets at weekends. This became a far more lucrative method of earning a livelihood than relying upon outdoor employment and by the time Annie was born, in June 1903, I now worked entirely on manufacturing my own merchandise, in addition to caring for my three young children in our tiny two-bedroom apartment, and in this way earned more money than Morris.

Then came a day that we could never forget. On the 8th of February 1904, the Japanese Navy treacherously attacked the Russian fleet at Port Arthur, without any declaration of war. The relative calm of everyday life in Russia came to an abrupt end, particularly for the Jewish community. Following the resulting defeat of the Russian Pacific fleet the civilian unrest started. With news of each Russian defeat at the hands of the Japanese rumour abounded on rumour and civil unrest increased. Reassuringly the public was led to believe that reinforcements would soon be rushed out to the Far East along the new Trans Siberian railway where the Tzar's superior forces would soon teach the perfidious Japanese that Russia was a major power not to be trifled with.

Each new setback and report was met with public incredulity. It appeared inconceivable that the small Nipponese offspring of Pacific island fishermen could vanquish Russia's fierce Cossack and Tartar descendants. No matter how the Russian censors spun the release of information, defeat upon humiliating defeat could not be concealed. Regardless of the description of loss of territory as 'a valiant strategic withdrawal', the sinking of several major warships with the accompanying horrific loss of life, were catastrophic defeats that no language could disguise.

Week after week further reversals were announced flowing like an unstoppable torrent of water, nurturing social and political unrest throughout Russia, ultimately shaking the Tzarist dictatorship to its roots.

With each reverse, gossip and speculation mounted, while each Jewish community was called upon to play the time-honoured role as the traditional scapegoat. This commitment had been honed over many centuries as successive Tzarist governments used this simple expedient to blame the Jews for all such calamities. Whether it was an epidemic, harvest failure, or some other disaster, the Yids were to blame; an uneducated population would be encouraged by State and Church to vent their spleen on the descendants of Abraham, once again permitting an archaic government to gain total absolution and remain in power.

In January 1905 came the loss of Port Arthur and, in May the ultimate military debacle.

With great fan-fare, the Russians dispatched their far larger Black Sea fleet, to redress the earlier humiliating defeat of the Tsar's Pacific Fleet by the smaller Japanese Imperial Pacific fleet.

This naval armada steamed across thousands of miles of ocean, round the Cape of Good Hope, to join and reinforce what remained of their Pacific fleet. The intention was to intimidate the Japanese and then by force of arms compel Japan to withdraw, with appropriate compensation paid to Imperial Russia.

With a far smaller number of capital ships the Japanese intercepted early radio signals from the Russian task force and tracking the fleet's progress had lain in ambush. As the unsuspecting Black Sea fleet steamed closer to its rendezvous with the remains of the Pacific fleet the trap had been sprung. In the brief battle that followed all but three of the Russian warships were totally destroyed and the damaged remnants of her once majestic armada limped into the safety of Vladivostock.

Riots erupted in almost every town throughout Russia when news was released of this further ignominious defeat.

In Odessa, the homeport of the Black Sea Fleet there were large-scale revolutionary riots and mutiny broke out amongst the crews of the remaining warships. The consequence of an unpopular war and the culmination of Russia's humiliating defeats resulted in what was later described as 'Bloody Sunday' and the 'Battleship Potemkin Mutiny'. The incredible destruction of the Russian warships by a far smaller Japanese force and the dramatic increase in revolutionary activity throughout Russia signaled the urgent need for a radical change.

Tzar Nicholas II decided that he needed to bring a rapid conclusion to the conflict and stop the simmering revolutionary ferment in every corner of his empire that increased daily, as the disastrous war against Japan continued. Government reforms were promised, including the introduction of a parliament. Many other pledges made under the duress of threatened insurrection were never implemented and the unrest was ruthlessly quelled. Suspected revolutionaries and troublemakers were arrested. Some were executed others imprisoned and exiled in Siberia. A few of the political leaders such as Lenin were able to escape arrest and fled for a time to Western Europe. Anti-Jewish riots occurred with sickening frequency and ferocity as the government deliberately incited the population, which needed little encouragement, to turn upon the Jews in their midst, blaming them for all Russia's many problems.

As the *pogroms* (rioting against the Jewish minority) ensued, the police were ordered not to intercede to protect life or property. Where a few groups of young Jews armed themselves for self-defence the army was brought in to ruthlessly stamp out such opposition. The Jewish population who had not fled the pogroms of the early 1880's was again in fear of life and limb. In far larger numbers, they again sought to escape their persecutors by emigrating westwards, heading mainly for America.

To prosecute her war against Russia, Japan had purchased British warships, utilized German military training and issued war bonds using financial houses in New York and London.

In the aftermath, the USA hosted a peace conference in Portsmouth, New Hampshire and subsequently President Theodore Roosevelt was awarded a Nobel Peace prize for his efforts in brokering the peace treaty that year.

Chapter 5

October 1905 -1908

*I*could barely remember my two older brothers who left home for the new world shortly after I started school. I did however recall how they'd romped, teased and spoiled me, turning me into what mother had laughingly called a regular '*kleiner lobus*' (little tom-boy). Now, after all those years, I would soon be seeing my eldest brother Abraham again, whose eldest daughter was barely nine years younger than me.

I slept and dreamed through these pleasant reveries, rocked gently by the train's motion until I became conscious that there had been a change in the tempo of sound emanating from the carriage wheels, which suddenly woke me.

There was no mistake, the train was slowing and the excitement mounted within me, in anticipation of joining Moisheka once more.

The carriage windows had misted over and I had to wipe mine with my sleeve to enable me to peer out. As I strained to see, I became aware of row upon row of shadowy dimly illuminated terraced houses, as the train slowly slipped by in the night air, indicating we were passing through the outskirts of a large city and nearing our destination. I roused Hilda and instructed her to wake the boys and dress them in preparation for alighting from the train.

Reverting to its earlier asthmatic gasping, the train slowed further, as it puffed unhurriedly into Liverpool Street Station, where, with a brief and final high-pitched metallic squeal of brakes, it stopped.

Passenger doors were swiftly thrown open. I stood up, wrapped my coat round myself and anxiously scanned all the waiting faces for the sight of Morris. Holding Annie and loaded down with my bags I carefully climbed down from the train. As we stepped onto the shadowy grey, gas-lit platform, I resumed my search for Morris and unable to see him, I became increasingly concerned. Clutching Annie, still sleeping peacefully, and with Hilda at my side I yelled at her above the noise,

"We're making for the barrier. Stick by me as though you're my shadow, and you boys hold tightly on to *meema* (aunt) Hilda, because if you get lost, we might never find you again!"

With that, we pressed forward, following the throng. The crowd, constantly jostling us, surged forward like a river in full flow, as further trains arrived to disgorge ever more passengers. We were propelled onwards towards the gateway through which, under the stern gaze of the uniformed ticket collectors, each passenger prior to exiting from the platform surrendered a green ticket. Nervously, I peered everywhere, hoping for a glimpse of my husband.

Desperately I turned over in my mind what I would do if for some reason Morris wasn't there to meet us, or if somehow we missed him in this horde. I had that carefully folded piece of paper, with the name and address of my brother, Abraham Chisick, safely tucked into a small linen pouch securely pinned to the inside of my blouse. That gave some reassurance, but I was terrified at the prospect of attempting to complete this last portion of our journey unaided, with no knowledge of English and no English money.

As the teeming throng of passengers proceeded towards the ticket barrier, we were bumped into more often. Suddenly I spotted Abraham, who I recognized from a recent photograph. The brother I'd last seen when I was six years old towered like a giant, almost two metres tall. Then to my relief, far shorter and thickset, his face wreathed in one enormous smile I saw Morris, frantically waving and shouting my name, next to him.

With both arms full and unable to wave back I called out as loudly as I could, as an uncontrollable damn of tears ran down my cheeks leaving pale trails through the grime of the previous hours travel.

Once through the barrier, midst hugs, smiles and noisy chatter, with the men carrying the older children, we hastened out of the station forecourt into the foggy, damp, London night air. There we soon boarded a waiting horse drawn cab, which rapidly sped us to Abraham's house.

In the warmth of his home, where arrangements had been made for us to stay, there was so much chatter and excitement. I met my sister in law, Betty (Beila), for the first time and waiting with her were my seven young nephews and nieces ranging from Louisa, the eldest, a young lady in her teens, to Kitty the year old baby.

The first priority was to give the exhausted children a warm drink, after which they were washed, changed into nightclothes, and tucked into bed. Seeing Morris again after so many weeks and meeting my brother, somehow gave me a renewed source of energy to talk and listen.

Abraham gave me the same advice he'd earlier given Morris.

"The first thing all of you must do is learn the language. Yiddish may be fine between us, but you must learn to speak English as soon as possible and while you're doing that, you'd best change your name. Make your name easier to sound and spell in English."

"Of course we'll learn English, but why do I need to change my name?"

"Take my word. You're starting a new life. You have to be as much like your neighbours as possible. Try to sound like them, dress like them, and copy them. If you don't, you'll always be an outsider and no better off than you were amongst those anti-Semites back home in Poland. If you're not prepared to change, then you might as well just go straight back to Warsaw, tomorrow, without unpacking."

"So I'll change. Instead of Zlata, call me Sophia, but I'm not changing my last name."

"That's up to you, but just you mark my words. You'll change it sooner or later. Meanwhile you must be exhausted by that journey. We'll get to bed and tomorrow morning, Lulu, my eldest girl, will start by giving you and the children your first English lesson."

Abraham was the eldest and I was the third surviving child of our parents, Pesach and Geitle Chisick. Pesach told us that he never remembered his real father. There had been a village disturbance, and with their simple wooden home ablaze, Pesach, a young child held securely in his mother's arms, looked on as his parent's and their neighbours helplessly watched the fire take hold. With a jacket placed over his head, his father had suddenly darted forward, before anybody could stop him and re-entered the family home to retrieve some forgotten family heirloom.

Within moments the supporting roof timbers collapsed. The blaze was now too fierce for any possibility of rescue as his father surrendered his life in the resulting funeral pyre. His grief stricken widow had died shortly after this, some said from a broken heart, and Pesach, an only child was adopted by his father's cousins, a childless furniture maker and his wife.

As he grew to manhood, he worked long hours as an apprentice cabinetmaker alongside his adoptive father. In 1859, when a shy introverted young man aged twenty, there had been an arranged marriage with his neighbour's daughter Geitle Blumensohn, the 'good one' who was also a cousin, related through her mother Genendla's father, Hersz Chisick. She was two years older than him and the eldest of nine children.

Our mother Geitle Blumensohn was intelligent and confident, but no beauty. She had acquired her mother Genendla's shrewish tendency, and in time polished this inherited skill to a flawless precision as she rapidly dominated her considerate, but slower, hard working artisan husband.

Pregnancies followed one after the other almost every year, in a rhythmic pattern, akin to the changing seasons, while nature cruelly culled the infant numbers with childhood ailments and epidemic infections. Even her first born in 1860 had died within hours of his birth when not a day old. These sporadic tragedies immured them to the harsh realities of everyday life amongst a largely hostile Catholic populace, where Jews were still considered unwelcome interlopers, in spite of living in Poland for more than seven centuries.

Periodically there were epidemic outbreaks of contagion from cholera, typhoid, typhus and gastro enteritis. The uneducated local population, in the absence of any understanding of the causes of these recurring disasters, sought revenge. Encouraged by the ranting of local priests, they embarked upon a series of mindless hostile acts against their Jewish neighbours, breaking and entering homes, pillaging, assaulting, maiming and sometimes even killing the cowering victims within.

Yet never stopping to rationalise that these long suffering Jews who were condemned for these outbreaks were victims in their own rights, similarly decimated by the contagions for which they were blamed.

Those empowered to enforce law and order did nothing to protect the victims, often standing by as onlookers, condoning acts of lawlessness against the suffering minority in their midst.

In 1881 Tzar Alexander II was assassinated by a revolutionist's bomb. Endemic anti-Semitism increased dramatically following this event. Riots followed throughout the country, encouraged, organized and sanctioned by a Tzarist government desperately clinging to a despotic feudal power base.

Terror, loss of livelihood and frequently death resulted, as Jews were persecuted and hounded from their homes, giving birth to a new word, 'Pogrom'.

The consequence was that thousands of refugees commenced migrating westwards from Russian territories, mainly to the United States, an exodus that was only halted with the advent of the First World War. In all, some 3,000,000 Jewish refugees sought sanctuary in the west, including all of our parents, Pesach and Geitle Chisick's children.

The first to leave was, Abraham, the eldest son and a cabinetmaker like our father. Born in 1861 he was a strapping young man, tall, strong and well built who had somehow survived the lottery of childhood ills and in some way also managed to endure four years of military service. After much soul searching he had decided to leave for America. Years of scrimping, saving and borrowing enabled him to amass the small fortune needed to pay for his transatlantic fare to New York.

Arriving in Bremen he was assured that he could save in excess of 15% of the fare and more than 3 days travel time, by journeying through London. He could sail to London and then travel overland by train to Liverpool and then by steamship to New York. Arriving in London in the spring of 1886, he presented himself at the rail terminal only to discover that he'd been given a platform ticket and that he'd been duped out of his transatlantic fare.

With no money, there was no alternative but to settle in London. Abraham Chisick, adopting the English spelling of his name, readily found employment as a cabinet-maker. Rapidly mastering the English language, he was able, as a skilled craftsman, to establish his own cabinet making business. Within two years he had also embarked upon importing lumber from Eastern Europe. Later that same year, in 1888, he met and proposed marriage to Beila Cohen a young woman three years his junior. Their marriage was conducted under a *chupah* (marriage canopy), by a rabbi in the garden of his bride's parents. None of the groom's family was present and without the presence of a registrar, the marriage was never officially registered. The day following these celebrations there was a day trip to Bolter's Lock, above Maidenhead, after which it was back to work, as usual.

Once alone with Morris, in spite of my exhaustion we talked and whispered excitedly long into the night.

"Moisheka, where have you found us to live?"

Morris told me how helpful Abraham had been.

"I walked round the streets for hours searching for somewhere reasonable to live. Without Abraham's help, I'd never have found anything suitable and wouldn't have been able to find a decent job either in such a short time. I've located a couple of rooms in a tenement block just off the Mile End Road, in Union Street, at a rent of four shillings a week.

"To secure a tenancy, landlords here insist that a tenant installs his own furniture. That way the occupier trying to make a moonlight flit owing rent would be more likely to betray their intention by first making provision to move furniture. Abraham helped by lending me beds, a table and chairs and some other furnishings, which he says we can pay for later, or return once we've bought our own things.

"He also helped me to pay for the railway and steamer tickets with an interest free loan. Without your brother it might have taken me a couple of years to bring you and the children out to London."

The following morning Morris went to his work at a nearby kosher butcher's shop, where he'd secured employment working ten hours a day, with only late Friday afternoon and Saturday off each week for a weekly wage of twenty-five shillings plus one plump boiler fowl.

Later that morning accompanied by my sister in law, Betty, we went by horse drawn tram to see our new home, leaving Lulu and Hilda to care for the children.

We climbed the drab, concrete steps with its accompanying cold, black, iron handrail. Our footsteps echoed dismally as we ascended, until we reached the door of Flat 23 on the fourth floor. While the key was inserted into the lock, I noticed the peeling brown paint. The door swung open to reveal the first of two cheerlessly small rooms, each with its empty fire grate ready to endow the flat with warmth once provided with dry wooden logs, or lumps of coal. To compensate for the cramped living accommodation was the thrill of gas lighting, a luxury that I'd not previously possessed in my Warsaw apartment. At the time I didn't notice the absence of double glazed windows which we did have in Warsaw, although later, as the weather grew colder I soon found we had to scrape ice off the inside of the windows with a knife each morning. A small brown stoneware sink with a pump handle and wooden draining board indicated the kitchen. The toilet was in a yard at the rear of the building, where there was also a locked cupboard in which our coal could be safely stored.

Two days later we moved into our sparsely furnished home. The front room, or parlour, had a kitchen table and wooden chairs, while along one wall was a sofa bed that would be used by Hilda and the two boys. It took very little time for me to discover that with Morris's wages and three adults and three children, with a fourth on the way, we were every bit as poor as in Poland. We were barely able to feed ourselves, pay rent and buy a seven-pound bag of coal. Purchasing a sack of coal of a hundredweight (112 pounds) would have been far more economical but was way beyond our means. Unless I could work, and I didn't need to be an economist to identify this necessity, I didn't see how we could possibly survive without the disgrace of accepting charity. We would be forced into becoming *schnorers* (beggars).

In spite of my poor knowledge of English, I soon found employment in the artificial flower and feather trade as an outdoor worker. I'd collect my materials from a manufacturer who paid me piece rate for my work. I was required to provide my own tools and was expected to purchase some of the raw materials I needed, such as wire and tape, which reduced my profit. It sounds immodest to recall that I was very dexterous, but no matter how rapidly I worked, I was unable to make any major contribution to the family income. The rate of pay for my work was abysmally low and worked out at less than thrupence an hour.

The need for shopping, cooking and supervising the children, also ate into my allocated work time.

The need to wander through the streets to purchase my supplies proved a blessing in disguise. It taught me where to make these acquisitions and compelled me to learn scraps of English as rapidly as possible, in order to negotiate the best prices for my materials.

Very early in the morning of 30th January 1906, I went into labour. I was almost three weeks overdue and Mother Nature was not prepared to wait until the dawn. Muffled in overcoat and hat, Morris, rushed out into the freezing winter's night to summon the midwife, leaving Hilda in charge.

In between the birth pains, that were coming every few minutes, I had time to reflect. I'm twenty-five and after six years of marriage I'm about to have my fourth child. In a strange land hardly understanding a word of English and with no mother to help me we're so poor that we can barely afford the luxury of eating and keeping warm at the same time. Before marriage I hadn't a care in the world and now we have absolutely nothing. Morris is a wonderful husband and companion, but somehow since his father passed away, he's been unable to make a proper living. If we weren't to find ourselves in the workhouse, I would have to do something. By the time Morris returned a few minutes later with the midwife in close pursuit carrying her maternity bag, my mind was made up. I'd have to go into business.

With the labour pains increasing, only a brief time elapsed before our first English child arrived. Our daughter Esther Sarah, or Essie as we called her had made her entrance. Since there were now four children for Hilda to supervise and care for, Marcus, who four months earlier had reached school age, was enrolled at the local infants school, where on his first day we admonished him never to take sweets from, or talk to strangers and to always look both ways, first right, then left, before crossing the road. Within a few weeks of Essie's birth I'd persuaded Morris that he should give up his job to concentrate on purchasing the household needs and materials I needed and then selling the hats, feather trimmings and artificial flowers that I designed and made. I would employ a young woman who I could train to help me, while Hilda would then have total care of the children.

During the day, the parlour was crammed with bags containing feathers. The kitchen table was turned into a workbench at which I worked with Molly my young Irish assistant, while even the children were put to work helping to sort feathers, according to size and colour. At meal times Morris helped prepare the food and Hilda cleared a small space at the table where the children could sit and eat, often with feathers blowing into the food. At this stage, our lives were work to eat and eat to give us the energy to work, with as little time wasted in sleeping as possible. We had bread to put on our plates, but never any butter and only a little *schmaltz* (dripping) when we celebrated a special occasion, like a birthday. The only recreation was on Saturday with synagogue in the morning for Morris, with the boys and walking to visit Abraham in the afternoon, where we would have tea and the ecstasy of butter and even jam on our bread. It was some years before we could afford these luxuries.

Morris soon discovered that the only avenue open to him to sell my merchandise in any quantity was through a wholesaler. Regulations were rigidly enforced that forbade him as a manufacturer selling his wares directly to retailers. The wholesalers were frequently difficult to satisfy. Invariably they wanted extended credit, which he found impossible to provide, and as a consequence was constrained to offer considerable discounts for immediate payment. Some wanted our goods on a sale or return basis. Others were reluctant to buy, since we were unable to provide the larger quantities they required, while yet others indicated that our wares were no different from many other suppliers.

"Moisheka, the only thing for us to do is to make our merchandise as distinctive as possible."

"Our goods are well made, the designs, good, but we're compelled to sell them more cheaply than our competitors because we can't give any credit. The only other way we can be really unique is to lower our prices so that we almost give our merchandise away."

"Don't be ridiculous. Let's do what we used to do in Warsaw. We'll use the French trimmings. That'll make our stock stand out and look far better value."

"But they came in directly by train from Paris and we could buy them locally. There's no direct connection with France and there's nowhere that I know in London where we can buy them."

"That's marvellous, we'll gain our advantage by going to Paris. You'll go there, buy whatever we need and bring it back with you."

"I'd thought of that, but you're overlooking a couple of things? The main snag is money. We don't have the fare, or the money with which to make our purchases in sufficient quantity, to make the journey worthwhile. In addition I don't speak anything more than a couple of words of French to negotiate a decent price. Lastly if we try to store anything more in this apartment the cat will need to find lodgings elsewhere, so will we, and even the mice will have to move out."

"You're being too negative, darling. Don't ignore the fact that we have a brother with a furniture factory. Go speak to Abraham tomorrow and arrange that he lend us the money. Make certain that he agrees, even if you have to offer him a little interest on the loan. Then tell him you must have a cupboard that can be locked or some other secure space in his factory for a few weeks until we can find a larger apartment. You speak Polish, Russian, Yiddish and German, besides a little English and French. Once you're in Paris, you're bound to find a *lantsman'* (an individual from the same town) and then you'll have no trouble at all."

Within days Morris had arranged a loan from Abraham with the promise of some storage space, before setting off for Paris.

With an early morning departure by rail from Victoria Station he arrived the same day in Paris, where he spent two days making contacts and purchasing the materials we needed.

On his return, Morris found the household in uproar, with me in tears, and our eldest boy in hospital under the surgeon's knife. The day Morris had left for Paris, Mark, had become unwell with a fever and abdominal pain. I'd summoned the doctor, who examined him and announced that the child was suffering from typhlitis (appendicitis) and needed urgent hospitalisation.

Taken to the nearby London Hospital he was operated on by Sir Frederick Treves, the surgeon who 3 years earlier had operated on King Edward VII the day before his coronation in 1902 for the same condition.

At the conclusion of Mark's surgery, a huge abdominal drain was left in place for seven days, which resulted in an enormous unsightly scar in the child's right loin as a permanent reminder of his successful tussle with death.

I resumed production of my hats and millinery accessories and with the advent of spring, business picked up, necessitating that I work from dawn to dusk and then well into the night. Morris's improved English enhanced his sales techniques, but within a few months it was obvious that I was again pregnant and Morris had to devote more of his time to shopping, cooking and generally assisting Hilda with the household duties.

On the last day of February 1907 the midwife was summoned once more through the freezing weather to our home, where I was delivered of a third healthy daughter. Although given the beautiful biblical name Rebecca she would always be called Becky, a name that she increasingly abhorred and which, when an adult she changed to Betty.

With three adults and five children in two rooms Morris had to prioritise finding a larger flat where fewer stairs would need to be climbed. A ground floor three-room apartment became vacant and he seized the opportunity of negotiating an acceptable rent with the landlord before we moved into flat 1 on the ground floor. Modestly larger, the convenience of living on the ground floor was enormous and with the additional room there was now space to employ a second girl to assist Molly and me with our work. We were still desperately poor, but we were starting to make progress.

As immigrants, the routine of our daily life was boring and monotonous. Morning, noon and night, day in and day out there was work, for I was determined that this was the only avenue whereby we could escape from our poverty trap. The greater we focused on our work the better the chance that we would succeed.

I increased my staff to two as Molly's sister came to help us. Harry started school the following year and both our boys were kept busy by attending 'chedar' (religious classes), three evenings a week plus Sunday mornings. Here, as was typical of the time, a tutor believed that optimal results combined with deference for ones teacher were best achieved by regular beatings.

In equal measure instruction and obedience was instilled with a cuffed ear or rap over unprotected knuckles from a cane or ruler. With this simple conditioning technique, discipline and respect for ones teacher was taught at an early age after which the next priority, which was to study and learn, soon followed at a remarkably smooth and rapid pace. A student never complained to his parents for fear that his father would consider the punishment had been justified and would then add his own tariff with an additional severe beating.

When Morris and the boys came home from synagogue on Saturday, I stopped my work and sat with them for lunch. Instead of resting, the family ritual was to walk, no matter the weather, to visit family. When conditions were particularly cold or wet we might need to stay home and as a special treat we'd allow the boys to attend a local hall where for a halfpenny each, which included a small paper bag of sweets, they could gain entrance to a silent film show.

We found that sanitary conditions in London were far ahead of those prevailing in Poland, although the vast majority of early 20th century dwellings had neither a plumbed in bath, nor a separate bathroom. Flush toilets had been introduced during the latter part of the 19th century, but very few homes were yet equipped with them. The majority had an outhouse; usually a wooden or simple brick built structure, with a wooden door, in which were ventilation holes. There was no toilet paper and newspaper was torn into squares for this purpose. Every home had one or more earthenware or metal pots for use whenever the night was particularly cold or in an emergency.

In the kitchen a stoneware sink with a small wooden draining board was where the family ablutions were performed, while the same sink was also used for washing dishes, pots and pans and clothes. Hot water had to be heated in a kettle on the kitchen stove. Many years later a small, ventilated gas heater made its appearance, removing the chore of heating water.

Whenever possible, we bathed at least once a week, on a Friday, in preparation for the Sabbath. The younger children were bathed in an enamel bathtub, which would be filled with warm water. The boys would accompany Moisheka to the local public baths, where, for two pennies they could luxuriate in a long deep marble/stone bath of hot water provided by a bath attendant from taps that were controlled outside the bathing cubicle. There, in steam and agreeably hot water, the pleasant fragrant aroma of soap and bath oils and the calls of "more hot water for number five", or calls from whichever cubicle needed water. The bathing was accompanied by echoing sounds of gushing water, and bathers happily singing or whistling in an atmosphere of steam and water condensing as tiny droplets from every cool surface. Voluminous soft white towels were supplied at the baths but bathers had to bring their own soap. Apart from this, every orthodox married woman attended the closest *mikvah* (ritual bath) each month for her customary immersion, as did the young bride to be, but I preferred a weekly visit to the public baths, where I could take my girls as they grew older.

Every day had its special designation of activities. Thursday was shopping day, when Morris bought larger quantities of food for the Sabbath and weekend, although small food items were purchased every day. Thursday night and Friday mornings Moisheka set aside time for preparation of these fresh provisions, while I worked.

Early Friday morning a *cholent* (meat stew) was prepared for the following day's lunch. Morris made this from inexpensive cuts of beef, which he cut into cubes and placed in a lidded earthenware pot together with potatoes, carrots, onions, haricot beans and seasoning. The pot was then taken early Friday morning to the local Jewish baker, who for ½d., or ¾d., depending upon the size, would place it in his banked up oven to slowly cook over a number of hours prior to being collected before the Sabbath. It was so hot that a pram was used to transport it home where it was then placed in the family oven to keep warm, over the next 18 hours to provide a hot Sabbath lunch. The Friday evening meal was always chicken soup, followed by boiled chicken, Saturday evening dinner was the remains of the cholent, while Sunday was invariably cold fried fish, or gefilte fish when we could afford it.

Monday was the worst day. Every conceivable item that needed washing was washed by hand on a washboard in the kitchen sink. I couldn't afford the luxury of a laundry, although for a modest charge there was the 'bag wash', where each week a driver collected, a sack which had been squeezed to bursting, full of dirty linens, then taken to a laundry and returned, washed and dry, but unironed.

Washday started early with water being heated and then emptied into the sink. With a wooden washboard and copious amounts of Lifebuoy brown soap and Lux Soap flakes, Hilda and I laboriously washed clothes by hand. The poor like me envied Abraham's wife, Betty, who had a boiler in their backyard. It was like a gigantic cooking pot with a tap at the bottom and a vented lid on top, in which a fire under the cylinder could heat water. It saved time and helped to avoid the tremendous build up of steam with the musty odours associated with washday.

Washed items had to be rinsed and wrung out to eliminate excess water, and again how I envied Betty, who had a mangle, which saved hours of work with hands immersed in cold water. Mark and Harry helped, Hilda and I wring everything out by hand and then everyone gave a hand in hanging everything out to dry and later collecting it all up again when dry to be ironed, folded and where needed mended and repaired on Tuesday and Wednesday.

Unless the weather was particularly favourable the process of drying might take two or three days since we had no garden in which to hang clothes to dry. Lines of stout string were hung over balconies, staircase landings, in bedrooms and kitchen. In the kitchen at such times there was a regular aerial ambush of knotted lines, supporting limp damp clothing hanging there and always the extended coiled brown ribbon of sticky fly-trap paper suspended below the ceiling light with various flying insects adhering to it on both sides, the latest adherents struggling in a futile attempt to escape. Interspersed with all this activity time had to be made for daily household tasks and, preparation of meals. Those who were better off were able to employ a *yokelta* (a washerwoman) to help with the washing chores and the more tiresome housecleaning, which included regular scrubbing of linoleum, wooden floors and external stone steps and how I yearned for the day that we could afford such help.

Wherever possible beds were made up with freshly laundered lightly starched white sheets and the bliss of sleeping within such bed linen on a warm evening had to be experienced to be believed. This together with the aroma of freshly brewing coffee or freshly baking bread was considered amongst the most joyous memories of our immigrant lives.

Each room had its own fireplace for heating. A coal fire would provide heat, or at least that was the intention, but a constant shortage of money meant that apart from the kitchen, nowhere else was heated. Even in the kitchen the fire served a dual purpose, when it was also used in part for cooking and keeping food warm. Hot drinking water suitable for making tea or coffee was kept in a large Samovar which when filled, contained many pints of hot water, and kept hot by a small gas burner at the base.

On a Saturday in winter the fire was re-kindled by a *shobbos goy* (a gentile who was permitted to work on the Sabbath), who would be paid a small sum of money on Friday to attend next day to build up the fire, but we soon gave this up from lack of money. Like Abraham's family, we became members of the Federation Synagogue, where Morris regularly sang in the choir, but while orthodox, in our dietary customs we were not averse to riding on the Sabbath and as time progressed, small lapses in our religious observances began to appear, as imperceptibly we commenced our process of assimilation into the English way of life.

I devoted as much of my time as possible to the design and manufacture of a range of millinery accessories and Morris, assisted by Hilda supervised the majority of the household duties, particularly the shopping and cooking, which he greatly enjoyed. Shopping was a time-consuming but pleasant daily task, but only when the weather was good. Most of the local shopkeepers spoke Yiddish and food stores carried a considerable range of fresh foods with tantalisingly mouth-watering aromas. Signs and posters in London's Eastend were largely in Yiddish and many newssheets were available with Hebrew letters in Yiddish and thus there was little need for immigrants like me to read or write English.

With Morris selling and my helpers assisting me to manufacture our millinery accessories our business enterprise slowly expanded, but somehow I still couldn't avoid becoming pregnant. On June 5th 1908 a further son, Solly was born, which meant creating bed space in the kitchen, since with Hilda there were now 6 children and three adults living in three rooms, plus my two helpers who worked with me.

Busily working, breast-feeding and often supervising many of the household chores I had no time to make clothes for my children. These had to be purchased, wholesale wherever possible. This in turn helped me improve my English, which I was told I always spoke, with an east European accent, and improved my negotiating skills as I cajoled, pleaded and argued to obtain a keener price. In time it helped me to become a very formidable bargain hunter and shopper.

One day Moisheka brought home one of the largest orders that we had ever received. I worked day and night with my helpers to make everything ready. When the finished goods had been packed in their cardboard boxes Morris delivered them, or rather attempted to make the delivery. The wholesaler was an anti-Semite and now refused to accept delivery other than on a Saturday morning, knowing full well that we couldn't work or carry goods on the Sabbath. There were ten large boxes. We overcame the problem by hiring a man to carry them and meet me outside the entrance of the wholesaler on Saturday at 9 o'clock when they opened. I walked into the customer's showroom and on my instruction my helper placed the boxes in the entranceway, so that nobody could enter or leave once I had gone inside. Once inside I enquired in a loud voice if there was anyone who could help a lady with a delivery of goods. That was the last time that client insisted that we deliver on a Saturday.

Chapter 6

1907-1910

*I*n the spring of 1909 we moved once again. As business improved, Morris found an old five-roomed house on two floors, with a yard in the rear, at 80 New Road, Whitechapel where we relocated. It was in very poor condition, but the rent was low and we desperately needed a large front room to use exclusively as a factory to give us more living space. With our new home, although we were always on the verge of bankruptcy, Morris and I felt that we were at last moving up in the world.

The living room was located at the rear of the house, beyond which was a small kitchen with access to an outside flush toilet and the yard. In the front parlour, space was allocated to create a factory, where we installed a machine to heat press fabrics, to create petals and leaves and another for steaming feathers. Along one wall we placed a long trestle table with wooden bench seats. On the other we installed a smaller table for packing, while in one corner was a small desk, in which Morris kept a ledger and could conduct his bookkeeping activities. We made storage space for bags and boxes on shelves, which lined the corridor and staircase, where it became a distinct advantage to be either thin, or short to negotiate a way through the narrow passageway, without knocking into some obstruction. Our family, now numbering six children and 3 adults, slept in the living room and the two first floor bed rooms, while everybody entering or leaving the house had to walk past the front room factory door.

One day I sent Mark and Harry on an errand to buy a pennyworth of horsemeat for the cat from the cat-meat man in the market, and before they set off I again warned them not to talk to strangers.

As they were walking down Petticoat Lane, one of the stallholders who sold an array of flowering plants, bulbs and herbs, from a barrow, called them over.

"You look like a couple of bright honest lads. How would you like to earn a tanner (six pence) fer five minutes work?"

Mark nodded his head up and down, since he'd been told repeatedly never to speak to, or accept sweets from strangers. This was surely a stranger, but nodding couldn't be counted as talking and he wasn't being offered sweets, but rather a princely sum for an errand of some kind. The stallholder continued.

"How old are yer?" Again remembering to abide by his mother's repeated prohibition, Mark held up seven fingers and, following an elbow encouragingly prodded into his ribs from his older brother, Harry followed suit a few moments later, extending his own five grubby fingers.

"That's perfect. Lost yer tongues 'ave we? Me 'elper's away; orff sick ee is, an' I've gotta see a man about a dawg, somefink awful. All you've to do is watch the barrer, see nobody takes nuffink, an' I'll be back in a jiffy."

The boys stood there and within a few minutes the stallholder returned.

" 'at's betta! Just 'ad to 'ave a Jimmy Riddle. Now I knows I promised yer a tanner, but you've bin sitch great 'elpers I'm gonna double what I promist." With that he stooped, fumbled in a large box, and then grabbed and withdrew a large bulb, which he'd concealed beneath some crumpled old newspapers.

"Now I sells this 'ere bulb only to me bestest, special custimers. It's real unique an' rare; it's a 'Voodoo Lily'. I only gits one a year an' if yew went up west to some of them posh stores like Selfridges or 'arrods it'd be at least 'alf a guinea, or more likely a pannd. Usually I sells it fer 'alf a crown but I'll give it yer fer a bob."(one shilling).

"We don't have a shilling."

"Well, tell me 'ow much 'ave yer got?"

"I've just got a thru penny bit. That's a penny for the cat meat, a penny for my brother and me to go to the pictures with a bag of gob stoppers this afternoon, and a penny change for mother."

"Boys, this must be yer lucky day. I'll tell yew what I'm gonna do. Out of the goodness of me 'art I'll give yew this magic bulb what's worth 'alf a guinea for thrupence cause you two 'ave bin such regula liddle troopas."

"Then what about the meat for the cat, the pictures and the sweets?"

"Yew take this 'ome to yer mum an' give it er! Just yew tell her 'ow valuable this 'ere plant is. Put it in a pot wiv a mugful of earth in a sunny place, give it a dropa water ev'ry week an' I'll warrant she'll be so 'appy she'll give ya another thrupence an' an extra penny besides fer being sitch a couple o' bright young lads."

Mark conferred momentarily with Harry. Unable to resist a bargain, even at that tender age, they decided to part with their small silver coin. The stallholder wrapped the bulb in newspaper exhorting them.

"Fer Gawd's sake don't tell no one where yew bought this, 'cause, if word gits arand, I'll 'ave a mob of angry custimers comin down on me like a pack of wolves on a lamb, demandin to knows how cum I can be givin sitch a rare plant away fer next to nuffink. There'll be riots in the street, so you must promist not to tell."

Nodding their agreement, Mark held the prized bulb tightly in his hands and as they withdrew, the stallholder called out:

"Rimemba boys, shtum's the word!"

Clutching their newly acquired Voodoo lily bulb, with its name label 'Sauromatum guttatum' recording its botanical name, the youngsters, minus their three penny, bit sped home in glee with their half guinea prize, prepared to guard it with life or limb if called upon.

Breathlessly arriving home, Mark and Harry proudly presented the prize lily bulb to me, telling me of its remarkable value that had cost them only three pence, a real metziah (bargain). I was not only unimpressed with their bargain, but I was furious that they'd ignored my repeated instruction not to speak with strangers.

"You must both be a bistle meshuga, and Mark, you should certainly have known better. You wasted three pence on this overgrown onion that's not worth a farthing. You remind me of Jack and the beanstalk selling his mother's cow for a bag of beans."

The upshot was that there was no extra penny for being bright lads. There was no picture money that week, no gob stoppers, no meat for the cat and they narrowly avoided a thrashing from me for talking with strangers.

Having resisted the urge to throw it out, I placed the bulb on the living room window ledge behind the buttoned brown leather settee, in a small pot where Mark dutifully watered it, each week, once shobbos (the Sabbath) was out.

Within a few days a small stem sprouted with a tiny furled leaf either side. The green stem with its white blotches grew rapidly taller like the spike of some plant from prehistoric times, its broad flat uncurling leaves left far behind as the stem fought to escape the bounds of gravity as rapidly as possible. A bulbous swelling appeared at the stem's apex, which slowly darkened as it filled out to a deep maroon colour. There was no doubting that the Lily would shortly exhibit one measly flower, which as I constantly reminded my eldest boys, was but little recompense for their misspent three penny investment.

It was a warm sunny day when we returned home following kiddush at the nearby synagogue. As the children pushed ahead of the grown ups to enter the living room it was apparent that something was seriously wrong. Morris was next to enter, following closely after the children.

"My heavens what a terrible smell! One of you children must have stepped into some dog poo!" Morris announced. There was a chorus of denials as each child stood and attempted to look at the sole of each shoe without falling over.

"That's enough! Outside into the street, the lot of you; take off your shoes and look properly."

Morris followed his progeny to see that his instructions were rigorously obeyed. When each child again reported clean shoes, he insisted that each shoe be removed for his personal inspection. Then the children gleefully ganged up on him and insisted that he remove his shoes for inspection. They then returned into the house, by which time I had equipped myself with a bucket of water a brush and a large bar of sunlight soap.

"I bet it's the cat!" He's become old and lazy. He's either brought in a dead mouse, or he's been messing somewhere and I'll not have it. Let's search!" I ordered. There followed a brief episode where everyone sniffed round the room, in every crevice and corner. The general consensus was that the smell seemed to be coming from behind the settee.

"Morris, help me move it out. You children mind away. Whatever happens, that cat has to go. And when I say go, I mean today, not tomorrow."

After a ritual scrubbing of the linoleum there was still no reduction in the smell, which could no longer be called awful, since it had now reached an 8 on the Richter scale of smells and could be designated as appalling, which was marginally just one less than completely intolerable and possibly almost life threatening. The older children were in revolt and demanded to be allowed out into the street for some urgently needed fresh air.

"All right you can all play outside, but don't go far! Mark and Harry, you're in charge of the younger ones. Morris, open that window before we all pass out."

It was as Morris struggled to open the window that the truth finally assailed him. As he sniffed, he at last realised that this dreadful odour was emanating from the maroon flower that had just blossomed from the children's Voodoo Lily. This member of the genus Araceae utilized the aroma of rotting meat to attract flies from miles around in its attempt at cross-fertilization.

The plant was expelled from the house and, with windows and doors thrown open wide, the smell gradually diminished over the following days. The only beneficiary was the cat, which, unaware of the closeness of his fate, achieved an unexpected stay of execution, as I commuted his death sentence with the words "We'll see how he behaves!"

At the end of May 1909, precisely one year after the birth of Solly, our fourth son Hymie was born. With blue eyes and fairer than his siblings, six-year-old Annie regarded him as her personal responsibility and playmate.

As with all the others I breast fed him, and he was growing into a fine healthy boy when I suddenly noticed him roll his eyes up and then his little arms and legs started shaking. After a couple of minutes he fell asleep and by the time he awoke for his next feed he seemed fine. He was just seven months old. It happened again the next day. His twitching limbs terrified me and I had no idea what was causing the problem, or how I was to deal with it.

Morris and I took him to see the doctor, who referred us to the paediatric department at the London Hospital. Following an examination the doctor explained.

"Something appears to be restricting the flow of cerebrospinal fluid in the brain, resulting in a build up of pressure, called a hydrocephalus, which has caused his symptoms. We don't know what the cause has been but we can give you some medicine to reduce the likelihood of further convulsions. It's not a cure and we'll need to wait and see if the problem is ongoing or not. Would you please make an appointment so that I can see your little boy in a months' time.

Our English still wasn't too good and we'd never heard many of the words the doctor used. There was no interpreter and we didn't understand most of what he was telling us, but we kept smiling and nodding our heads yes, as though we did. We felt too intimidated in the strange environment of the hospital, with its odours of carbolic and antiseptics, to ask further questions.

As we walked home on that cold winter's morning just after the New Year, Morris carefully held the large bottle of red medicine with its cork stopper we'd been given from the hospital dispensary, and I held our baby. All we'd understood from our visit was that the movements we'd seen were like epilepsy.

We thought that the doctor had said that while the medicine would help, it wouldn't cure Hymie's problem, and that they wanted to see how he was progressing in a months' time. We were still terribly worried and decided that on our next visit we would ask my brother Abraham to accompany us to explain what the doctor was saying.

I gave Hymie his medicine, half a teaspoon-full, four times a day, as we'd been told, as regular as clockwork. It seemed to make him very drowsy, but at least there were no further convulsions that we could see and we felt reassured.

It had started out as a normal school day at the end of the third week of January. Anne was at school seated in a diminutive wooden seat at the front of the class of some forty children. She clutched her black slate board in one hand and a short stick of white printing chalk in the right, with which she diligently printed her letters and words on the slate. Anne always sat in the front. In winter there was the advantage of the warmth from the coal fire that blazed behind the teacher seated at her desk, but that was not the reason. She had discovered that the further back she sat, the writing on the blackboard appeared more blurred, while, at the very rear of the classroom, farthest from teacher's austere gaze and favoured by most of the children, she found it impossible to see the writing.

Unexpectedly the primary school head mistress walked into the classroom and every head looked up. Without preamble she sternly enquired:

"Is there an Annie Podguszer in this class? Would you please raise your hand."

Anne looked up, and still clutching her chalk, obediently raised her hand.

"Annie, I've just received a message that your mother needs you at home straight away. You're excused from school. Your mother is expecting you, so no playing, or dawdling on the way.

"You're to get your coat from the cloakroom and hurry home. Do you understand child? Just go home at once without delay, so make haste!"

"Yes Miss." Anne lifted the lid of her desk neatly replaced her slate and chalk within, and then left the room. Puzzled, she donned her coat, hat and gloves and, with a scarf her Aunt had knitted her for Chanukah wrapped, round her neck she hurried into the cold January afternoon and skipped home. She always preferred to skip when speed seemed important since she had the impression that she travelled faster when both feet were off the ground at the same time, as though she were flying.

At the front door, unable to reach the knocker, she customarily stopped a passing grown up and, smiling coquettishly, would politely ask if they would knock for her, as she was still too small to accomplish that task. The timber door acted as a sounding board to the bang of the black knocker and the sound that reverberated within the house was as grotesque as any clap of thunder.

The response that day was unusually rapid. The door was thrown open and there unexpectedly stood her aunt Beila, dabbing her eyes with a handkerchief. From within came the muted sounds of wailing and crying, from a multitude of voices. Not understanding the cause of so many anguished sounds and suddenly confused, Anne stood there momentarily motionless, her lip quivering until, sensing that something terrible must be wrong and without understanding the reason, she too began to cry.

Suddenly darting forward, she dodged nimbly round her aunts' outstretched arms as they unsuccessfully sought to encompass her, and ran into the house sniffling and crying uncontrollably, her tears now blurring her vision, calling. "Mummy, Mummy, where are you?"

Having nimbly slipped past her aunt's bulky presence, she rushed up to her mother in the rear kitchen where, unaccustomedly disheveled, she was seated rocking backwards and forwards, howling like some demented being. Her hair and clothing were in disarray as she clutched the baby asleep in her arms, surrounded by a roomful of tearful relatives and friends.

"Mummy. What's happened, what's happening?"

People were talking, crying, gesticulating, but she didn't understand why. At first uncomprehending, as the words sank deeper into her mind she started to understand, as her six-year-old universe stood still.

How could her beautiful, flaxen-haired brother have left her so suddenly? Why had he been taken to heaven so that she would never be able to sing to him and play with him ever again?

Mummy had told her repeatedly not to believe what they had told her at school about the baby Jesus, before Christmas, when she had returned home singing Christmas carols. Was this to be her punishment for not believing? If she said in her prayers to God that she did believe, would Hymie be returned to her?

Secretly she made her resolve. Fervently she prayed every moment of the day to God that she believed in Jesus and that she was sorry to have ever doubted that he was his only son and saviour who had died for all their sins.

"Dear God, now that I really love Jesus, and promise always to be good, could you please bring my baby brother back to play with me and make Mummy happy again?" After a few days, seeing that her prayers were of no avail and remained unanswered she gradually stopped. With the cessation of her prayers there was disappointment and finally anger, from which grew the dreadful resolve that she would never again believe in baby Jesus, no matter what the teachers taught in school.

Once the mourners had disappeared, Sophia entered that unseen fog of melancholy that is the refuge of the bereaved. She sat in tears during the first days, and thereafter remained seated motionless, cheerlessly staring out of the window looking upwards into space. She gazed intently, as though she might detect in the beat of a distant bird's wings, or the flutter of a butterfly early emerged from its chrysalis, or even the burst of reflected light at some cloud's edge, just something, anything, that might reassure her that her darling child had joined the host of angels, as the rabbi and mourners had guaranteed would assuredly happen.

There was no solace to be found for her anywhere other than at night when asleep, and even then, Morris would awaken periodically with Sophia's anguished tears and repeated questions.

"Why my little boy? Why him and not me?"

As he attempted to assuage her pain and grief she would admonish him.

"Leave me alone Moisheka. I'm to blame. I failed our little boy. As his mother I had a duty of care and I let our poor Hymie down. I was too engrossed in work to realise how sick our little angel had become."

"Sophia, nobody's to blame. It's just that these things sometimes happen. My mother and grandmother all lost young children as yours did. You've got six beautiful healthy children and that's the most important thing now."

"Morris, as a mother, even if I had twenty six children, every single one would be precious to me beyond measure. Not only did I let him down, I've still got his teddy that I meant to put into the coffin to keep him company so that he mightn't feel so lonely."

And the same interminable tearful conversation went on; night after night and days without end, for weeks, until all track of time had been lost.

Unable to cope with her family or work, life at home drifted endlessly. Whenever it appeared that the worst was over and that there might be a turning point Sophia would again break into a sobbing deluge of tears, which in turn caused her children to follow suit. Her sister, Zelda, who'd arrived recently in London and was living in a tenement building in Flower and Dean Street, turned up each morning with her two youngest toddlers to help cook and assist in the care of Sophia's young children.

Sophia, pole-axed by lethargy and depression, was unable to work or supervise her employees. To save money Morris decided that the three young women who assisted her should find alternative employment and were encouraged to,

"Keep in touch so you can return to work here again when Mrs. Podguszer is a little stronger."

With no merchandise to sell Morris was in a terrible quandary. He decided to open a small millinery shop. He acquired the lease of a vacant shop at 165 Whitechapel Road and within days commenced buying and selling other manufacturers hats and accessories.

Once six months had elapsed, without any change, it was feared that Sophia might need to be hospitalised, but Morris was resolute in his determination to cope and care for her at home, to avoid any possibility that she should enter one of those dreadful asylums. Further months passed before there was any sign that Sophia was in the early stages of being able to throw off the invisible burden of her depression.

Almost a year slipped by before Sophia was well enough to resume the care of her children and then a few weeks later to concentrate on re-establishing her workshop. Imperceptibly she re-entered the life style that had been work, from early morning until late at night. At first this was a slow transition, but little by little and then with renewed vigour, Sophia resumed her former role as the dominant breadwinner in her family.

To a casual observer she was the same Sophia, but something had changed. Following the traumatic loss of her baby the industrious mother had now been transformed. She had acquired a maturity that had been previously absent and had at last discovered how to limit the size of her family.

The loss of her infant and her inability to be able to affect the outcome of his illness had devastated her. As she slowly emerged from the invisible cocoon of grief in which she had been imprisoned, she felt particularly vulnerable, as she realised once more that the welfare of her family and the income with which to support them, depended mainly on her.

The children idolised Morris, who was a good husband and father, whom she loved dearly, but in the world of commerce he was primarily a figurehead. She knew that she was the brains and the motivator and she needed a strategy to conceal this aspect of her relationship with Morris. As their business prospered, primarily under her direction, she became increasingly dominant and manipulative.

With practise, she became a consummate actress on life's stage and evolved the role of the sweet naïve wife and mother who knew little of the world; constantly permitting others to help her; giving her husband credit for the management of their business, and encouraging others to believe this. In reality she was an intelligent vixen who knew what she wanted and with great determination would do all in her power to achieve her ends. Behind her benign, attractive feminine exterior, she became a schemer, developing an almost obsessive need to succeed in a man's world that constantly attempted to deny her any expression of the mercantile talent she possessed.

Unknown to Sophia, her elder daughter, Anne, was a keen observer of these changes and later displayed the same traits as her mother, reaching greater heights of economic success.

Morris with his easygoing charm did not possess her commercial prowess. If their enterprise were to prosper, he needed to accept that he lacked the qualities Sophia displayed and must acknowledge a more subordinate role as more of a figurehead. Fortunately he was sufficient of a realist to permit this role reversal in the office and factory, and between them, they developed a partnership where she never undermined his authority with the children or in work and to the casual observer, she never appeared anything more than the docile submissive wife.

Sophia had evolved a simple philosophy. In life one had many choices, but to succeed, one needed a stubborn yearning to make ones own good fortune. The secret ingredient that she constantly added was a light touch of chutzpah. She developed an almost fixated need to work and succeed for the sake of improving the lot of her children, for whom she considered an education was a vital priority. Unfortunately this was largely unavailable as economic deprivation meant that in the early years of their immigrant struggle all the children left school at the age of 14 to assist in providing money for their burgeoning family expenses.

Amongst members of her family there was the acknowledgement that here was a woman, who stubbornly fought over any and every matter, no matter how trivial, relating to the welfare of her family. In addition she was a charitable woman, and regularly helped support her family in Poland until this became impossible with the advent of War in 1914, and again in 1939.

Morris had applied for citizenship in 1910 and on 27 June 1911 became a British subject, as did his wife and children. In the summer of the following year Sophia's niece Louisa, Abraham Chisick's eldest daughter, was married. He had sent his parents rail tickets to persuade them to visit hoping that, with three of their children living in London and with a brood of grandchildren they had never seen, they might be encouraged to extend their visit and settle in England.

Pesach and Geitle attended the wedding celebrations and were feted daily by their children and grandchildren, but all this however was of no avail. They felt unable to leave family and friends to adapt to living in a new, alien culture. With promises to return in two or three years for a further visit, they returned to Poland. The Great War intervened and they were never to see their family again.

On 7th Sept 1913 aged 26, after 8 years caring for her nephews and nieces Hilda, giving her occupation as a milliner, left the Podguszer household to marry Solomon Schwartz, a 28 year old tailor in the New Road Synagogue, Whitechapel, ultimately to bare four of her own children; Max, Netta, Morre and Beatrice.

Chapter 7

1915

With few exceptions, the newly arrived immigrants from Eastern Europe were impoverished Jewish manual workers. They lived in squalid overcrowded conditions and in spite of long hours of work, mostly labouring in sweatshops where they were underpaid, they invariably had to rely upon the succeeding generation to assist them in improving their economic conditions.

Sophia from the outset realised that relying entirely on her husbands endeavours she and her family were doomed to follow the same path. She dreamt that she could break this pattern of deprivation and raise herself and her family to a middle class status if only she could manipulate her husband into accepting her leadership in commercial matters. She understood that this would require tact and guile to ensure that Morris felt and was seen by others to remain the titular head of household without realising that he was little more than a marionette while she controlled the strings.

Sophia was blessed with an engaging quality of wit and humour and with her mercurial temperament became a strong-willed fighter. Her ambition drove her to work from dawn to dusk, never seeming to tire, never resting and with little thought of recreation, or making friends. She worked well with her husband as they struggled to raise a young family, and was meticulously careful never to be seen to cross the Rubicon of undermining Morris's authority.

Morris who'd never displayed his wife's energy or ambition to prosper accepted Sophia's controlling ways and frequent tantrums as she fought to raise herself and her family from the squalid conditions in which they had initially found themselves.

Morris, a gentle good-natured man known for his wit and bonhomie, became increasingly rotund as he contentedly accepted the role he'd exchanged with his wife. He attended chiefly to the family domestic and culinary needs, and in Messrs. Podguszer and Company dealt mainly with sales, foreign purchases and accounting matters, while Sophia's responsibilities related to workroom production, which included recruiting, supervising and training staff, together with designing each new season's range.

In addition to running and developing a business Morris and Sophia had to contend with a boisterous family of children who not only lived in extremely crowded conditions but whose numbers had increased almost yearly until 1910. As a consequence of living in constant close proximity there were frequent squabbles amongst the children, with an ever present rivalry for the attention of parents whose principal daily consideration appeared directed towards running a production line where goods had to be manufactured and delivered on time if the family were to eat, survive and prosper. In later years these rivalries would continue amongst the three older children to the detriment of each, as the fabric of family unity was torn apart.

In 1915 staff shortages in wartime London had became a major problem and experienced staff were urgently needed if the Podguszers' were to remain in business. Sophia had talked the matter over with Morris and they decided that the simplest means of overcoming a skilled worker shortage was to headhunt staff. This was to be achieved by Morris chatting up employees leaving competitors work places, to determine who the most eligible milliners might be so that they could be approached with the offer of a better job with Podguszer and Company.

Jacob Cohen, a middle aged orthodox Jew, with a thick greying beard and a black skullcap perched on the crown of his head had returned home from work that May evening in 1915, tired and hungry.

His evening meal of *gedempta* (braised) meat balls, and kasha had been set on the kitchen table by his wife, Sarah, and he was in the midst of washing his hands at the kitchen sink prior to eating, when there were two staccato knocks at the front door. Dressed in his dark grey waistcoat with the sleeves of his white shirt rolled up above the elbows, he hurried forward to open the door, clutching the towel with which he was drying his hands.

There in front of him stood a smartly dressed, portly, middle-aged gentleman with cropped blond hair and blue eyes.

"Yes; how can I help you?"

"Is this number 1 Great Garden Street, the home of Reb Cohen?" He enquired in Yiddish with a disarming smile, extending the business card that he had been busily fumbling to retrieve from his jacket pocket.

"Yes it is. I'm Jacob Cohen, how can I be of service?"

"As you can see from my card my name is Morris Podguszer. I'm in the millinery accessory business and I've come to speak to the father of Miss Annie Cohen, a young lady who I'm told works in the millinery trade."

"I'm her father. What seems to be the trouble?"

"It's a pleasure to meet you Reb. Cohen. There's absolutely no trouble; please be reassured on that point."

"Then why are you here disturbing me; you're keeping me from my meal?" Jacob Cohen interrupted.

"This may take a few minutes to explain and if it's not too inconvenient I'd like to come in to talk to you."

"Well Annie's not here at the moment, but feel free to come into the parlour, but only for a minute mind you, because my supper's on the table."

Once in the front room when both were seated, Jacob Cohen exclaimed.

"Nu, what do you want from me?"

"As I said, it's a long story and I know you must be hungry after a busy day so I'll be as brief as possible. My wife and I have a factory in City Road, where we manufacture artificial flowers and feather hat accessories. We've been trading for ten years and while business is tolerably good, we have a problem."

"I'm sorry to hear you have difficulties, but there's a war going on and there are a lot of people with appalling troubles. I'm famished and while your story, if you ever get to the end, may be interesting I'd like to eat my evening meal before I leave you to discover you're talking to a corpse who died of hunger."

"Well I'll not take up too much more of your time."

"Excellent, that's what you said before, so now I can bid you good evening."

"But Mr Cohen, I've not finished yet."

"Nu, so get on with what you have to tell me and say it quickly, my supper's getting cold."

"There's a war on and it's become increasingly difficult to find staff."

"I think we've already agreed there's a terrible war on which is causing great hardship. So if you follow me, I'll show you out and then have my supper."

"I understand that your daughter Annie is a very skilled milliner and I'd like, with your permission of course, to offer her employment."

"Mr.......er what did you say your name was?"

"Podguszer, Morris Podguszer, it's on my visiting card."

"Mr Podguszer, my daughter already has a job. She's in the third year of a five-year apprenticeship and has a contract. So, if you'll pardon me, I'll say good evening." Standing up he ushered his guest to the door.

"I realise that she has a job, but I'm hoping that I might be able to offer her something close to £1 a week."

"Mr Podguszer, it's taken you a long time, but at last what you're saying is beginning to sound interesting."

"The salary would be in a contract and would depend on your daughter's age and work experience. Could you tell me how old she is?"

"She was born in December 1896, six months after I arrived in England."

"So that makes her eighteen. Well for somebody of that age I could offer her nineteen shillings a week."

"Did my ears deceive me? Didn't you say £1 a week?"

"Reb Cohen, I said close on £1, but I assure you that if her work is satisfactory we would certainly increase her wage to that sum.

"Well that makes a very tempting offer, but I think Annie should be involved in this discussion and as I said before, she's not home."

"If you could tell me when your daughter will be back, I could return later and we could look at the possibility of giving her an agreement to work for my company at an initial salary of nineteen shillings a week."

"Come back tomorrow at the same time and I'll see that Annie stays home to see you."

The following day Morris Podguszer called again at the Cohen's terraced home, where he met Annie with her father.

"Miss Cohen, let me say how delighted I am to make your acquaintance. I've heard from some of your colleagues at work that you're considered a particularly skilled millinery worker and one of the best apprentices your employer has ever trained."

"Thank you." replied Annie, blushing.

"Could you tell me what a talented apprentice like you might be earning at present?"

"Well it's not really any of your concern, but she receives five shillings a week. And whether it matters, I know that before the war some apprentices received no salary at all." chimed in Jacob Cohen.

"The war has changed a lot of things and as more men enter military service it's created a severe labour shortage. A skilled worker is hard to find these days, particularly in the millinery trade. I've come here to meet you and offer you a job. I can give you a contract to work for me at nineteen shillings a week and you have my word that if your work is satisfactory and from what I've heard I'm certain it will be, your salary will be increased to £1 after one year. If you're in agreement, your father and I can sign a contract to that effect this evening and you could start work next Monday.

The offer of such a huge rise in salary proved irresistible. A hand-written agreement was signed and a few days later Annie commenced working in the Podguszer factory in City Road. Three months later Annie was summonsed to appear in court for breaking her apprentice contract and had to pay a fine of £5 plus court costs.

On the first day of her new job Annie met her employer's wife who managed the small factory workforce.

"So you're the new millinery worker my husband just hired. What's your name?"

"Annie Cohen."

"Well Annie it's now five minutes past eight and you're late. Wasn't it made clear that we start work at eight o'clock and stop at six, with an hour's break for lunch?"

"Yes Madam. I arrived well before eight and as I came through the house I heard the piano being played by a boy. He played so beautifully that I couldn't resist stopping for a few moments and I quite forgot the time."

"That was our eldest boy Mark. He practises each morning before leaving for school, but I don't employ you to listen to my children practising piano each morning."

"I'm sorry, I shan't let it happen again."

"Now your place is at the end of the work bench. I've left all the materials you'll need and a pattern to copy so let me see what you can do. Just call me over when you've finished."

Within a few minutes Annie summoned her employer.

"That was quick." And after a few moments inspecting her work "Yes that's very good indeed. Now tell me a little about yourself."

"What would you like to know?"

"I'm always interested to know a little bit about my staff and their family. What does your father do? How many brothers and sisters and so on?"

"Oh, I see. Both my parents' work. Father's a master tailor and mother helps people who need to write letters home. She can read and write in Russian, Polish and Yiddish. Not only does she write letters, but she also spends ages giving advice and counselling them whenever they ask her for help. She's so busy that my sisters and I have to attend to most of the housework. I'm one of eight children. I've two older sisters, Bloomah and Millie, who married two brothers and each of them has a baby boy. I've an unmarried older brother Abe who's a tailor and then I've two younger sisters Hannah and Minnie and a younger brother Sam at school and then there's my baby brother Phil who's just two. We make all our own clothes and Hannah, although she's only twelve, is a wizard at dress making."

"That's good. Now if you continue to work like this and can arrive on time, I'm certain that we'll get along like one big happy family."

As the day progressed Annie discovered to her astonishment that when her employer was confronted with the slightest problem, Mrs Podguszer's response was to shout irascibly and scream at the staff. When Annie in turn was rebuked in that manner her employer overheard her, as she confided in a whisper to the woman seated next to her.

"That woman must be a 'bissle meshugga' (a bit mad) to rant and rage like that."

As a result she was called into Morris Podguszer's office.

"Miss Cohen, my wife tells me that, when she rebuked you, you turned to your neighbour and in a voice that the whole workshop could hear accused her of being mad. Such comments are totally unacceptable and you must apologise."

"Mr Podguszer, I've never been screamed at like that and I'd done nothing wrong. I've never heard such a tirade over so trifling an issue. She shouts like that at all the staff. I've never seen or heard such irrational behaviour. My comment was whispered in private to a fellow worker and as such doesn't warrant an apology."

This was a difficult predicament for Morris. Good workers were difficult to find and now that this lively young woman also had a year's contract, he was in no position to dismiss her because of something that Sophia had overheard. The matter was resolved by extracting a promise from Annie Cohen that she would never again make such an utterance about his wife while on the premises, or in public.

This fudged solution did not satisfy Sophia, and an atmosphere of animosity was created in Sophia towards her husband's new protégé. While seemingly contained, it never disappeared and smouldered to resurface from time to time, ultimately with devastating consequences.

In addition to recruiting new staff, Morris had been searching for larger premises, which he ultimately managed to locate in Kingsland Road. This consisted of a dwelling behind which was an extensive garden in which the children could safely play and most important of all, a spacious factory attached to the rear of the house. The main disadvantage to the property was that access to the factory could only be gained by walking through a corridor in the house. Since they'd lived with a similar difficulty before, Morris felt that the problem was acceptable.

Later that year they moved into their new home and factory. As the employees constantly walked through the ground floor of the building, it gave them ample opportunity to meet and get to know the Podguszer children and visa versa. The firm of Podguszer and Company was to remain at 336 Kingsland Road for eighteen years.

Chapter 8

Mark's Story I

1905-1922

Apart from a few Polish words, I remember nothing of my life in Poland, or of the pogroms that finally drove my parents, along with tens of thousands of fellow Jews, from their homes. Nor do I recall the dreadful journey to England my mother so often described to me and the initial sorrows and difficulties experienced when adapting to our new life in London. Only an old stained linen photograph, frayed at the edges, of me seated, naked on a bear rug, in a photographer's studio in Warsaw was left of that earlier life. Perhaps it was kept to remind me that I had once lived somewhere other than London for clearly scrawled on the lower corner of the photograph below the studio address was 'Mark Podguszer 1901'

My earliest memories were of the terror and pain when I was admitted to the London Hospital with appendicitis. Perhaps it wasn't the hurt that I remember, so much as the revulsion to the two huge scars that I have been able to see and feel ever since; the abdominal appendix wound over McBurney's point, named after Dr. Charles Mc Burney who in 1889 working at the Roosevelt hospital in New York first described typhlitis, later termed appendicitis and the second far larger scar in my right loin from the drainage tubes inserted by Sir Frederick Treves the renowned London Hospital surgeon.

In 1902 King Edward VII experienced severe abdominal pain two days before his coronation. He consulted the surgeon Sir Frederick Treves, who diagnosed typhlitis and advised the king to postpone his coronation to undergo surgery. The King was reluctant to accept this advice until Treves assured him that if he delayed there would be a funeral in place of the coronation. The following day the operation was successfully performed at Buckingham Palace and the coronation postponed until a few months later.

Somehow I survived my operation to continue my education to become an English gentleman. Speaking mainly Yiddish at home, I learned English at school and Hebrew at *chedar* (religious classes), where a succession of Hebrew teachers cuffed my head, boxed and twisted my ears and tormented me three evenings a week and every Sunday morning as they did my younger brother Harry and the other boys. I escaped these ordeals when I became Barmitzvah at 13 years and enjoyed that fleeting moment of glory when the women threw down raisins and sweets from the synagogue gallery and later that evening we had a modest celebratory chicken dinner at home with my parents and close family.

When reviewing some of my childhood escapades, I often chuckle, at memories of those in company with my younger brother Harry. He was less than two years younger and was a constant stalwart, until my military service and, marriage gradually eroded our boyhood camaraderie. I could never have dreamt in those years of my childhood that during the last nine years of my life Harry and I would never speak to each other again.

It was the custom among the newest immigrants, regardless of religion or previous nationality, to belong to one of the many local pre-teen Eastend street gangs. Should we wander into another gang's territory, unless accompanying a parent, there was always the likelihood of being chased. We would need to run like hares to escape being pushed and punched, or to avoid the more distant ill aimed broadside of catapult missiles and over ripe fruit. There were also the periodic scraps, following encounters with those none gang members, who called us,

"Dirty Jews!" and "Christ killers!" with the resulting torn and dirtied clothes and occasional bloodied nose; Few amongst us seemed to realise, or worry about our desperate poverty. While we strove for an education our parents worked every available hour, mainly in sweatshops, to improve our lot as they also struggled to master the rudiments of the English language. But all in all it was a happy childhood in London's Eastend with its teeming mainly eastern European immigrants.

Only when looking back over half a century to those early émigré days do I realise that two predominant things that we took so much for granted are now missing. Those were the all-pervading smells and every conceivable kind of raucous noise.

Each morning before ones eyes opened the smell of the bedside chamber pot, plus odours of unwashed bodies overwhelmed us. There was always the morning chore of carrying chamber pots and emptying them in the outhouse while fastidiously holding ones nose with the other hand, without spilling too much of the contents in passageways and on stairs. It was better than a trip to the outhouse in the dark and cold of night.

Where there were infants and young children, as in our home, the stinking smell of ammonia from nappies engulfed the whole apartment every moment of the day and night, seeping out under front doors into the communal stair-well, to mix with the stale stench from washed clothes, unwashed clothes, unwashed bodies, over-cooked vegetables and the vomit that hadn't been cleared up from the gentile neighbours' previous night's alcoholic pub binges.

Of course there were pleasant aromas from pantry and kitchen, whether freshly baked bread or brewing coffee, and in the streets every small grocery shop had barrels of pickled cucumbers, pickled herrings and spices which at times even masked the ever prevalent stench in every road of the yellow brown droppings left by the horses that laboriously pulled every size and shape of wheeled vehicle. There was the daily sight of urchins and men who rushed out with buckets and shovels to garner up this free golden harvest to fertilise flowerpot and garden. Close at hand were market smells and the all-pervading pong associated with discarded rotting fruit, vegetable and animal matter. There was the stench and odour of washdays and the ever-present reek of coal delivered by the sack load, or purchased by the poor, like us, in bucket or bag, and black smoke from steam engines and countless chimneys. Accompanying these constant assaults on nasal senses was the unwavering cacophony of sound from horse's hooves, street vendors, the name calling and screams amongst families and the nocturnal cries of those distressed by pain, and the regular alcoholic fights and beatings, both outside and within the home. Always in close attendance upon this noise and stench were the pestilential buzzing flies, cockroaches, body and head lice, bed bugs and the enormous rodent infestation, necessitating that cats be kept by almost every household, which in turn produced more noxious odours and nocturnal screeching.

In those early years we seldom enjoyed the luxury of a daytime visit to the countryside, let alone an annual vacation. The closest approach we had to nature was a visit to Black Lion Yard, off Old Montague Street, where the local dairy was situated along with a plethora of jewellery shops, visited by those about to be married busily selecting engagement and wedding rings. There, farmyard smells encompassed us. In childhood wonderment we watched as the cows were milked in their stalls, following which we were given a deliciously warm glass of fresh milk to drink, with no thoughts of pasteurisation. As we drank we could gaze at buckets of milk being poured into large urns, secured on either side of the back of a donkey, which would then be led into the street by a milkmaid to be sold by the jug or pot-full as she walked through the nearby streets, alleys and lanes.

Our fondest recreation was a visit to one of a number of early makeshift cinemas, where a halfpenny would secure admission to sit on a wooden bench with a small bag of gob-stoppers, which were included in the price of admission. Even then, we would leave our seats feigning a need to visit the toilet and allow a waiting friend to enter unseen through the exit door, saving the price of admission.

Our gentile neighbours, particularly when there had been too much to drink, which was a regular occurrence on Friday evenings and weekends, believed in strong corporal punishment. The cries and sounds we clearly heard were the horrendous evidence of what went on, often at night. Fortunately as children our parents never beat or abused us. Father was far too calm and gentle and mother was never nimble enough to catch us, although she often managed some formidable tongue-lashings.

Apart from Saturday afternoons, Mother had little time for socialising. She considered that each minute spent on such frivolous moments meant less bread on our plates. It came as a pleasant surprise when our next-door neighbour announced they were having guests to celebrate their daughter's marriage and could mother please lend them our cutlery for the wedding dinner. All the cutlery was taken next door and mother assumed that at the very least she and father would be invited in for the traditional pre-nuptial drink and to admire the bride in her white dress before the bridal party set off for the wedding.

That mealtime we ate our food with our fingers. When mother saw and heard the wedding party return without her and father having been invited in to toast the bride, mother was furious. Harry and I were sent next door into the wedding party where we were instructed to announce as loudly as possible that Mother needed our cutlery back straight away so that we could eat our dinner and on no account were we to return until we had all our cutlery. We waited as the distraught neighbours collected up the knives, forks and spoons before marching triumphantly home. It didn't matter that they didn't speak to us again, because we moved to our new home some weeks later.

Once Harry and I were almost caught red handed when somebody spied us on the roof of the local *mikvah* (ritual bath house) looking through the glass skylight as we endeavoured to catch a glimpse of the naked ladies performing their ritual bathing below. As we made a hasty escape Harry lacerated his hand on a nail. There was blood everywhere and that was the red hand! Mother dealt with the wound by covering it with a cobweb and using a strip of cloth as a bandage. I had to bribe Harry with a capful of foreign postage stamps to guarantee his silence in anticipation of mother's expected interrogation as she investigated how he'd cut his hand so badly.

Just before the war, Harry and I joined Uncle Abe Chisick, mother's eldest brother, a big man well over 6ft tall, on a visit to the races. With individual compartments on the train, there was no room in our compartment for uncle, who sat in the next section and said we should wait for him on the platform when we arrived. A friendly man in our compartment showed us the three-card 'find the lady' trick. It was so simple and he soon relieved us of every penny in our possession, including our return fare money. At our destination we tearfully confessed our folly to uncle Abe, who immediately asked that we point out the rogue before he disappeared in the crowd rushing for the exit. We identified the cardsharp, ran after him and left it to uncle Abe who then accosted him. With the persuasion of two huge menacingly clenched fists and a promise to give him the biggest thrashing of his life, the trickster gladly returned his ill-gotten gains to us.

In early August 1914, just a few months before I was due to leave school the world seemed to turn upside down. There were street riots where shops and offices bearing any semblance of a German name were broken into by mobs intent on looting. Even Dachshund sausage dogs were irrationally stoned and attacked in the streets. German shepherd dogs were renamed Alsatians while, the aristocracy from the King downward found it prudent to anglicise German names. England and France, allied with Russia and Italy, were at war with Germany and the empires of Austro-Hungary and the Ottomans.

My formal education at the Davenant Foundation grammar School in Commercial Road, where I was considered a promising pupil, finished in December, shortly after I turned fourteen, as did my piano lessons, where I had gained a modest proficiency, enabling me to entertain relatives and friends with a few set pieces. My parents didn't have the financial resource to let me proceed further and once school was over, I became fully employed helping my parents in their small but busy factory 'Messrs Podguszer & Co.' making artificial flowers and feather accessories for hats. My first job was attempting to make these flowers, but lacking the skill and dexterity of some of the young women who worked there, I was soon given the task of packing and then delivering goods to various hat manufacturers and wholesalers.

Within a few weeks, dressed in a new dark grey worsted suit and clean white shirt with stiff collar and tie, I looked quite the man about town and accompanied my father when he visited existing and potential customers. He instructed me to watch and observe, as full of bonhomie he taught me to sell. He showed me how to present our merchandise and the various wiles needed to encourage clients to buy our products without us needing to discount prices more than was necessary and at the same time to persuade those with outstanding accounts to pay, without causing offence and encouraging them to place further orders. Following each visit, father would discuss what had transpired and at the end of each day, we would chat over dinner about the day's events, which made me feel increasingly grown up and important.

"Mark, remember that providing you've bought or made your merchandise at the right price, you'll always find a market to sell it."

It seems immodest to admit that I was considered bright and mature for my age. Blessed with a slim pleasing appearance, with cleft chin, ice blue eyes and modest speech without trace of a foreign accent, I was frequently able to persuade our customers to place orders with me, where they might otherwise have prevaricated when father was alone.

With men volunteering for military service in large numbers and women being implored by the government to undertake munitions work in factories, an increasingly severe labour shortage developed. As a consequence, when hardly more than a few months had elapsed since I'd left school I graduated to become a fully-fledged salesman when not yet fifteen.

News of the war was very dispiriting, with no end of the conflict in sight. Following a year of hostilities with mounting numbers of dead and injured, conscription was introduced, as we experienced the first terrors of aerial bombardment from German Zeppelin airships. In April 1918, six months before my eighteenth birthday, the government introduced food-rationing coupons while I received my call up papers notifying me where I was to report for my basic military training. In many ways it was a relief to enter the army. Since I always looked older than my years, housewives and mothers had plagued me by presenting me with those embarrassing white cowardice feathers wherever I went.

When I left home mother's weeping was of little avail as she extracted repeated promises from me to write regularly, and to stay out of danger.

As a newly arrived conscript with a foreign unpronounceable name and as a Jew I rapidly discovered that I was the one who had been chosen to be as much of a victim as the Huns we were being trained to fight.

Stockily built, and having grown up in some of the roughest areas of London, I soon taught my adversaries that I knew how to take care of myself. Following a few rough tussles, the message was passed round that this was one private who couldn't be easily intimidated after which my training progressed without major incident. We drilled repeatedly, as we learned to handle a rifle and bayonet proficiently, even when wearing a gas mask. We learned of the 'creeping barrage' of artillery shells with their high pitched whistle as they passed invisibly overhead that we would follow as we advanced, silently praying that none would fall short, and the use of the 'Bangalore torpedo', an explosive-filled drain pipe that when detonated was supposed to clear a path for us to walk through the tangles of enemy barbed wire, but seldom did.

In October our troop were given a 48-hour pass, as embarkation leave. My parents were sick with worry as we parted for what, judging by the casualty figures, might be the last time. We reported to our port of embarkation, where my comrades, none of whom had ever travelled abroad, thought that this was going to be an exciting adventure. On November 4th, the Austro Hungarian portion of the Axis powers sued for an armistice. While this clearly meant the war was approaching its end there were still fierce battles to be fought, with all the resulting bloody carnage. Two days later, fully kitted out and unaware of our final destination we boarded a cross channel steamer at Harwich. This had been our family port of entry in 1905. In the third week of October 1918 newspapers had reported that Ostend had been liberated with minimal damage to the town and port facilities. A few hours later after embarking on our cross-channel troop transport I was vindicated in guessing that Ostend was most likely to be our destination.

On arrival in Belgium we bivouacked under canvas and simply hung around. Peace rumours abounded and flew around as rapidly as the birds circling and gathering noisily overhead in preparation for an annual migration to some warmer clime.

The war had been going well since the allies' new offensive in mid August. The Germans were being driven out of Flanders and although the trench battles were virtually at an end, the Boche, was still fiercely contesting the war, and the casualties were unabated.

After a delay of several days spent in the wet and cold, our spirits sinking with the progress of autumnal mists and chill, our transports arrived in the form of mud-spattered camouflaged brown double deck buses, which without roof and windows were completely open to the elements. We motored inland on solid tyre wheels for the best part of a day and as we proceeded I became aware of the trucks and horse drawn wagons coming the other way, each with a large red cross painted within a white background on either side; These ambulances carrying the maimed and injured, the dying and the dead, represented the horrendous price of heroism in war. At home, their families, as yet unaware of the fate of their soldier husbands, fathers, brothers and sons who were once whole men, waited for news as these loved ones, benignly written off with the term 'casualty', or the 'fallen in battle', and were no longer called soldiers.

The few trees that lined the road stood as silent sentinels, not merely without leaves, but mostly with shattered trunks and mutilated stumps of absent branches. Mud and water was everywhere. Whether in a hamlet, village, or even a church or a solitary farm, every building revealed varying degrees of pockmarked devastation.

Dusk was fast approaching as, cramped and weary, we arrived at a hamlet, which was used both as a staging post and casualty clearing station. Shirt- sleeved doctors and nurses cared for the wounded brought in by orderlies. There we disembarked, and stood in line to receive a welcome hot meal, following which we were provided with an issue of bully beef and biscuits, our food rations for the next 48 hours.

As we stood about in groups, dirt and fatigue masking our fear of the obscene horrors of war that we had seen and knew lay ahead, almost every man smoked one or more of his issue of Woodbine cigarettes. We were ordered to bed down on straw mattresses in one of a couple of barns and were notified by our sergeant that we'd be moving up to the front at first light.

Early next morning, with barely a chance to have a hot drink and a stale roll, we formed up in single column in the mist and proceeded towards the front. We marched and slithered forward on the slippery mud-caked duckboards that were in place to stop us wallowing ankle and sometimes knee deep in mud and to avoid the evil liquid putrescence that partly filled the countless craters. Helmeted and in our khaki long coats, each infantryman bearing a 60 pound pack on his back, we moved slowly and inexorably towards Ghent, which was still in enemy hands. Loaded down with our packs, gas mask and rifle at the ready, we passed the wounded returning from the front. Bandaged with stained field dressings, moaning and crying out, some walked but most were conveyed on stretchers, as we stepped into the mud to allow them to pass. As the hazy autumnal sun unhurriedly climbed higher above the horizon, slowly lifting the mist, our spirits sank lower. We now realised that what we had believed might be the roll of distant thunder was the increasing crescendo of howitzer and cannon as the smell of cordite drifted in the air. Our progress was unbelievably leaden and slow, with no shelter, or place to sit or rest even momentarily. As the morning wore on, the sergeant in charge told us that we would reach the forward line before mid-day, when, if we were lucky, we could have our break and some food before entering the battle line.

Some of the lads sang 'It's a long way to Tipperary' and other songs to keep our spirits up, but in my mind the only thought was of the sands of time that might be running out.

Suddenly there was an unexpected quiet. No thunder from guns, or explosives, only the sound of our boots squelching and slipping on wooden boards. All around, spreading along the column like a midsummer bushfire was the rustling clamour of "What's up? What's going on? What's happened?" Within minutes a regimental runner arrived at the head of our column with the miraculous news; an armistice had been agreed and the war, thank God, was at an end. This was 11 a.m. on the morning of November 11th. There was to be a peace conference the following summer in Versailles, a token army of occupation in the Rhine, and just victory parades.

With the armistice the remainder of the day brought celebrations, such as we had never seen before. We were over the moon, and by the day's end, as we joined in the general merriment, not one of our platoon retired sober to bed.

I was demobilised in the late spring of 1919. I had been in military service for one year and left at the height of the Spanish Influenza epidemic, which appeared to be particularly lethal to young adults, particularly when living in close proximity as happened in camps amongst military personnel.

When I entered the army in 1918 I was a boy of 17, but a year later with copious exercise, fresh air and the horrors of war fresh in my mind, I had matured and grown in physique.

When I returned home I resumed my employment as a salesman for my parents. Mother, while overjoyed at seeing my safe return, refused to acknowledge that I had become an adult in my own right, intent on making my own decisions. School friends who hadn't seen military service were now a thing of the past as I mixed with a group of older companions, of whom mother strongly disapproved, particularly my non-Jewish girl friends.

Only years later did I discover the devious scheme to which mother resorted, with father's connivance, to encourage me to date a Jewish girl rather than these 'shicksa's (non Jewish girls).

Mother's plan, of which I was totally unaware, was to encourage me to start escorting Annie Cohen, an attractive young Jewish woman in her employ. At some later date once she'd had time to research and make her arrangements, she would make me end the relationship. She would then see that I was introduced to a more suitable young lady endowed with a large dowry whom I would finally marry.

This *shiddach* (arranged marriage) would be organised through contacts of family or friends, who knew of an eligible young woman. Eligibility meant money. In return for marrying his daughter, no matter what her appearance might be, the wealthy father would guarantee setting me up with a comfortable home and a business to match.

I'd met and talked regularly to Annie Cohen, who'd worked for my parents for the past four years. She was single, and although a slim and pretty young woman, she was many years my senior and I had never paid her too much attention.

Mother recognised her as a well brought up young woman from a poor orthodox Jewish family, who was far too old to be interested in her son, since there was almost a four-year age difference. Mother intended that, introducing me to her employee, Annie Cohen, would be the bait to entice me away from my many non-Jewish girl friends. Poor Annie was unwittingly to become the attractive lure to condition me to accept escorting a 'nice Jewish girl' as normal behaviour.

This would then give Mother a brief period of respite in which to find a suitable moneyed shiddach for me. Once this had been achieved mother would break up this temporary relationship. Annie would be sent packing, like some returnable unwanted merchandise, while I would be expected to dutifully follow what Mama said, and marry the young lady selected for me.

Fortunately neither of us was aware that we were about to become pawns in my mother's design. My parents regularly attended the Yiddish theatre, and doubtlessly mother had borrowed this scheme from some romantic fiction they may have seen there. Predictably, a strategy of this complexity was bound to fail, and it certainly did, with the most terrible repercussions.

On my return home just after Easter 1919 as I changed from uniform into civvies, it became clear that I'd filled out and that none of my clothes fitted me properly. I was urgently in need of a new suit, particularly for work, and it was decided that I should visit the tailor to have a suit made. Mother invited Annie Cohen to accompany us for her advice in the choice of material and style, since her father was a master tailor. Any person connected to tailoring, or fabrics, no matter how remotely, was automatically designated a *maven* (an expert) when a suit was to be made. Annie could be included in this category even, though it was her father who was the tailor, and a ladies' tailor at that.

Amongst the most recently arrived Jewish immigrants, whenever it was intended to make any major purchase; there was an accepted formula to be followed. A strict observance was called for of the unwritten eleventh commandment that was akin to a biblical imperative.

'You shall only buy goods trade, or wholesale!'

Nobody knew its origin, passed down through the generations but only gentiles, the most affluent, like the Rothschild's, or the feeble minded ever bought retail. Secondly the individual needing to make the purchase never went alone. The unabridged commandment read;

'You shall only buy goods trade, or wholesale and shall always be accompanied by companions, there being safety in numbers, one or more of whom must be a maven. Bind this instruction to thy cash belt and wallet as a covenant, that thou might always obtain best value for money.'

The shopper would always solicit the help of a number of family experts. The more the better, amongst whom would be the *maven* (expert) and another the negotiator.

Even though one was buying trade there would still be a margin that could be more finely honed to obtain a keener price. There might even be another maven to advise on the style and cut. In short a small retinue was involved in any purchase of more than a few shillings, and the experienced salesperson, knew the complexities of these immigrant-trading patterns.

Within a matter of days following my demob, it didn't come as an unusual surprise to Annie Cohen or me, when mother announced:

"Mark's in urgent need of a new suit for work. As your father's a master tailor would you join us this afternoon to give me your opinion on the fabric and cut of his new suit?" Anne was flattered and agreed.

My mother certainly didn't need Annie Cohen to give her advice, but this was the opening gambit in her complicated scheme.

As we proceeded into the tailors shop we resembled a small platoon on manoeuvres, with mother as the officer in command, fearlessly leading from the front. In addition to the maven, other family members had been invited to join us including all my younger siblings and a small tribe of older relatives. It was felt that with the reassurance of a large group of family and friends, there was some advantage to the shopper.

It took time for our entourage to enter the shop behind mother and, as those of us in the rear arrived we could hear the commencement of the opening reconnoitering probe.

"Good afternoon! How can I help you madam?" politely enquired the smartly dressed salesman in his three-piece suit, as he rushed forward, uncertain of the size of the group he was about to confront.

"We're only looking thank you." Sophia replied, in a well-practised nonchalant manner, in her unashamedly broken English. She had spent the past 14 years in a ceaseless guerilla battle to ambush the English language as only she knew how and there can be little doubt that Sophia, and many like her, finally enriched the native English tongue with many useful expressions in Yiddish and Polish in what could later, best be described as an unofficial truce.

"Look around," invited the salesman.

"How much are you going to charge me to make a three piece suit for a young man?"

"As you can see our sign says that we charge nineteen shillings and eleven pence madam."

"I don't read English so good, and anyway I can't afford such fancy West End prices. Could you make me such a suit for a little less, like, maybe twelve shillings, which is what I had in mind?"

"Madam that would be absolutely impossible, but if you were to purchase your material here, then I think we could accommodate you with a price of nineteen shillings."

"Accommodate, shmaccommodate, maybe if you can make it for fifteen shillings then we can do business."

"Madam, that's impossible. Eighteen shillings and sixpence is absolutely the lowest price."

"Had you said that at the start, we could have agreed straight away on fifteen shillings and six pence and not wasted so much of my time."

"Madam if you could agree to meet me half way at seventeen shillings and six pence then I think I can help you, but not otherwise."

"You drive a hard bargain, but at seventeen shillings it's agreed, as you said."

"Madam I didn't say seventeen. It was seventeen and six."

"If you're suggesting that I'm lying, I have witnesses and I'll need to speak to the owner of this establishment."

"Very well, seventeen shillings." agreed the salesman, as he attempted to avoid further confrontation.

Zoshia, smiled having won the opening foray with a price reduction of 15%.

"I'm looking for material for a man's suit; something smart and hard wearing." "This must be your lucky day madam. Only yesterday we received a shipment of navy blue serge pinstripe. It's the first we've received since the end of the war and it's been selling like hot cakes. Fortunately I've just half a bolt of cloth remaining."

"Alright, show me this fine material that sells so well."

Reaching up to a shelf behind the polished wood counter, the salesman lifted a roll of material down. Spreading it on the counter surface he smiled invitingly, as he claimed,

"This is one of the finest weaves of material that you can find anywhere in London. It's not only as fine as you can see and feel, but it's particularly strong and durable."

"Nu! What do you think?" enquired Sophia, as she turned to Annie with an encouraging smile.

"They may say it's hard wearing, Mrs Podguszer, but I'd have my doubts. I've seen material like this that initially looks good, but starts to shine where it's been worn and even begins to fray at the edges." Another family member, not to be outdone, chimed in with the observation.

"I think you've got a point there, and, anyway, I've seen better goods at Feingold's shop down the road."

"Well, if I was to choose this inferior piece of material for a suit for my son here, who's just been demobbed from the army, and I'm not saying I would choose it, how much would it cost a yard?" Sophia enquired, turning her attention again to the salesman.

The psychology of the moment was distinctly in the customer's favour.

"The price of the material is four shillings and nine pence a yard madam," the salesman announced with a smirk, more akin to the smile a shark gives, as it takes a bite from an unsuspecting passing walrus.

A senior relative explodes with indignation with this announcement.

"Either they're crazy, or they must take you for being a bissle meshuga! (a bit mad). Only the other day I saw the identical pin stripe material in Levy's round the corner. It was almost two shillings a yard less than this *gunuf* (thief) is quoting you for this *shmutter* (rag), and furthermore I'll wager it was probably of better quality."

The salesman unwilling to lose a sale and ignoring the insult continued:

"I want to assure you madam that this material is manufactured exclusively for this tailoring establishment. Whatever your friend may have seen elsewhere is undoubtedly a cheap copy that would fade in the sunlight, or shrink when cleaned, and would only have been cheaper because it was sub-standard. On the other hand I would be prepared to cut our profit to the bone, forego my commission and would practically be giving the material away by reducing the material by six pence a yard to four and thru' pence, if you agree to make your purchase to-day."

For the novice, the transaction would have ended at this juncture with the purchaser agreeing to the reduced price, but not my mother. For her, the game was afoot, and she was enjoying the chase. One of the maven knowingly asserted in a loud stage whisper to her:

"Better quality material giving better value for money you can find elsewhere! While they mightn't have the identical pattern, there's bound to be something close to it. I'll show you. Just follow me. It's not far."

With a curt,

"Thanks but not at that price." directed at the salesman, Sophia pivoted through 180 degrees towards the door. Without any indication of instruction, or the presence of a drill sergeant, her entire entourage simultaneously turned together, as though in a rehearsed trooping of the colours, and started to move in slow time towards the door, in pursuit of the maven. The salesman, experienced in such matters, rushed forward attempting to place himself between this interfering family busybody and the door as he declared:

"Wait, why be so hasty? If you really have your heart set on this particular fabric, let me go into the cutting room and speak to my boss. Maybe he'll see what can be done. After all we don't want to disappoint our brave young war hero do we?"

Sophia waited, with a knowing smile on her face. After a brief disappearance the salesclerk returned declaring,

"My governor tells me that he can let you have the material at four-pence a yard less, which makes it three and eleven, but that has to be the final offer."

"Well. I think it's only worth two and eleven, a shilling less than you've priced it." announced Sophia, sensing the concluding skirmish was about to begin.

"That's impossible! It costs us more than that to buy it," retorted the salesman. At that moment he was joined by reinforcements from the cutting room, in the form of the proprietor and one of the cutting room staff, both of who then nodded in synchronised agreement.

"That's my final offer. Take it or leave it!" Sophia snapped, indicating in her voice that this game had tired her and she had better things to do with her time for her weary troop.

Seemingly in deep distress the salesman shook his head from side to side replying, with appropriate negative nods from his colleagues.

"It just can't be done at that price."

With a shrug, followed by a silent nod from Zoshia indicating it was time to go, the tribe gave every indication of trooping to the exit once more, while some of the younger members, bored by this negotiating ritual, had deserted the field of conflict and gone through the door to escape to the pavement, teeming with more interesting activity outside.

The owner, having surreptitiously edged round the counter in a pincer movement to position himself between the door and departing customers spoke for the first time.

"At the original price the material is wonderful value. If we take a further three pence off, making it three and eight, we'll not be making any profit, but at least, if you accept and promise not to tell anyone else of such a bargain price, we'll know that to-day, before we close the shop, we'll have created one more satisfied customer. What do you say?"

Sophia stopped. A hurriedly brief top-level conversation ensued with the *maven* (expert) and Mark, before she turned moments later and brightly announced.

"Alright. Three shillings and eight pence is highway robbery but we haven't any more time to waste shopping elsewhere today. The children are getting restless and want their tea. so it's agreed."

The battle may have been won but there was still the final skirmish with the booby trap. The negotiations started afresh concerning the amount of material that would be needed to make one jacket, one waistcoat and one pair of pants for that young man, with mother emphasising young, implying the need for less material even though I was a full grown muscular adult 5 feet 7 inches tall. As those further discussions ensued, the younger family members were herded back into the shop where they dutifully felt lengths of material with sticky dirty fingers in spite of the repeated adult admonitions.

"Don't touch!" and "Behave, or else!"

At last the quantity was agreed. Three yards of material would be required. As discussions ensued concerning the style of suit, the salesperson smugly convinced himself that those three yards would generously provide sufficient 'cabbage' (material left over with which to make a further garment) to make another jacket, possibly for his own son, and even a waistcoat for himself.

Without ever realising that she suffered from a mild nominal aphasia when under stress, Sophia always found herself needing to run rapidly through the names of all her progeny whenever she felt rushed to find the correct child. Stridently she summonsed her youngest son. "Marky, Harry, Annie, Essie, Becky, Solly! Solly, where are you hiding? Come here child and stand still where I can see you!" As her ten year old dutifully stepped forward, she released the catch on her oversized handbag removing her purse and then extracted and methodically counted, in Yiddish, the money that would be the deposit on the new suit. Tantalisingly clutching the coins in clear view for the salesperson to see as she continued:

"Since my youngest son here is so small, surely with the material left over and at the same price you could make this young boy a pair of pants?" enquired mother innocently releasing the booby- trap.

With the money so temptingly close and yet not quite within his grasp, it would be foolhardy to jeopardise this sale for the sake of one pair of child's trousers. Such a small garment would cost very little to make, use a negligible amount of material and, providing the cloth was cut really carefully, might still leave sufficient for that waistcoat.

"Madam, you drive the hardest of bargains, but agreed."

The deposit was paid and the date agreed for the first fitting.

"And don't forget to leave a big hem in the jacket sleeves and in the pants for both boys so that there's plenty to let out as they grow." emphasised Sophia. Turning to her employee she then announced.

"Annie Cohen, you can take the rest of the afternoon off, and Mark, you escort the young lady to Lyons for tea, while I get back home with the children and see what's happening at the factory."

"But Mrs Podguszer, there's still lots of unfinished work. I need to go back with you."

"Nonsense, you deserve a little time off for having helped this afternoon. Have tea with Mark and if you feel it's necessary you can always stay a little later tomorrow evening." Game, set and match!

Within days the suit was ready for the first fitting and Annie Cohen was invited on this and each subsequent occasion, followed by time off to go to tea with me.

I admit I was a little nervous at escorting an attractive young lady, so much older than myself, even if it was only to have a cup of tea and share a pastry in one of the Lyons teashops with their waitresses in white caps and pinafores scurrying to serve the customers seated at the marble topped tables. Within a few moments I soon realised that age was not a hindrance. We had known each other for almost four years. She knew all my family and it felt as if we were old friends chatting, laughing and making small talk together, without any hint of embarrassment.

With my return to work as a salesman for Messrs Podguszer and Company, business picked up in the wake of the post war euphoria and I earned substantial commissions from my sales. With more money in my pocket than I'd ever had before I could indulge the passion I had acquired from my father for the opera and ballet. I bought a record player, with its huge brass trumpet horn, purchased a small but growing collection of records and soon regularly attended the Royal Opera House Covent Garden and the Stoll Theatre, always sitting in the least expensive gallery seats.

I disliked attending these productions by myself and invited Annie Cohen, who had never been to an opera. Having escorted her to the theatre I would accompany her home safely and, in this way met her parents, brothers and sisters. Her parents, who knew my father, made me welcome.

There were some major differences immediately apparent between the Cohen household and the Podguszers. Jacob and Sarah Cohen were far more orthodox and their home was always so hushed and peaceful. There was none of the shouting and frequent boisterous arguments that were a part of mother's Chisick inheritance. Mr. Cohen always had his head covered, had his own *shteeble* (small synagogue) in a room on the second floor of his home, while Mrs Cohen, a well educated lady who wore a *sheitle* (a wig, worn by very orthodox married Jewish women), had developed her own enterprise, counselling, translating and writing letters for a great number of illiterate immigrants.

I enjoyed Annie's company right from the start, and she mine, in what was entirely a platonic friendship. My parents approved of our friendship and seemingly encouraged it. After we'd been to the theatre two or three times, I invited her to accompany me to a Henry Wood promenade concert at The Queen's Hall.

"Mark Podguszer! You see me every day at work and you keep inviting me to accompany you to all these theatres and concerts. Are you asking me to 'walk out' with you?"

"Now that you mention it Annie, I do enjoy your company, so the answer's a resounding yes. How does that appeal to you?"

"Well I'm flattered but I've a couple of things to consider. My parents have to approve."

"Yes and anything else?"

"Once you stop calling me Annie and call me Ann without an e after the double n then I think we can agree that we're walking out."

We walked out or dated for more than a year. During that time I learned more about her family and met all her brothers and sisters but one.

"Ann, I've met every one except your older brother Abe. Doesn't he live in London?" I enquired.

"That's a rather sore point."

"Why's that?"

"Father has forbidden us to see him, or even talk about him at home."

"What's the mystery?"

"I wish it were as simple as that!"

"What do you mean?"

"If you feel that you must know, and you promise not to talk about it in my home, I'll explain. The truth is that he married out. When the war started he went to work in a clothing factory making army uniforms. He met Annie Sage, a girl who worked at the next workbench and who wasn't Jewish. They fell in love and went out together for six months. In April 1915, although none of us had ever met her, they were secretly married in a registry office and he still continued to live at home. Soon afterwards he received his call up papers and, because of poor vision, went into the pioneer corps. Without any of us knowing anything about it Annie had a little boy in December 1916. They called him Leonard and Abe never breathed a word about his marriage or his little boy to any of us. It was all a big secret.

A few months ago Abe was demobbed. He obviously couldn't live at home, with his wife and son living somewhere else, so he finally brought Annie and little Leonard round to our home to see my parents. He was a lovely little fellow and looked just like his daddy. We all sat down to tea and to begin with mother and father said they were very upset because he'd married without telling them. Then Abe explained that the reason was that Annie wasn't Jewish, but that she was prepared to convert.

Everyone went deathly quiet. Father was furious and said some awful things to Abe. Then mother started to cry and so did my sisters and I. It was horrible. Father shouted and told him he was no son of his and that he'd brought disgrace on the Cohen family. He ordered Abe and Annie out of the house. He said that he never wanted to see or hear from him ever again and that he was going to sit *shiva* (seven days of official mourning).

Abe and Annie and then little Leonard all cried. It was all too terrible for words. Abe left with his family and that's how it's been these past months. Leonard was such a sweet innocent little boy and none of us have dared say a word about any of them in front of father. So I think it's best that we just don't talk about my brother, or his family in front of my parents for the time being."

Ann and I had been dating for almost nine months when I decided it was time in the late summer of 1920 that I asked Ann's father for his consent to become engaged to his daughter. Smiling he gave us his blessing as he took out a bottle of wine, then made us all sit at the table where we drank a toast that he made to our health and happiness 'Lechayem'. I explained to Ann that I intended speaking to my parents that evening. As I returned home I felt so happy it felt as though I was walking on air and, although I could barely contain myself, I decided to wait until after supper to tell my parents. We were all seated round the dinner table when I told them that I'd spoken to Ann's father and that he'd given his approval to our engagement.

Had I dropped a Mill's grenade bomb into the living room that evening, the resulting bloodless tumult could have been no less explosive. It was my mother with her Chisick inheritance who did all the raging and shouting, interspersed when she stopped for breath, with father's more reasoned talking. Could a verbal assault be worse than a physical battering? After that evening I would say categorically that anybody who knew my mother at that time could never have been in any doubt. Yes.

In a more reasoned context their disapproval centred upon several mainly false assumptions. Annie Cohen, one of their workers, was a mature woman endeavouring to seduce the boss's son, who was four years her junior, into marriage only to improve her working class station in life. Their eldest son was an inexperienced boy, who at nineteen had no knowledge of the world, or a woman's wiles.

Yes I agreed that Ann was an employee and there was no denying she was older and possibly more mature than me, but there had been no seduction and believing I had my parent's approval, I had chased after her and not the other way round. I disagreed that I was an inexperienced child and explained that anybody who'd spent even a few days as an infantryman in Flanders could never be accused of having no knowledge of the world. That experience alone had provided me with enough nightmares to fill a lifetime.

Worse than the hand grenade was my parents' insistence that I give up all thought of an engagement, since they had, over the past week, arranged a shiddach with an influential moneyed family. The following week I was to meet Millicent at the home of Jason and Sally Rothstein who lived in an apartment in George Street in the West End. Rothstein was in a big way in the ladies couture gown business and had only one daughter. My mother screamed,

"You'll meet her and you'll get to know her! She's too thin and needs feeding, but she's pretty enough. You'll get engaged and then married and Mr. Rothstein will take you into his business. You'll have a magnificent home, maybe with servants, and there you'll raise children. You'll never have financial worries or want for anything. That's all that really matters in this life. It's been arranged, so I want no more arguments."

I lived at home, and worked for my parents. I was too young at 19 to marry without parental consent. I couldn't function independently in spite of my bravado. Unable to withstand my mother's angry words and gesticulatory stormy tantrum, I felt that I had no other option than to break my engagement with Ann and so I reluctantly agreed.

The following afternoon at the conclusion of work I was in a terrible state. I had to break the news to Ann and I didn't know how to tell her, poor girl.

"I want to walk you home. I've something terribly important to tell you." I said.

As we started our walk, arms entwined, Ann enquired,

"You sound so serious Mark. Is there anything amiss?"

"Yes, you've hit the nail on the head. There's something terribly wrong and that's why I need to speak to you in private."

"Don't be so secretive, darling, tell me what it is."

"Ann I don't know what to say, but I must tell you, even though you're going to hate me forever."

"Darling nothing that you could possibly say or do would make me change my feelings and love for you. What's troubling you?"

"It all started last night after I told my parents that I'd asked your father for permission to marry you and that he'd agreed. It was supposed to be one of the happiest moments of my life, but it wasn't. It turned into the worst nightmare of my life."

"What in heaven's name are you saying? Tell me Mark! What on earth happened?"

"All hell broke loose. I've heard my mother rant and rage, but never the histrionics last night. She said some really terrible things. Until I'm 21 the law states that I can't marry without parental consent and she said that she'd never in a million years give her consent to me marrying you. I can fight and die in uniform but the law say's that I'm still a minor."

"Well then, we'll wait until the end of next year when you're 21 and their consent won't be needed."

"It won't work. They insist I break off any engagement, official or unofficial, with you, because they've already arranged a shiddach. It's with some girl from a wealthy family that I've never met and they approve of."

"I can't believe what you're telling me! What are we going to do?"

"Ann, I'm still under twenty. I've no capital, I live at home with my parents, work for my parents and I'm beholden to them for my accommodation, my clothes, my food, in fact everything. I adore you and shall never love anyone else, but try to see it from my point of view. I'm in no position to disobey them or go against them in any way."

"Are you trying to tell me that our engagement is over?"

"Yes. My parents insist."

"I can't believe my ears. You simply don't love me. You're a sham. Nothing more than a spineless mummy's boy, while I thought I was engaged in marriage to a man. Somebody who wouldn't just care for me, but for the children we might have one day. It's lucky you didn't give me an engagement ring, because it saves me having to throw it back at your feet."

"Ann, you've no idea how my mother can bully and shout. She's a tyrant who rules and manipulates our household as she chooses. I'm in no position to contradict her wishes. But it's you I love. I worship you and the very ground you walk on. I'll always love.."

"Oh do stop it Mark! Stop! You're driving that bayonet blade deeper inside and twisting it with all your false protestations of love."

"I stand by every word I've said. I adore you but I simply can't fight my parents."

"You're willing to wound me horribly and completely ruin my life, but afraid to strike a blow against your parents for the right to secure our happiness. I can't take any more of this. Please leave me alone. Just go away and don't talk to me anymore."

"Look I know how upset you must be, but I want to go home with you to explain the situation to your parents."

"No Mark. You don't know how upset I feel. Perhaps you never will until someone breaks your heart. But don't worry on my account. I'm not quite an old maid just yet and I assure you there are plenty of other fish in the sea."

"At least let me see you home."

"Thank you. No! That really won't be necessary. I'd prefer to walk alone and when I get home I can do my own explaining. I'm an adult, which is more than I can say for you. Go home! I wouldn't want to keep you from Mummy and the shiddach she's arranged for her little boy."

There's no point denying that there weren't a few tears, but as she turned and briskly walked away with those short-mincing steps that I so adored, I could see how upset I'd made her. Slowly I walked home feeling a deep sense of shame at the great hurt I'd caused the woman I truly loved. I'd behaved like an utter heel.

Candidly I was amazed that she turned up for work next morning, as though nothing had happened, although there were the telltale despondent rings of red round both her eyes that couldn't be concealed. She continued working for my parents, where it was something of an embarrassment for us to keep meeting every day. She never once lost her composure or gave any indication of the humiliation to which she'd been subjected, simply treating me formally as though the past year of our friendship had never existed. For my part, I was completely devastated.

Reluctantly I met Millicent Rothstein on a number of occasions with both our parents' approval. The Rothstein's lived in a magnificent apartment in George Street and seventeen year old Millicent, a delightfully pretty slim brunette had no interests other than to go dancing and visit the cinema several times each week. While I thought of her as slim I was somehow reminded of those civilians I'd seen in 1918 who'd been freed following the German occupation of their towns and villages. They had been on short rations for years and were emaciated and hungry. Millicent certainly wasn't starved, but I did notice that, when we dined together, she would only order a salad and ate no more than a few lettuce leaves.

After a courtship of several months our engagement was announced. Mr Rothstein agreed that now I was to become his son in law, I should join him in his business. I left my job with my parents and started working for Rothstein Gowns of Mortimer Street. As Jason Rothstein explained, I would need to learn something about the business and could only do so by performing some of the more menial tasks before progressing up the managerial ladder.

Enthusiastically I entered into the spirit of my new work but soon noticed one or two things that perturbed me. Ladies couture clothes were designed and made on the premises. Assisting in the design and modelling of these intricate garments were many young ladies who were frequently in various stages of undress.

It soon became apparent that J.R., as he wished to be called, who designed most of these creations, considered these young models, many of who were teenagers younger than his own daughter, his private serfs living in his domain to be used as he wished.

But there was more. I noticed that most afternoons J.R. appeared to have a problem with his gait. Not only did he have difficulty with his walking, but at times, his speech was slurred and occasionally he would fly into an unaccountable rage, following which he would disappear completely for the remainder of the day. I realized that my future father in law was a womaniser of the worst kind, taking advantage of girls who were younger than his daughter and he was also a secret shickerer (alcoholic). While these matters were really none of my business I felt that this was hardly the sort of family circle I wished to enter, or have any part in, in spite of my mother's approval of their business and affluence.

Matters finally came to a head one afternoon when a problem arose in the workroom and J.R. was, as usual, nowhere to be found. An important order of tulle material that had been expected the previous week had not been delivered and certain garments required for the following day remained unfinished.

I contacted the supplier who complained that he hadn't been paid. Not only had he not been paid for deliveries over the past month, in spite of assurances given by J.R. but also money had remained outstanding over many months. The supplier was adamant that no further material would be delivered until these accounts were settled. I assured him that J.R. was an honourable man and that I would check the accounts to see where the error lay.

I went into J.R,'s office to check the bank statements and there soon found the cause of our predicament. Not knowing of any problem J.R.

might have had, apart from his drinking I was confronted by something that at first I couldn't believe.

Lying on the top in his desk drawer were documents, which I quickly read. Letters from the bank and many of his suppliers revealed that all of them were threatening to call a creditors' meeting, unless they received immediate payment. In simple terms Rothstein Gowns was probably insolvent, with the chief executive officer an alcoholic and a womaniser. In no way was I prepared, even at the behest of my meddlesome mother, to marry into a bankrupt family with an alcoholic father whose daughter was anorexic. It was all too much.

I delivered a letter to Millicent terminating our engagement. I explained that, since I'd never learned to ballroom dance and didn't enjoy film shows, I felt we had too little in common to continue our relationship. She never returned the silver band engagement ring, engraved with its floral and heart design that mother had provided, and I secretly hoped that it might at least provide the wherewithal for her to purchase as many lettuce leaves as she might need for the foreseeable future.

I returned home that evening and told my parents what I'd done.

Initially mother didn't believe me. However once I'd convinced her of the facts she was of course disappointed that her scheme had gone awry, but told me not to be too upset, as she was convinced that within a matter of days she could explore London and would have found me another suitable 'shiddach'. It would only be a matter of time.

I resumed employment with my parents where my broken engagement became common knowledge. Plucking up my courage I decided to ask Ann out once again. I practised for days the words and phrases I might use to confront her expected rebuff. Then I invited her to an opera at Covent Garden.

I told her that I'd been given two tickets. As I expected she refused at first, but after considerable persuasion agreed to accompany me, just that once, my having convinced her that if she didn't join me the ticket I was offering her would go to waste. By the autumn of 1922 Ann and I had resumed our former friendship and, once again assuring her of my love I told her that I would like us to become engaged, but that this time I would first speak to my parents.

Again I broached the subject and once more their parental opposition to the suggestion was no less vehement.

"No! no! no! That girl's not good enough for you. I should better have a kidney stone, maybe even two stones, one in each side, than that young woman as a daughter in law," raged my mother.

I was now 21, and determined that Ann should become my wife, but with my parents vehement antagonism, how was this ever to be achieved?

Arnold Powell

The Family Tree Of Sophia Podguszer

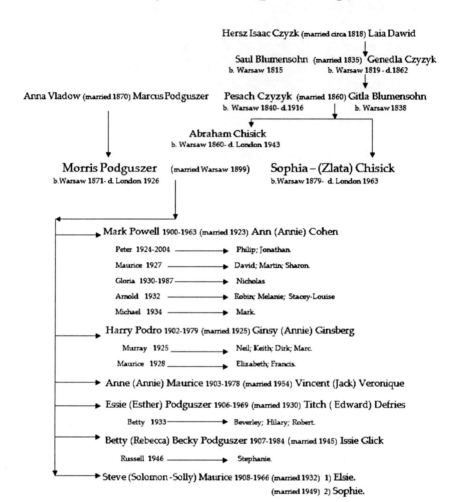

Hersz Isaac Czyzk (married circa 1818) Laia Dawid

Saul Blumensohn (married 1835) Genedla Czyzyk
b. Warsaw 1815   b. Warsaw 1819 - d.1862

Anna Vladow (married 1870) Marcus Podguszer   Pesach Czyzyk (married 1860) Gitla Blumensohn
                                                b. Warsaw 1840- d.1916   b. Warsaw 1838

Abraham Chisick
b. Warsaw 1860- d. London 1943

Morris Podguszer   (married Warsaw 1899)   Sophia – (Zlata) Chisick
b.Warsaw 1871- d. London 1926   b.Warsaw 1879- d. London 1963

Mark Powell 1900-1963 (married 1923) Ann (Annie) Cohen

    Peter 1924-2004 ————————▶ Philip; Jonathan.

    Maurice 1927 ———————▶ David; Martin; Sharon.

    Gloria 1930-1987————————▶ Nicholas

    Arnold 1932 ————————▶ Robin; Melanie; Stacey-Louise

    Michael 1934 ————————▶ Mark.

Harry Podro 1902-1979 (married 1925) Ginsy (Annie) Ginsberg

    Murray 1925 ——————— Neil; Keith; Dirk; Marc.

    Maurice 1928 ——————▶ Elizabeth; Francis.

Anne (Annie) Maurice 1903-1978 (married 1954) Vincent (Jack) Veronique

Essie (Esther) Podguszer 1906-1969 (married 1930) Titch (Edward) Defries

    Betty 1933————————▶ Beverley; Hilary; Robert.

Betty (Rebecca) Becky Podguszer 1907-1984 (married 1945) Issie Glick

    Russell 1946 ————————▶ Stephanie.

Steve (Solomon -Solly) Maurice 1908-1966 (married 1932) 1) Elsie.
(married 1949) 2) Sophie.

Ann Powell and Sophia Podguszer on 1st Dec 1957
Celebrating at the Mayfair Hotel

Sophia Podguszer
(Warsaw circa 1899)

Circa 1947 Essie Defries & Sophia Podguszer seated.

Standing Steve Maurice, Anne Maurice,
Betty Defries and Titch Defries in dinner suit.

Issie and Betty Glick
April 1973

Harry and Ginsy July 1925

1913 Wedding of Louisa Chisick to Louis Hart

Taking the bride as the starting point. On the right her husband Louis Hart. On the left is her mother Betty and to her left Betty's husband Abraham Chisick.

On his shoulder is the hand of his sister, Sophia Podguszer aged 34. Above and to the right of Sophia is her eldest son Mark aged 12 also with a hand on his shoulder. To Sophia's right (behind the bride and her mother) is her sister Zelda and husband Sam Kelter Returning to Abraham. To his left is his mother Geitle and to her left, at the end of the row, with the white beard is Pesach Cyzyk. Immediately behind Geitle and Pesach is their son in law Morris Podguszer aged about 41. Pesach Cyzyck is holding Solly Podguszer aged 4 (later Steve Maurice) and to the right is Annie Podguszer aged 10, pertly holding a finger to her cheek (later Anne Veronique). Sixth child to the right of Annie is Essie and seventh child, Becky Podguszer. Blurred In the right hand corner, is Harry Podguszer.

Chishick Wedding 1913. Enlargement of photo from previous page. Front from left, Pesach and Geitle Cyzyk, their eldest son Abraham Chishick and his wife Beila. Rear, Left Morris and Sophia (née Cyzyk) Podguszer; Zelda (néeCyzyk) Kelter.

Steve and Sophie Maurice Wedding 1950

Ann Cohen & Mark Podguszer
Summer 1919.

Mark and Anne Powell Sept 1955

Mark Powell April 1947

Abraham Chisick and Sophia Czyzyk Family Tree

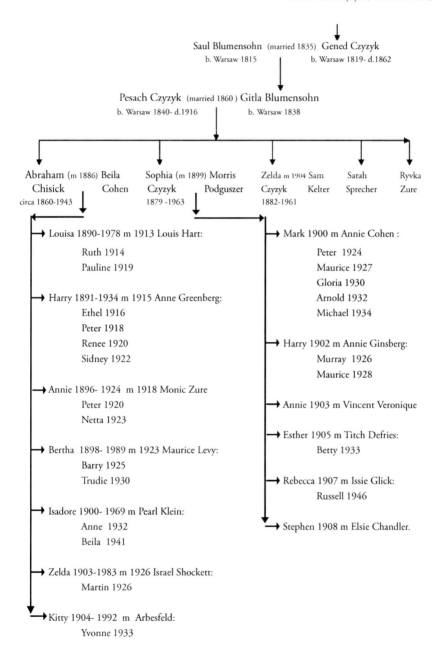

Hersz Isaac Czyzyk (married circa 1818)

Saul Blumensohn (married 1835) Gened Czyzyk
b. Warsaw 1815   b. Warsaw 1819- d.1862

Pesach Czyzyk (married 1860) Gitla Blumensohn
b. Warsaw 1840- d.1916   b. Warsaw 1838

Abraham (m 1886) Beila   Sophia (m 1899) Morris   Zelda m 1904 Sam   Sarah   Ryvka
Chisick   Cohen   Czyzyk   Podguszer   Czyzyk   Kelter   Sprecher   Zure
circa 1860-1943   1879 -1963   1882-1961

Louisa 1890-1978 m 1913 Louis Hart: Mark 1900 m Annie Cohen :
    Ruth 1914   Peter 1924
    Pauline 1919   Maurice 1927
                  Gloria 1930
Harry 1891-1934 m 1915 Anne Greenberg: Arnold 1932
    Ethel 1916   Michael 1934
    Peter 1918
    Renee 1920   Harry 1902 m Annie Ginsberg:
    Sidney 1922   Murray 1926
                  Maurice 1928
Annie 1896- 1924 m 1918 Monic Zure
    Peter 1920   Annie 1903 m Vincent Veronique
    Netta 1923
              Esther 1905 m Titch Defries:
Bertha 1898- 1989 m 1923 Maurice Levy: Betty 1933
    Barry 1925
    Trudie 1930   Rebecca 1907 m Issie Glick:
                  Russell 1946
Isadore 1900- 1969 m Pearl Klein:
    Anne 1932   Stephen 1908 m Elsie Chandler.
    Beila 1941

Zelda 1903-1983 m 1926 Israel Shockett:
    Martin 1926

Kitty 1904- 1992 m Arbesfeld:
    Yvonne 1933

Chapter 9

1962

I'm still waiting, this time in the lounge. In fact when I'm not sleeping I always seem to be waiting. There's no communal activity, nothing to keep my wits active and nothing to do except wait, or watch some mindless television programme, eat a meal, or sleep. Almost all the other residents have either received their visitors, or gone with them for a visit somewhere, but I'm still waiting. In fact I'm no longer conscious of waiting, as I've dozed off to sleep. It was either that, or stare at that infernal television set with its more often than not, flickering screen, as though one had a seat in the silent movies.

Apart from the TV the only other activity is to chat with ones neighbours. Such scintillating conversation you shouldn't wish on your worst enemies! Most of them here don't know the time of day; let alone the day, or the month. The few that one can talk with keep repeating the same stories and supposedly amusing anecdotes, ad-nauseam, day after dreary day. There's not even any-one here with who I can pass away the hours with a game of cards.

My main fear is not death, but that I should be losing my mind like most of the people here. Even that isn't so terrible if you don't know it's happened, but to realise that one is losing ones mental faculties, and can do nothing about it, is one of the worst aspects of aging.

"Wake up Sophie, wake up, you've got visitors!" Slowly I awaken. I realise I'm being gently shaken and roused from my deep slumber by a carer. As I open my eyes I'm surrounded by a number of smiling faces, seemingly leering, or are they smiling at me. Initially there's not one that I recognise.

It takes me a few moments to clear my mind and, as I'm doing so, one of the voices that belong to a man keeps repeating.

"Say hello to grandma and give her a kiss!"

Ah ha, a clue. Providing they've got the right person it would seem that one or more of these people are grandchildren, but I don't seem to recognise any of them. One of the strangest aspects of ageing is that many of us somehow start to look alike and it's quite possible they've found the wrong old lady. Should I go along with this mistaken identity and enjoy a brief visit from people I don't know, hoping they may take me out for a drive in the country, or possibly to tea, or should I explain they've found the wrong person?

Suddenly salvation is at hand as one of the carers who has been shaking me gently by the shoulder repeatedly saying,

"Wake up Mrs Maurice! Wake up, you've got visitors." offers me a lifeline.

"Wake up Mrs Maurice and say hello to Peter."

Now Peter Chisick was the name of my old father. I last saw him 50 years ago at my niece's London wedding, when he looked better than I probably do now, and I'd recognise him anytime, but this was a far younger man. Rapidly I go through all the family names and realise that this must be my eldest grandson.

They say that when an individual is drowning their whole life flashes before them. In my case it seems to happen when someone wakens me from a deep sleep and involves my association with the person who initially rouses me. It's a bit like starting a petrol engine on an icy cold morning. The first whirring of the starter brings the motor into brief spluttering life, but, after a few coughs and rattles, it soon fades. Then, with the introduction of the choke, the engine catches and soon settles into a gentle rasping as the engine oil warms.

Before my befuddled mind can summon any speech, I smile like a young baby seeing its mother after a brief absence, as my brain rapidly scans its inner cortex bringing all the facts associated with the person in front of me to some central area for analysis. It all happens in a few microseconds and as I'm doing this one of the voices, which belongs to the man standing over me, keeps repeating, as though he's a gramophone record stuck in a groove;

"Say hello to grandma boys and give her a kiss!"

I'm not fully awake and in this twilight zone my mind briefly wanders.

Out of the blue I recall it was Easter Sunday, 1925, and my husband Morris and I had been invited to our friends the Levines for tea. We entered their apartment and visiting there, seated round the tea table was our son Mark, his wife Annie Cohen, and in a high chair our grandson, Peter, almost a year old.

I'm mortified to admit that we hadn't seen my son for almost a year and a half and this was my earliest sighting of our first grandson. On seeing us Mark leapt to his feet as it rapidly dawned on him that our family friend had ambushed him.

"Come on Ann, we're not hanging about here. Let's go."

"Mark, you're staying where you are. You and your parents have been invited to tea because somebody has to put an end to this absurd state of affairs." Mrs. Levine said in a firm, no nonsense voice that would brook no opposition. Meanwhile the chubby eleven months old Peter with an enticing smile was attempting to feed himself with a spoon pushing mashed banana and cream into his mouth, coating every surface around that orifice with the gooey white mush, while beaming at the adult audience who were looking on in rapt approval.

That was how the ice was broken, and Moisheka, and I eventually saw and held our grandson for the very first time. It seemed unbelievable that we had waited almost a year to see and then hold our first darling grandson.

Then more memories filled my mind, so many, so fast that I couldn't halt them.

Following their wedding on Derby Day, Wednesday June 6th, which was also my birthday, Mark and his wife returned to work the next day. Mark was on the road as usual collecting orders as our salesman and his bride, Annie Cohen was in her usual place in the factory workshop. Their honeymoon, four days later, was a Sunday trip to the seaside.

A few days later there was a bust up between my daughter in law and me in the factory. I can't remember precisely what happened, but words were spoken between us. I know if there were words, then they were in all probability mine and I must have shouted a little, for when I was younger, I always had that tendency when angry. She jumped up in tears, crying.

"You're always trying to find fault with everything I do. You're making it absolutely impossible for me to work in this mad house."

"Just because you're my daughter in law it doesn't mean that you're above criticism. When your work is unsatisfactory I've every right to tell you so."

"You treat me like some sort of skivvy and deliberately embarrass me in front of the other staff. You've no right to behave in this abominable manner. After all, I'm your daughter in law."

"If that's the way you feel about it, you don't need to stay. Pack your bags and be off with you." I said, imperiously pointing to the door.

Normally my husband would have calmed the situation as he'd done countless times before, but on this occasion he was out of the office. Ann stalked out, and I was absolutely certain she'd come creeping back, timid as a mouse, as she'd done many times before.

When Mark arrived home his wife complained about me. Naturally she gave only her version of events and that evening he visited us, and was he in a foul temper.

"Ann's at home, crying her heart out, telling me that you're always finding fault with her, and she's so upset she tells me she can't work with you any more. No matter what she does, you do nothing but criticise, even though we all know she's your best worker. Don't you see what an impossible situation you're creating for me?"

"Mark you've only heard her side of the story, so now listen to me. I can't supervise a workplace on kindness alone. If there are faults then I must ensure they're corrected. If Ann takes exception to my supervision then I'm sorry, but I have to maintain a rigorous quality control and can make no exception because she's your wife. If her work is substandard then I must say so."

"Ann's work is excellent and you know it. Incessantly picking on her like this and finding imagined faults places me in an impossible position. Every time you quarrel with Ann an intolerable situation of divided loyalties is created for me. It has to stop and you must apologise to my wife for the upset you've caused today."

"There's no way I'm going to grovel and apologise to one of my workers even though she's married to my son."

"For heaven's sake mother, she's your daughter in law, not just any worker. If you don't make amends then Ann certainly won't work for you again and if she doesn't work here then neither can I."

"As you please Mark, but I've made my position quite clear. I'm not apologising and I assure you that if Annie Cohen doesn't want to work here then I can easily find a replacement."

"I can't believe this. Her name's Ann Podguszer and she's my wife and you still refer to her as Annie Cohen as though she's not your daughter in law. You realise that I can't work where my wife's not welcome. Do you really know what you're doing? It means that neither of us can work for you ever again. We'll have no choice but to start out on our own."

To his credit Moisheka wanted to mediate.

"Zoshia, Mark, both of you calm down. Let's have a glass of tea and talk this thing through."

"Morris, I'll thank you not to interfere. I run the factory. On the work floor Annie Cohen is just another worker, not my daughter in law. When work's finished she can resume being my son's wife. I'm not prepared to make favours for her or anyone else when we're working, because if I do where will it all lead?"

"If that's your last word, then there's nothing more to say other than I'm through." At which Mark turned on his heels and stomped out, slamming the door.

"I'll go after him and get him to calm down."

"Moisheka, you just stay where you are. Give those young hotheads a day or two to calm down and when they've eaten a little humble pie they'll soon come crawling back, you'll see. You can be sure that she's put him up to this. Mark knows on which side his bread is buttered and Annie Cohen will learn soon enough."

Three weeks passed and we heard nothing from them, then at the end of the fourth week, Morris was on one of his customary visits to one of our customers when he learned that Mark had called on them with an excellent new range of merchandise which had impressed them sufficiently that they had given him an order. Over the ensuing weeks, time and again, Morris learned from clients that Mark had called a few days earlier with samples and had secured orders that might otherwise have gone to us.

This was intolerable. I'll admit that Annie Cohen was the best millinery worker I'd ever had, and Mark was a first-rate salesman, but our order book was down as a direct consequence of our children poaching our clients. If we lost our customers we'd be out of business and our children would starve, which would be just too unbearable. This had to be stopped, but how?

Moisheka said he would talk to Mark and Ann so that we could patch things up, so that we could work together again, but, out of foolish pride, I forbade him to make any such contact.

I learnt that they'd taken a room in Ann's parents' house, where they were employing women to manufacture their merchandise. I decided to inform the factory inspector that a factory had been set up in a domestic dwelling at 1 Great Garden Street.

The inspector called and I soon learned that instead of closing them down he'd permitted them to continue on condition that they employed no more than four employees in the room they were using and caused no obstruction to the passage way, or staircase. When I found out, I made a formal complaint and was informed that the inspector had elected to review the case in a further six months. My own son was stealing my clients from under my very nose and the factory inspectors would do nothing about it to close them down. I was livid and to my eternal shame did something in my anger that was unforgivable and which I've always bitterly regretted.

Without telling my husband, I marched round to Great Garden Street the very next morning and knocked on the door. They were taking the very bread from the plates on which I fed my children and I was incandescent with rage.

Old Mrs Cohen answered my insistent knocking. When she opened the door, she exclaimed in Yiddish.

"Mrs Podguszer, what an unexpected surprise. How are you?"

"Azoy, (alright). I need to see my daughter in law straight away. Where is she?"

I could see that she was undoubtedly astonished at my bad manners in not enquiring after her health and that of her husband and family, but the devil had a hold of my mind and gripped my heart in the palm of his hand and was squeezing.

As she told me Ann was working on the second floor in the front right room, my very blood was boiling. I pushed past her, and rushed up the stairs. I threw open the door and there she was sitting at a trestle table working with three other women, with bags of feathers on the floor and a series of shelves on the far wall supporting an array of boxes. As I burst in she stood up in astonishment.

"Mother in Law! Whatever are you doing here?" There was little friendliness in her greeting and I could see that she was pregnant, but this didn't deter me.

Heaven forgive me, I'd lost all reason. An unquenchable fire was raging within me.

"First you steal my son from me, and now you rob me of all my customers!" I shouted.

"That's nonsense. I never stole Mark from you. No matter how often I rebuffed him he was like a bee in search of nectar, always chasing after me, and we're not poaching your customers. There's more than enough out there for all of us."

"Liar! All lies, but I'll teach you to show me a little more respect." With that I sprang forward like a tormented beast battling to protect its young and with one heave upended the table, scattering all the feathers and equipment on the floor. The girls screamed and in the general pandemonium, I rushed over to the shelves and flung the boxes on the floor. Ann advanced to stop me, but I was a good four inches taller and also far heavier than her. I pushed her aside, and in doing so, caused her to stumble over a box. She fell heavily to the ground. I'd unintentionally knocked her down, and still raging, yelled that if she and my son didn't stop poaching my clients, I'd be back and next time it would be far worse. The women in the room were mortified and impotent with fear, they made no attempt to stop me.

The room was in turmoil and I saw that Annie Cohen was in tears. I smiled with satisfaction and totally unimpeded, rushed out of the room, down the stairs, then past Mrs Cohen, who'd come out of her kitchen when she heard the commotion, and out through the front door into the street. There I stood momentarily, to catch my breath and straighten my clothes, my heart beating like a sledgehammer, as I willed myself to calm down.

That evening, Mark called. We were sitting at the kitchen table just after supper, with Moisheka, unaware of what I'd been up to that day.

"Mother, I don't know what you thought you were doing this morning, but one thing I can promise you. If you ever come near our place of work, or touch my wife again, I'll not be responsible for what follows. Sending the factory inspector round was bad enough, but what you did today was unforgivable. Think yourself lucky that you didn't injure Ann badly, or upset her pregnancy, because had you done, so I swear I'd have preferred charges against you for causing grievous bodily harm.

"So far as my wife and I are concerned we're going to have nothing more to do with you ever again. Just forget you ever had me as a son, or Ann as a daughter in law." With that he stalked out, slamming the door, leaving me to explain to an astonished Morris and my children, all that I'd been up to that day.

"Peter, is that you?"

"Of course it is. How are you Zoshia? I've brought my boys Philip and Jonathan to see you. Boys say hello to Grandma and give her a kiss."

Fortunately he pointed as he named them. The elder, an 11 year old, was the image of his father and reminded me a little of my late husband, while the younger one, more closely resembled Doreen, his mother.

"Hello children. Come here and give grandma a kiss." I said, as each uncertainly stepped forward to give me a reluctant kiss. It's surprising how the very young seem to be frightened of the elderly. Could it be the wrinkles or the odd liver spot skin blemishes? Maybe it's my false teeth, or my hearing aid. I know I pong a teeny bit at times, but I can't help it. That comes from having a weak bladder, the price of too many children and lifting heavy parcels. The doctor says its stress incontinence, but I call it peeing in my pants when I cough, or laugh too heartily.

"Peter, where's Doreen?" I enquired.

"Have you forgotten so soon? You know we're in the process of divorce and I'm going to marry Helen."

Now it all comes back to me. Helen is the korva (whore), who Peter's going to make his second wife once his divorce comes through and who I've no wish ever to see.

Peter married Doreen Jacobs in Leicester, in June 1951. That young couple were so in love, and what a happy occasion the marriage of my first grandchild proved to be. The whole family travelled to Leicester to enjoy a marvellous celebratory wedding dinner at the Bell Hotel.

They set up home in Edgware and within less than a year, Philip, the first of my great grandsons arrived and three years later Jonathan came along. Marriages may be made in heaven, and sadly, whatever the chemical potion that magically makes two people adore each other, and marry, sometimes changes and turns, to bitter gall. Unfortunately that's what seemed to have happened to Peter and Doreen.

As I thought of Doreen, the first thing that sprang to my mind was the matter of her stockings and all the trouble they caused. I'd have gladly given her a dozen pairs of those wretched nylon stockings, and as many pairs of shoes to go with them, to have avoided all that then ensued. A single pair of stockings worth no more than ten shillings completely broke up my family, and made them look completely dysfunctional.

It happened nine years ago, when in the post war period nylon stockings were all the rage amongst young women, replacing silk stockings, which had become old fashioned. They were still in very short supply, and difficult to obtain. Because of this, when a stocking developed a minor fault in the knitwear, it was possible to have it invisibly mended, for a charge of two shillings, rather than discarding it. My son, Harry had installed a machine in his shop to have nylon stockings invisibly mended and Peter had left a pair of Doreen's stockings to be repaired.

The following afternoon Harry's wife, Ginsy, phoned Peter's mother, Annie Cohen and ferociously berated her, because Peter had left a pair of Doreen's stockings for repair that she claimed were unwashed and disgusting. Ann explained that she knew nothing about the matter and that neither her son's, nor her daughter in law's behaviour, had anything to do with her, since they were adults in their own right. She further made it clear that if she or Harry were experiencing any problem they should speak directly with the individuals concerned.

I'm certain that Ginsy made her phone call because she was doubtlessly very upset, but she should have only complained to Peter or Doreen. Her accusation was misdirected and greatly offended Ann. Had the matter stopped there, this might have remained a brief family tiff, but it didn't.

That evening Ann related the exchange to Mark, which as later events unfolded proved to be a ghastly mistake. Greatly incensed Mark immediately phoned his brother Harry and all hell broke loose. The conversation became very heated when Harry made the accusation that Annie Cohen was always stirring up trouble in the family and had always done so ever since she first worked for his parents. He then slammed the receiver down.

The next weekend was Essie's daughter's wedding. Sides had already been taken and it was clear at the wedding reception that Harry, Anne, and Essie were no longer on speaking terms with Mark and Ann, over the incident. Over many years I'd foolishly and unthinkingly heaped vitriol into the ears of my children concerning Annie Cohen and pay back time had arrived!

Mark's younger son, Arnold, a Sheffield medical student came down to London by train on a day return ticket to attend the wedding. Unaware of the quarrel that had arisen, he went over to chat with his aunts and uncles during the reception. He then bade farewell to his father since he had to leave early to catch the last train back to Sheffield. Mark asked him;

"Did your uncle Harry say anything derogatory about me or your mother?"

"Not at all," replied Arnold as he attempted to conceal the true nature of Harry's bitter outpourings.

"Then what was he talking to you about all that time?"

"I haven't seen him in more than a year and we were just chatting."

"I can't believe that."

"We were simply having a chin wag and if you don't want to believe me then there's nothing more that I can say."

About an hour later, at the conclusion of the meal, Mark walked over to Harry. "Harry, what did you say to Arnold about his mother and me?"

At that point, something must have snapped. Harry let out a stream of invectives describing Annie Cohen in the most uncomplimentary terms for all in the vicinity to hear.

Mark summoned Peter to come over.

"Peter your uncle Harry's been bad mouthing your mother in front of all these guests because of those wretched stockings. What do you think of that?"

"Harry. Were you insulting my mother?" asked Peter belligerently.

"Yes. Everything I said was true. Your mother's been a bl**** trouble maker ever since she came into this family and I want everyone here to know what a…." As Harry was delivering a further diatribe against his mother, Peter interrupted him with a blow, which sent him sprawling across the floor.

Within moments there was a scuffling melee accompanied by shouts and threats, as with some difficulty the family combatants were separated.

Essie was in tears, distraught that her daughter's *simcha* (celebration), should be interrupted and spoilt by her brawling brothers and nephews.

It was awful that a family quarrel should have been aired in public like this. That my sons and grandsons should fight like primary school children was unbelievable, and I felt the resulting disgrace very keenly. It would never have taken place had my two elder sons exercised a little self-control. That single blow destroyed all that I had striven for in my relentless pursuit for my family's social ascent.

My children blamed Mark for this disgraceful show of bad manners, although I felt that both my sons were equally at fault and sadly the damage inflicted within my family was irreparable. Apart from Solly, none of my children ever spoke to Mark or Ann again, which later had the direst consequences for me.

Peter and I chatted for only a few minutes before his children became bored and restless. With promises that he would return in a week or two to play a game of gin rummy they departed, and I was again left to my own devices. Having no other visitors my thoughts turned to Peter and his failed marriage.

Peter had inherited my volatile Chisick temperament, which he clearly demonstrated when he struck Harry, but unknown to any of us, he and Doreen, were having serious difficulties within their marriage. Peter gambled at cards and on the stock market, which caused many an upset.

Matters seemingly came to a head when Doreen went to Lido di Jessolo, just south of Venice, in Italy, for a summer vacation without Peter. She and her boys were in the company of her best friend, Helen Brown, who was likewise vacationing without her husband as they were in the midst of a divorce. Doreen was to return to London for Peter's youngest brother Michael's wedding. Helen encouraged her to ignore the wedding and remain a further week in Italy, as she put it,

"Doreen, stay here and teach your husband a much needed lesson."

I shall never understand why Doreen followed this malicious friend's advice. She must have realised that her absence and that of her children could not be concealed and would be a terrible insult to her husband and his family. No explanation or apology could redress the humiliation delivered to Peter before family and friends. Their marriage might have survived earlier problems, but this affront proved to be the last straw.

That *korva* (whore) Helen, who'd encouraged her friend not to attend her brother in law's wedding, had secretly been ingratiating herself with Peter for several months. Displaying all the qualities of a femme fatale and throwing caution aside, she made it clearly apparent that she intended to steal her friend's husband. An otherwise sensible young woman, Doreen would appear to have been the only one who at that time trusted her friend. If there's a moral to this story it must be that no woman should ever trust her girl friends with her husband.

How true is the saying that love is blind! As Dorothy Parker might have written;

'When it rains you can stay home or, going out, use an umbrella.
But never trust any gal under 80 with your fella.'

They finally set up home in a small apartment, making no provision for either Peter's boys or Helen's daughter even to stay the night with their parent. All Helen seemed to care about were expensive clothes, jewellery, smoking and having a good time, although to her credit she did work alongside her new husband and proved to be a good if extravagant companion.

Chapter 10

Autumn 1926

One of Morris's sisters and his younger brother Lev immigrated to Paris in 1922 with their children. The French had lost so many fine young men during the war, that they were delighted to welcome any immigrant of military age or who had young sons who in turn would soon be eligible for military service.

Morris visited them at least twice each year when he travelled to Paris on his buying trips and Mark, who invariably accompanied him had the opportunity to meet his father's family with whom he communicated in a mixture of Yiddish and French. While in Paris Morris and Mark never missed an opportunity to visit the opera where on occasions they heard Enrico Caruso, the famed Italian tenor sing.

On two occasions Morris also journeyed back to Warsaw to visit his sisters and their families. Both his sisters had large young families and were struggling to make ends meet. He gave them money and pleaded with them to leave Poland and settle in England or as Lev had done, in France.

On his return he told me how disappointed he was to see their continuing poor standard of living and of his alarm at the level of virulent anti-Semitism his family continued to endure. He invited them to visit him in London for a vacation at his expense to experience the differences in standards of living and the friendlier attitudes of the people, but they were adamant that Poland was their home and given time, with Poland's new found independence, economic conditions would improve and the level of anti-Semitism would correspondingly diminish.

Morris and I worked long hours and in this way our business prospered. England was at peace with her neighbours and we were in the midst of a period of post war prosperity. My brother, Abraham, had seven children; my sister, Zelda, had a similar number and all our children were growing into fine young men and women. My sister Sarah was married, with two children and had settled in Lille and my other brother lived in New York but somehow we had lost contact with him.

My sister, Rivkah and her husband, Harry Zure, stubbornly remained in Warsaw. They had two sons, one of whom, Monic, had arrived in England just after the war in 1919 and stayed with my brother, his uncle Abraham. There he met and then fell in love with Abraham's third child, Annie Chisick. They married the following year and later had two children. Annie developed influenza in 1925 and within four days had tragically succumbed to pneumonia, and we were devastated.

Monic who'd been troubled with a chronic cough for years had been diagnosed with consumption and hospitalised in a Tb sanatorium. With the death of his wife his condition rapidly deteriorated and he died within a few weeks. During this time their two young children were cared for by their grandparents Abraham and Betty, who shortly afterwards adopted them.

In June 1925, our second son, Harry, married Annie Ginsberg, a young woman two years older than himself, in the Dukes Place Synagogue, where Chief Rabbi, Dr. Adler officiated.

At this time we not only had 3 Annie's in my family and two nieces with the same name, but my daughter also had a very good friend, Annie Langley. To avoid the mix-ups that always seemed to be taking place, we agreed that my daughter would be called Anne, Mark's wife Ann would be called Annie Cohen and Harry's new wife would be called Ginsey, while Annie Langley would be addressed as Langley.

A year later Harry and Ginsey's first son, Murray, arrived. Morris and I were elated. Now with two grandsons we felt we'd entered the happiest period of our lives. Apart from our constant concern for our family in Poland, to whom we regularly sent money, Morris and

I considered that we could anticipate many years of happiness and continued success ahead of us in a city we had chosen as our home. I was soon to discover how deluded such dreams are and the folly of becoming so complacent.

It was in November 1926, a few weeks after Murray's arrival when everything changed. The autumnal days had grown shorter and cold, cloaked with dense morning mists and fog, often accompanied by frost as a pale, watery sun emerged above the horizon and barely raised the temperature sufficiently until noontime to clear any remaining ice. Cobwebs festooned the garden with glistening gossamer threads and everywhere could be seen those few remaining red and gold leaves tenaciously clinging onto bare branches, before falling from their deciduous perch. As they fluttered down, blown hither and thither with each passing breeze, they finally settled to join ever growing mounds of brown leaves, the detritus of past, glorious summer days.

Flocks of chattering starlings would periodically rise suddenly into the air wheeling in coordinated unison darkening the sky, before settling in their thousands on branches and overhead cables, waiting for some unseen signal to head towards some distant warmer foreign clime.

It was on such a day in early November that Anne arrived home from her secretarial job a little earlier than expected. Happy to be home, she bounded into the house, pleased to evade the late afternoon's damp cold air, intending to make a cup of tea to dispel the chill from her hands and feet. To her surprise, she discovered that her father was not in his factory office where he would normally be found mid afternoon, but was lying on the living room couch, clutching a hot water bottle to his abdomen. With Mark and Harry married, Anne at 22, was the oldest of our children living at home.

"Father, are you alright?"

"No, not really, I've had this terrible bellyache since late morning and I just can't seem to shift it."

"Maybe it's something you've eaten."

"I shouldn't think so. I've had the same as everyone else in the family."

"Well if you rest a little while longer it's sure to be better soon."

"I certainly hope so because it feels as though it's getting worse. In fact it's getting so bad I can scarcely bear it."

"Maybe I should call the doctor to see you."

"No, Don't worry. I'm certain I'll be better soon."

"Well I was just going to make a cup of tea and I'll make a fresh cup for you. That should help settle your tummy."

"I don't think I can manage one. Your mother made me one not half an hour ago and I just vomited. Since then the pain seems worse."

"That settles it. I'm going to ring for the doctor."

Within the hour the local GP arrived. Anne requested that she be permitted to remain in the room as the doctor first questioned and then examined her father.

As the doctor concluded his examination, with his patient's consent, he called Anne over. Indicating a large blue discoloured swelling that protruded from Morris's umbilicus he announced.

"This I believe is your father's problem."

"That looks terrible. Whatever is it?" enquired Anne.

"That's a large umbilical hernia. Your father says he's had it as long as he can remember and normally he can push the swelling down, but now it simply won't budge. I've tried but it just won't go back." Then turning to the patient he enquired. "How old are you Mr Podguszer?"

"I'm 53."

"Have you had any previous operations?"

"No, never."

"Well Mr. Podguszer you certainly need one now. You've what we call an irreducible hernia, which I believe left unattended could strangulate. I advise that you be admitted to hospital straight away for an urgent operation and it's important that we don't waste any time."

"Is this very serious Doctor?" Asked Morris.

"Not necessarily, but if there's any delay, it could become very serious indeed. Without surgery the bowel could become gangrenous which could produce a far nastier problem. In my opinion the sooner you undergo surgery the better. I'll make all the arrangements for your hospital admission this afternoon."

The household was suddenly thrust into confusion, as they awaited the arrival of the ambulance, which had been summoned to take Morris to the Middlesex Hospital where later that evening he underwent surgery.

Following his operation, although he was considerably overweight, there were no apparent complications. As was the custom, the patient remained in bed to recuperate. No attempt was made to encourage a patient to sit out of bed, walk, or participate in any early mobilisation.

Hospital visiting hours were strictly adhered to, with only two adults at any time permitted between 3 and 4 pm. alternate weekdays. Solly arrived at the hospital on the sixth post operative day carrying a bunch of flowers for his father,

When the ward doors were opened to visitors, Solly promptly walked briskly over to his father, so as not to waste a moment of precious visiting time.

Standing at the foot of the bed, Solly found his father dozing. He called out, "hello father, wake up, I've come to visit you."

Morris blinked as he opened his eyes and smiled, saying

"Hello," as he responded to his youngest son's greeting. He then sat up, but just as he opened his mouth to speak he suddenly uttered a gasp and fell back on to his pillow, where he stopped breathing. Solly called out in alarm.

"Nurse! Nurse! Help. Something's happened to my father!"

As the nurse arrived, followed a short time later by the house doctor, the patient's sightless blue eyes, stared vacantly upwards, indicating that the patient was now beyond help.

Adhering to the Jewish practice of prompt burial, we interred Morris the following day at the Federation cemetery in Edmonton. Harry registered his father's death but the certificate never made mention of the surgery he had undergone six days earlier or of the pulmonary embolus that had so abruptly taken his life.

After Morris's death my world fell into chaos and my joy for living came to an abrupt end. Days earlier Moisheka and I had somehow foolishly tempted fate with our happiness. The pleasures we had enjoyed together now became no more than fond memories. Morris and I had been a team and while I may often have believed that I was the stronger, I relied on Moisheka for advice and used him as a sounding board before making every important decision. My strength had been a delusion as I found myself without a partner to confide in and unable to make decisions for what previously had been simple run-of-the-mill problems. Morris had been my rock and support. Without him I was suddenly uncertain of myself. The flexible wooden bow is not stronger, nor weaker, than the limp cord, which when stretched and released then projects the arrow, for one without the other is useless.

What ambition I possessed was for my husband and family and now with Moisheka no longer at my side and my eldest two sons married all my drive and enterprise evapourated like the heavy morning dew that appeared each autumn morning, only to vanish as the sun rose higher in the sky.

I attempted to immerse myself in work to blunt the despair that had appeared as my unwanted daily companion. I still had three single daughters and an unmarried son at home and I resolved to make and save as much as possible for my daughter's dowries. Harry had just opened a leather goods shop where he also manufactured handbags, so was unable to help me, but Mark agreed to purchase all my requirements when he travelled to Paris on his own account. Having discovered his new cousins, who were of a similar age, Mark journeyed there at least twice a year, combining business with the pleasure of meeting his cousins, many of whom were furriers.

Personally I preferred never to wear a fur coat or one of those fashionable silver fox skins complete with head, tail and paws that were the fashion for some twenty years from the mid 1920's. Most men enjoyed flaunting their affluence by providing their wives and ladies with mink and other fur coats. Many family and their friends took advantage of the fact that we had family in France who could provide such luxury items at considerably less cost than could be purchased in England. Some of those who had a mind to do so could wear the coat when entering the UK from France, without declaring it as new, thereby avoiding a hefty purchase tax and import duty. This lead to an amusing incident when one of Anne's friends decided to play a trick on one of the acquaintances they knew who had recently purchased her fur coat in France without declaring it to the port authorities. She had her husband telephone the lady, pretending to be an officer from the customs and excise stating that they had reason to suspect that a fur coat had been smuggled into the country without the appropriate duty being paid. This he explained was a serious offence; punishable by a fine and a custodial sentence of up to five years and that officers would be arriving shortly to search her home. In what could only be described as a blind panic, she immediately took her coat into the garden and burnt it with garden waste in the incinerator to destroy any evidence before the customs inspectors arrived.

In March 1927, Mark and his wife had a second son who they called Maurice and twelve months later, Harry and Ginsey, also had a second son, who they also called Maurice. Since Ginsey had no mother I jumped at the chance of looking after their eldest child, Murray, during those first weeks to give her a much needed rest to cope with her new baby. Mark was in hospital with a kidney stone when the child was named, and Annie Cohen attended the ceremony by herself. I took the opportunity to goad her by saying.

"I shall always think of this one as the real Maurice, and not yours."

What devil entered my soul that day to make me utter those words I shall never know, but once voiced there was no means of retracting it. There was no salve that could have been magically applied to heal the wound that those unkind, illogical words caused. That one spiteful and unnecessary comment came back to haunt me in the years that followed.

In 1930, the first of my daughters was married. Essie, as we called her was the first of my children born in England. In temperament and appearance she was the feminine double of my husband, even down to her beautiful soprano voice. With fair auburn hair and beautiful blue eyes she had a very pleasing personality and like her father was short and had a tendency to be overweight.

Essie had met Edward Defries, a widower with a young son Eugene. Edward was one of the kindest men one could ever wish to meet and preferred to be called Titch. His family had arrived from Holland more than a century earlier and was mainly connected with the wine and spirit trade. He came from a family of publicans and managed a busy public house, The Duke of York in Rathbone Place in London's West End, off of Goodge Street. There he earned both a very good livelihood and lived in an apartment above the pub, provided by the brewery. In September 1933, they had a daughter, Betty, who was to remain an only child. All went well for three years when out of the blue, Eugene developed leukaemia and died. Titch and Essie were heartbroken and this presaged an unhappy turning point in their lives, for the following year found them without a home, and with Titch unemployed.

It was always the manager's responsibility deal with any disturbance in the pub as soon as possible. A customer had arrived in the pub, approached the bar and asked for a beer. The barman seeing the man was clearly very drunk amicably suggested;

"Look mate, I reckon you've already got a tankful on board and for your own good I don't think you should have any more."

An increasingly loud argument ensued. Titch walked over attempting to calm the situation, explaining to the customer that they were within their rights to refuse to serve any more alcohol if it was felt a patron had already had enough to drink.

Without warning the inebriated man picked up a glass, smashed it on the counter and aggressively lunged at him, plunging the glass into his face.

He was rushed to the nearby Middlesex Hospital with serious facial and eye injuries, which required urgent surgery. The vision to his eye was seriously impaired and later there followed one of the first successful corneal graft transplants. Unable to work for several weeks another manager was appointed and he was relieved of his post. Without a job and without a home, Anne stepped into the breach by providing a home for her sister and her family. When well enough and with a loan from Anne, Titch purchased a small garage with lock up facilities near his new home. He then embarked on a new career in road haulage and entered into a contract with Anne's assistance, to deliver furniture for H. Lazarus.

Shortly after the outbreak of war, Anne acquired a house in Lent Rise, Burnham where I could live with Becky and Clara to get away from the bombing, while the Defries family moved into the home I vacated in Overlea Road where they remained well into the 1950's.

Shortly after the end of the war, Clement Attlee's labour government nationalised the road haulage industry. The derisory compensation was delayed by red tape, which meant that Titch was again unemployed and without funds. There was a tremendous shortage of motor vehicles in the post-war period and again with loans provided by Anne, he entered the second hand car market where he was able to make a very adequate living.

Steve lived in a flat in Streatham High Street with Elsie and obtained employment as a ship's steward with the Cunard Steamship Company. In the late 1930's he decided to remain in New York, but returned to London with the outbreak of war when Steve felt it was his duty to help

England in her hour of need. He joined the NFS (National Fire Service) and was employed as a fireman during the worst period of the blitz, having first acquired a small flat close to where I lived in Lent Rise. As they had no children, Elsie continued to work as a sales lady in the gown department of one of the large stores. In 1942, all my children except Becky changed their family name by deed poll. Anne and Steve chose the name Maurice; Mark chose Powell; and Harry, Podro. This was the very action my brother had recommended to me that first night in 1905, which I had stubbornly rejected. The reason for this change was that no English person could spell or pronounce our name and since family members were entering military service we all felt that this was the most sensible thing to do.

In late 1942, Steve left the fire service and joined the merchant navy. He reassured me that he would never be in any real danger since merchant ships always sailed in convoy with naval warships providing an escort. He reported for training and duty and on January 16th 1943 he sailed from the Clyde on the merchant cruise ship Dempo.

The SS Dempo had been built in Rotterdam in the late 1920's as an 18,000 ton passenger ship working the Holland to Java route in the Dutch East Indies with accommodation for 634 passengers. It was chartered by the Ministry of War Transport in 1941, and converted for troopship service that same year.

As it left its berth it inauspiciously collided with one of its tugs, which postponed the sailing by a further week for repairs before proceeding on its journey to India.

In December 1943, two British destroyers and the US destroyer, Bristol were torpedoed, and sunk off the coast of Algeria, by U boats amongst which was the German submarine U371.

In mid March 1944, the SS Dempo, carrying a large complement of American servicemen sailed with convoy SNF.17 with its destroyer escorts into the western Mediterranean, where unknown to the navy department U371 was again lying in wait.

From that point onwards Steve suddenly disappeared. There was no contact of any kind, which was most unusual, and we had no idea where he might be. There was no means available to discover his whereabouts, or the reason for his lack of communication. Then early one morning somebody rang Elsie's front door bell. She opened it to find a naval officer standing there.

"Are you Mrs. Maurice?" he enquired.

"Yes. Is there something?"

"Yes. I'll be very brief. Your husband's quite safe. His ship was torpedoed and sunk. He's not in any position to contact you, and the navy department agreed to communicate with you on his behalf, because of the delicate state of your health." As the officer delivered his message, he constantly looked at her midriff, seeming to mentally undress her, which made her feel most uncomfortable.

"Where is he?"

"I'm afraid we're not allowed to say. All I've been authorised to tell you is that he's well, and when he finds another ship, he'll doubtlessly be home."

Some weeks later when Steve at last returned home on leave, the mystery was unraveled.

His ship had been sailing in a convoy in the Mediterranean off of the coast of Algeria when the submerged U371 attacked. Without any preliminary warning, the US Maiden Creek, a freighter in the convoy was torpedoed and sunk. Within minutes the SS Dempo was struck by a torpedo and rapidly started to take on water.

The crew were well disciplined and had regularly drilled muster, and abandon ship procedures. Steve was made to take his place as helmsman in one of the lifeboats and a small quantity of water and rations were issued. They believed themselves to be 40 miles off the coast of Algeria and were instructed that they were to row to the nearest land. As senior crewmember he was issued with a loaded rifle in case any need to maintain order arose, which made him most uncomfortable.

As they pulled away from the sinking vessel, they set a south-westerly course. They noticed other lifeboats had followed suit both ahead and behind them and an escort vessel had approached close alongside the stricken liner.

Once they reached dry land they were picked up by naval vessels and taken to Gibraltar. There they were required to wait to be assigned to another merchant vessel but were not permitted to write home or telephone. There was no way in which any message could be dispatched. Steve requested permission to see the commanding naval officer, to whom he explained that his wife was pregnant and was imminently expecting their first child, and that she would be worried out of her mind with the absence of news. The commanding officer agreed that he would have somebody contact his wife to reassure her that all was well. That explained why the officer delivering the message some weeks earlier had been inspecting Elsie's silhouette so closely.

While in Gibraltar Steve learned there had been no loss of life amongst a crew of 333 persons, although there was no specific information available concerning the loss of life amongst the troops on board. Considerably later it was revealed that a total of 498 military personnel were lost. Surviving crew members were mystified that this had been the case, and attributed this to panic and inadequate abandon boat emergency drill amongst other factors.

In May 1944, two months after these events four destroyers managed to corner a U boat in the western Mediterranean. The U boat, which turned out to be U371 badly damaged one of the attacking destroyers, the USS Menges, before it was finally depth charged into submission. The German crew safely abandoned ship and was taken into captivity.

At the end of the war Steve divorced Elsie on the grounds of her marital infidelity. They had been married sixteen years and there were no children.

Entering civilian life he again obtained a position with the Cunard line as a ship's steward on the transatlantic run between Southampton and New York. His second wife, Sophie, whom he married in 1950 was a dentist's widow with a married son living in Birkenhead who was also a dentist.

Most consumer items were in very short supply in post war England and Steve was able to supplement his income many-fold with all that he acquired in New York, which could be sold for a handsome profit in England. On one occasion in early 1949 he was even able to obtain a new wonder antibiotic Chloromycetin, which was unavailable in England, which was needed to cure Annie Cohen, who'd picked up typhoid fever when vacationing in Italy some months earlier.

Chapter 11

1933 to 1945

My retirement in 1933 meant that I now occupied my time visiting family, taking the grandchildren out on special outings, or escorting them to visit a doctor or a hospital specialist when any-one of them was sick. The rheumatic pains I experienced periodically in my knees had not evolved into the severe disabling mobility problem that I later experienced, although they gave me a more reliable indication of any imminent weather change than the forecast on the wireless.

In September 1933, Essie gave me my second grand daughter, a pretty baby named Betty, which kept me busy and they became regular visitors in my new home.

I enjoyed the occasional afternoon game of cards, usually gin rummy or kalookie with friends like Mrs Levine. The local shops were of little interest since I preferred the kosher stalls and shops in Petticoat Lane where I could indulge in the enjoyable ritual of bargaining to obtain the best prices for food and the other items I needed. At least a couple of times each week I would drop in on Harry and his family who lived above the handbag shop they rented in Wentworth Street and then shop for food. I would regularly buy salt beef at Strongwater's and smoked salmon at Mossy Marks and periodically I'd visit Yanovsky my corsetiere in Whitechapel Road. Somehow the one thing that I really missed most was the exhilarating challenge that my work used to bring. As each week passed, I increasingly craved the hurly burly of commerce, almost like a drug.

More and more I gravitated towards visiting Mark, who now had four children, including my first grand daughter Gloria, named after my mother Geitle. While visiting Mark I would surreptitiously enquire whether there was any work that I could help with in the workshop, just in case anybody was away sick, or there was an urgent order. I turned up regularly each week and although Mark insisted that he pay me for any work, I always refused since my daughter, Anne, generously ensured that money was a commodity I was never short of. I even took work home with me where I could listen to the wireless or records on the gramophone and create, at my own pace, the feather and floral designs Mark wanted. For the first time in many months since retirement, I was at peace with the world and myself and enjoying life once again.

Our Chisick family had inherited a spirited temperament from our mother Geitle, which could best be described as volatile. The slightest perceived provocation and whoosh! Those involved were in the centre of a maelstrom of capricious anger. Always of brief duration the family had a reputation for being easily upset and *broigus* (angry, not on speaking terms). The Podguszer temperament was the complete opposite. Morris and his family had a nature that was at all times placid and calm and my husband always provided his more gentle calming influence, particularly in the work place, and between us there were seldom any unmanageable upsets. Of our children, Mark and Anne and to a lesser degree Steve and Harry were like me in temperament, while Essie had more of her father's make-up.

Then one afternoon, without warning, all hell broke loose.

Anne visited me unexpectedly at home with the intention of joining me for a glass of tea and found me at work surrounded by feathers. While I'd been told she drank the occasional glass of whisky, smoked cigarettes and could swear like a trooper, she had never done any of these things in front of me.

"What the bloody hell's all this rubbish? Damn it, where did all these feathers come from?"

"There's no need to swear and shout like that. I'm just doing a little work for Mark to help him out. No more than a simple favour."

Rushing over to the phone she asked the operator for Clerkenwell 7391. and as she waited she drummed her fingers with her well-groomed fingernails impatiently on the table, until after a few moments she barked out.

"Mark, you bastard; Get over here right now and take your dammed bloody feathers away. I've undertaken to look after mother and she doesn't need the money you're paying her. She's worked hard enough all her life and she's no need to ever work again."

I heard him trying to say something in response but she slammed the phone down and then turned on me. Sweeping my feathers onto the floor she raged at me that I'm retired and she's giving me an adequate enough allowance so that I don't need to work and that if I need more money I only need ask. Lighting a cigarette she continued to rant and rage and as she gesticulated with her hands, I was fearful that she might unintentionally set the feathers alight with her cigarette.

"Must you smoke? It's a detestable habit and very unladylike." My comment was like a red rag to a bull.

"Mother, it's time that you realised that a woman can smoke and you'd best get used to the idea that this is one gal who's going to do what she damn well pleases."

I tried to calm her down and decided that the best thing was to make a pot of tea. The one thing I couldn't make her understand then, or at any later time was that I was bored and wasn't working for money. In fact I'd gladly have paid Mark to let me do a little regular part time work. As a modern intelligent woman Anne showed little insight into the psychology of ageing.

When Mark arrived to collect his feathers he was as bewildered as me. Anne was waiting and pounced like a wild tigress. The most terrible scene imaginable followed. She shouted abuse and raged at him and wouldn't listen to any attempted explanation. Both of them had inherited my mercurial Chisick temperament. Momentarily their anger knew no bounds and I thought, for a moment, that they were close to exchanging blows. Only my tearful shouts and entreaties stopped them. I remostrated with Anne about her conduct in my home only to receive her angry rebuke.

"This may be your home but it's my house. I'm running things now and don't you forget it! I don't ever want to see you working again."

Mark collected his feathers and then stormed out of the house and I had to contend with Anne who could not accept that her brother, on this occasion, was entirely blameless. To make matters worse Becky and Harry sided with Anne in this family spate, while Essie and Steve at least appeared neutral. The resulting animosity that ensued between them was entirely my fault. It went on for ages and there was nothing that I could say or do to make any of them understand the resulting predicament was entirely of my making.

It was then that I started to realise the heavy price that was being exacted in return for accepting my daughter's generous largesse. Since adolescence I had always been determined to make things happen my way. Some might call it ambition, but I knew how to exploit whatever advantages I had been given and now I had unwittingly placed myself in a trap that eroded my ability to determine events for myself.

No longer was I mistress of my own destiny, since I had unintentionally made myself completely beholden to a well-intentioned daughter, who was even more ambitious than I had ever been and who had little concept of what an older woman really needed in life. To be fair to Anne I hadn't much idea either. We were both learning and I was frustrated that no matter how often I tried, I found it impossible to convey my thoughts and ideas to her. I had imagined that I would have earned the right to a little self-indulgence to do as I pleased when I retired, but this had to accord with Anne's concept of retirement.

Following that dreadful episode it was many years before I again took work home with me and then only clandestinely, although I still visited Mark at his factory. Ostensibly this was to visit my grandchildren, but I would take the opportunity to put in a few hours work a couple of times a week, to keep my hand in. Work was not simply a means of earning a livelihood; it had become an enjoyable therapeutic way of life. It had made me financially self-sufficient and provided status amongst those who knew me.

The remainder of my leisure time weighed heavily upon me. I would shop at Norman's wholesale shoe establishment buying shoes for all my grandchildren and elsewhere for their clothes. I took any grandchild with an appointment to visit the dentist or to be seen by a specialist in hospital. The nurses soon learned that I was not prepared to stand or sit for hours on rigid wooden benches in dark waiting areas to be seen, and soon the word passed round "Let Granny in with the children." The medical people also rapidly realised that they had a formidable guardian to deal with, who was not amenable to being fobbed off with the usual bottle of useless coloured medicine at the end of a brief consultation, or the delaying tactic of a referral to be seen in six months time. Should any grandchild of mine have a medical problem I wanted an answer to the nature of that setback and how the condition was to be managed to restore the child back to health as rapidly as possible. If the response weren't to my satisfaction I'd request a second and even a third opinion.

In January 1936 King George V died and the body lay in state at Westminster Hall for several days. I decided to take my three eldest grandchildren Peter, Murray and Maurice to see the lying in state. On arrival we were greeted by the sight of tens of thousands of warmly clad mourners, huddled against the winter cold, queuing in orderly fashion, the line four deep extending along the embankment, with a wait of up to six hours. Rising to the challenge I hit upon the strategy to approach one of the police guarding the entrance to the hall.

"Excuse me constable. I've been waiting with my grandsons for hours in the freezing cold. I had to take them to the toilet, I couldn't let these little boys go alone, and now I've lost my place in the queue. What should I do? Can you help me;?"

"Certainly Madam. Just you follow me." With that he escorted the children and me to the entrance, announcing loudly. "Make way for grandma!"

Old Street was part of the ancient Roman road that linked Watling Street, now part of Edgware Road, with Bethnal Green and the street crossing over the River Lea.

In 1924 Mark had acquired the lease on 117 Old Street a property at the corner of Old Street and Ironmonger Row owned by the Ironmonger's guild. It was a spacious building with a double fronted shop on the main road. The remainder of the ground floor provided extensive accommodation for a factory with an entrance off Ironmonger Row overlooking the magnificent early 18th century St. Luke's church, while on two upper floors was the living accommodation.

In addition to a factory housing The Ostrich Feather Company, manufacturing millinery accessories, hats and artificial flowers, Mark established a successful sweet and tobacco shop where he also sold home made ice cream. He expanded this retail confectionary and tobacco enterprise with the acquisition of three kiosks at the entrance to tube stations, where items of confectionary and tobacco were sold.

The Wall Street crash of October 1929 was a turning point followed by years of severe economic depression. To boost sales of his tobacco merchandise and to assist those out of work to be able to buy cigarettes while on the dole, he cut the price of his cigarettes. Within a short time he was taken to court by the cigarette company, accused of violating the law which permitted a corporation to stipulate the minimum price at which its goods could be sold under 'The Retail Price Maintenance Act'.

Realising that when he appeared in court he would be found guilty he hastily organised his financial affairs, by disposing of all assets and shares, by gifting them to his wife. Once found guilty he appeared in the Bankruptcy Court in Carey Street and entered into voluntary insolvency, thereby denying the cigarette company the considerable financial damages they had been awarded.

With the stigma of bankruptcy was the reality that he was unable to sign a cheque, hold a bank account or accept the directorship of any company.

All attempts that he made over the following three years to discharge his bankruptcy were of no avail until unasked, I set myself the task of assisting him. I made an appointment to see the registrar. It was a cold winter's afternoon and when shown into the office the registrar invited me to warm myself in front of the fire and offered me a cup of tea, which I gratefully accepted. Seated in front of him at his desk I explained the purpose of my visit. He listened without interruption and then informed me that no assistance could possibly be forthcoming. Calmly I stood up, walked over to the fire and deliberately poured my tea over the coals, extinguishing the warming red embers. I then turned to find him in a state of shock as I explained,

"I've extinguished your fire and as your room grows colder I'd like you to reflect on what my son's wife and five young children experience each day. They have to endure terrible deprivation and hunger in the cold until you have the humanity to permit him to earn a proper living by allowing him to discharge his bankruptcy."

"Mrs Podguszer, I think you've made a rather valid point with your illustration and I assure you I shall do my best to be of whatever assistance I'm able."

Fortunately the children were neither cold nor hungry as I implied, but within a few weeks my action had the desired effect and the bankruptcy order was discharged.

I'd been able to demonstrate to my son that his mother still knew a thing or two when it came to dealing with one of those faceless bureaucrats who self-importantly sits behind a desk preferring to say no, than to make any positive decision that might ultimately result in an early retirement and loss of pension.

Harry, unlike Mark had declined to enter the millinery business, claiming that hats simply didn't interest him. Just after the war in 1919, he'd met Jules Rose, a young fellow from Belgium in the leather trade who'd decided to settle in London. They seemed to hit it off and Jules taught Harry how to design and make quality leather goods. Harry was an apt pupil and rapidly became very skilled in his new trade. Before long he was manufacturing handbags and attaché cases, which he then sold to local shops and stores and was able to make a reasonable living.

He had met Annie Ginsberg a young lady two years his senior at a local dance and before long I was having the same trouble with him as I'd had with Mark. I had my eye set on a young woman from a well-to-do family, which would have been just right for him, but like his older brother he wouldn't listen. Defying parents in these matrimonial matters was like a contagion spreading from one son to the next.

All they could see was a pretty face and a shapely pair of legs. Of course I agree that such things are important to a young man, but living in a fine house and paying bills on time requires money. It's just as easy to marry an attractive, young woman from a wealthy family where life could be so much easier, than to marry a pretty, young woman without a '*nudin*' (dowry), where existence becomes a struggle often leading to great unhappiness. After all, there's an old saying; 'When money walks out the door, love flies out the window.'

"I've found a marvellous '*shiddach*' (arranged marriage) for you with a girl from a very fine family who can set you up in business." I explained to Harry.

"Mother, I've discovered that I can earn my living making leather goods. I know you and the way you think. When you say fine, you mean rich and I'm just not interested. I've met Annie Ginsberg and I want to get engaged and married to her. I've persuaded her to break off her understanding with Jack Solomons, a fishmonger, to marry me and she's agreed."

"You don't know what you're talking about. What if a family is affluent? Since when has that been a crime, or something to be ashamed of? My parents arranged my marriage. I accepted, as young people had for countless years, that their parents had greater experience in these matrimonial matters. That's why I accepted their recommendation. It's no different now and I expect you to listen to your parents in the same way."

"That may have worked years ago in Poland, but this is England. It's the 20th century and times have changed."

"Because things change it doesn't mean they've changed for something better. Tell me what does this fine young woman's father do for a living?"

"Simon Ginsberg is a fruiterer and green-grocer. He owns his own shop in Wentworth Street and says I can set up a market stall outside the shop to sell my leather goods."

"You may think that's good enough but believe me, you can do a lot better. The girl I have in mind for you has a father who's one of the biggest pearl importers in the country."

"Money's not the most important thing in life."

"Health can be more important, I agree, but why not give it a chance to see how much better life can be with money."

"Mother I don't care how rich a girl might be, or about her father's pearl business. I want to marry Annie Ginsberg. Anyway when Mr. Ginsberg heard that you were my mother he started to raise a few of his own objections to his daughter going out with me. He said you've a bad reputation in the market for stealing fruit"

"What nonsense. Before I buy fruit I want to taste it, and if it's no good, not only don't I buy, but I let the stallholder know in no uncertain terms what I think of his poor quality merchandise. In my opinion that's not theft, and it's a pity a lot more shoppers don't do the same thing, because that way we'd have some better quality food on sale.

"Anyway, I don't care what your Ginsberg, the green-grocer thinks of me. Any son of mine is far too good for his daughter. Your father and I forbid your engagement to that young woman. Send her back to her fishmonger friend Solomons, and you'll get engaged to the young lady we've found for you."

"I'd rather top myself than have to give Annie up."

"You're just infatuated with the girl and talking childish nonsense. You'll do as we say and in a few days you'll get over her and see that your parents are right."

"All right just you see. I'm going out right now to throw myself off the bridge and drown myself. You'll read it in tomorrow's papers, and then you'll know how serious I was about Annie."

So saying, he stormed out of the room. It was a Sunday morning and I screamed out "Annie, Essie, Becky, Solly: Quickly. Run after Harry. He says he's going to throw himself off the bridge. Stop the headstrong boy before he does himself any harm.

They managed to catch up with him and after some half-hearted resistance from Harry succeeded in persuading him to come back home. When he returned Morris had a long father to son talk with him, the upshot of which was that we agreed that he could announce his engagement to Annie Ginsberg.

Putting the best face possible on this loss of parental authority I had no alternative but to arrange to meet the young lady's parents and it was then that we learned that Simon Ginsberg had lost his wife during the dreadful 1919 influenza epidemic. A few months after their engagement, Harry married Annie Ginsberg, in the Dukes Place Synagogue on July 17th. 1925.

Since she was the third Annie in the family we all agreed she would be called Ginsy. Her father permitted Harry, as he'd promised, to set up a market stall outside his Wentworth street premises where he was able to make a good living.

A couple of years later the LCC (London County Council) made a compulsory purchase of the whole block where old man Ginsberg lived. They then immediately rebuilt the buildings with up to date shops on the ground floor and self-contained modern apartments above. Harry and Ginsy then rented number 35 from them. The shop had a small factory at the rear where Harry could manufacture his goods, and there they prospered and started to raise their family. They had two fine young boys, Murray who came along in 1926 and Maurice in 1928 and later, both attended the local Jews Free School as did Mark's son Maurice.

Simon Ginsberg was a very orthodox young man who when aged 17, had arrived in London from Riga in the 1890's, leaving his wife and two young children behind. Penniless he'd made his way to Spitalfields fruit market and persuaded one of the wholesalers to give him some fruit, which he could pay for at the end of the day. This went on for a number of days until Simon persuaded the wholesaler to lend him a wheelbarrow. Within a year he'd been able to send for his wife and children and a few years later purchased his own property in Wentworth Street.

Shortly after the outbreak of World War II old Simon Ginsberg completely lost his vision and had to enter a nursing home. I was present when his daughters removed him from his home. As he was about to enter the car that was to take him on this unwanted journey he threw up his hands and remonstrated with his daughter. With tears flowing from his sightless eyes and his nose running, he cried out despairingly.

"You're only doing this to me because I gave you my house with the shop. Had I never given it you, you'd have looked after me better than this."

Those final words rang out to haunt both Ginsy and me for the rest of our days.

Although I missed my husband dreadfully, these were happy years except for one personal matter that rankled deeply. My daughter had found a lover in her employer Hyman Lazarus. Outwardly I was always courteous and amiable, as he was to me, but inwardly I hated the man. Given the opportunity I could have gladly poisoned him; not because he was wealthy and successful, but because I despised him as the married man who'd seduced my daughter.

Anne was an intelligent young woman, a match for any man and yet she had permitted a man almost old enough to be her father to bed her. It ruined her opportunity to settle down to have children as part of a normal married life.

Lazarus had a wife and two fine children and everything that money could buy. He'd even been mayor of Tottenham, yet he had to make my daughter his mistress. I could have tolerated this situation, however reluctantly, had they indulged in a brief infatuated relationship.

But this went on, unashamedly for years, until brought to an end by his death.

I could understand him falling for my daughter. She radiated personality from her slim figure, to her elegantly slender fingertips. Always immaculate in appearance, heads would turn to follow her when she entered a room. Although not a ravishing beauty, her appearance, with bobbed hair and rimless glasses was elegant, with a dress sense that month by month competed with the models in Vogue. Ambitious and shrewd, she was a formidable negotiator who always paid great attention to detail and was fastidious in the manner in which she prepared her work. She tended to take after me in her intransigence. When she had a point of view and was convinced that she was correct, she would argue without giving way. To all these qualities could be added her discretion, her no nonsense attitude to life and her loyalty to friends and family. I believe she had everything her ambition had striven for, except her own children. She always denied ever wanting them, but I knew better.

Of course she had her faults as we all do, chief of which was a fierce short fused temper, but this trait was adequately compensated for by her generous caring disposition.

Her employment gave her everything that money could buy. There were designer clothes, an exquisite apartment in 55 Park Lane, a smart black American Packard saloon with Ambrose, her uniformed chauffeur. Unknown to Anne who would have been totally opposed to his political views, he was a communist sympathizer, who had been befriended by Peter Kerrigan a communist organizer for the International Brigade. Kerrigan was responsible for recruiting impressionable young people to fight against the Nationalist fascists and their leader, General Franco in the Spanish Civil War. Under his influence Ambrose threw up his job in 1937 to fight against Franco in the Spanish Civil War.

"Miss Podguszer, I'm sorry for the inconvenience, but I have to give in me notice. I'm leaving at the end of October."

"I'm sorry to hear you're going. You've been driving me for four years and I always thought that you enjoyed your work."

"Oh I do Miss, but I've a conscience and I don't think I've any choice. I'm going with some of me mates to Spain to join the International Brigade to defend Madrid from those fascists."

"I hope you know what you're letting yourself in for. There are reports of unofficial Italian army units that have been sent in by Mussolini, and

Hitler has sent in his Condor air division with scores of bomber aircraft to help Franco. It's a very nasty, dangerous situation."

"That's why we're going. Old Uncle Joe Stalin's sent General Kleber, one of the Soviet Union's best military men to rally Madrid's defence and we're going to help."

"I'll be happy to give you a reference as a first-rate driver, and of course, if you want your job back when you return, you'll let me know."

Ambrose left and went straight to Madrid with some of his left wing friends, where not many weeks later, he surrendered his life.

As we proceeded into the late 1930's the rise of fascist hatred and nazi anti-Semitism spoilt the contentment that I might have enjoyed in my retirement. In 1938 there was an amateur singing contest in the Paramount cinema in Tottenham Court Road, when my eldest grandson Peter, aged fourteen, sang in front of a huge audience. He was awarded second place and Mark was encouraged to take him to audition before Benjamino Gigli, when he appeared in London for a concert performance the following month. The greatest tenor of the day recommended that the boy be sent to Italy for proper voice training in Milan. At the time, Mussolini, the Italian Fascist leader, had invaded Ethiopia and also sent troops to support Franco in Spain and there were League of Nations sanctions in place. Mark felt that to send a young boy to Italy under those circumstances was unwise and I agreed.

I did my utmost to influence all my grandchildren and encouraged the boys to study.

"You'll only be able to make something of yourself if you attend to your school work. Games like football and cricket are a waste of time and will get you nowhere. You must study hard." I don't know how helpful this advice was but I hoped that it might have some beneficial effect. Two of Mark's boys listened to me. Maurice attended teacher's training college and Arnold, Sheffield University.

We should have realised that Hitler and his Nazis were not the usual run of anti-Semitic vermin when Mark and Harry joined a committee to meet German Jewish children at Liverpool Street Station who were being sent to England for safety by their parents. That together with

Crystal Night in November 1938, should have been warning enough for the world, even though Prime Minister Chamberlain had come back earlier from Munich claiming,

"Peace in our time," while waving a useless piece of paper signed by Hitler.

We thought the worst aspect of those infamous days of the Nazi pogrom was the burning, looting, imprisonment and humiliation of tens of thousands and torturing and killings of hundreds, but that was not all. The German government forbade the sale of food to Jews for nine days. Women and children were deliberately starved in a civilized European society, while the world looked on, and did absolutely nothing.

We begged our family in Poland to leave, but to no avail; Years later we discovered that all but two members of my family had perished. My niece Annette Vagenfish was one who survived. She was the daughter of my husband's sister Kraindel who was a hairdresser in Warsaw who had married Efraim Vagenfish with whom she bore four sons and two daughters. Annette was also a hairdresser and had accompanied a contingent of young Polish athletes to Paris for the 1938 Maccabbi games, where her French family persuaded her to remain in France.

In 1940 she fled to Bordeaux and managed to board a ship sailing to England, where two years later she married Alf Marks, an accountant. Her brother Kalman Vagenfish fled eastwards during the second week of September 1939 and fortunately found himself in the area of Poland invaded by the USSR. He was sent to Siberia where in spite of terrible privations he survived the war. After the war he escaped to Palestine and settled in Ramat Gan, where he had a family.

When the Soviet Foreign Secretary Molotov signed a non-aggression pact with Foreign Minister Ribbentrop their Nazi archenemies in the third week of August 1939 the agreement clearly left a feeling of foreboding. Something awful was about to happen. The ink had barely dried when the Nazis invaded Poland, on September 1st. As in August 1914, a far larger bubble was about to burst. On the 3rd of September, England and France declared war on Germany and in mid September Russia treacherously moved into eastern Poland to a line on the River Vistula secretly agreed with the Nazis the previous month.

Early in 1940 Mark was instrumental in helping my nephew Sylvain Podguszer to escape from Le Havre by smuggling him and his cousin,

Max, onto what was the last civilian cross channel ferry, while his brother in law, my niece Anna's husband, was wounded and killed guarding the French 'Maginot Line' fortifications.

My first cousin Charles Blumenson, my mother's nephew, arrived in London immediately before the First World War. Once married, he and his wife Annie opened a small tobacconist, confectionary and newsagent's shop in Kennington. In the mid 1930's they moved to Edgware where they raised their three children, Bella, Harold and Jack.

Apart from Christmas day, Charles would leave home each day at 5 am to travel the short distance to Kennington, where he would open his shop and sort out the day's newspapers for delivery. Once the children were grown up Annie would relieve him at lunchtime often accompanied by their daughter Bella, at which time he would return home for a rest before returning later in the day to finally lock-up.

Shortly after lunch on the 31st of January 1941 when Annie and their 22-year-old daughter were alone in the shop there was an air raid. A high explosive bomb fell close by, which demolished the shop killing both mother and daughter. Just three weeks earlier Annie Cohen's youngest brother Philip had also been killed in Great Garden Street during an air raid.

Of course I attended the funerals and it was this last tragic event that finally gave us the impetus to seek somewhere safer to live, away from central London and the intensive bombing to which the city was subjected, day after day.

Anne found a small house in Lent Rise near Maidenhead for us. Mark located a house in Cockfosters and Harry and Ginsy leased a spacious house in Golders Green and a weekend retreat in Lansing.

Charles Blumenson's two sons distinguished themselves during the war. Harold, who had trained as a ladies' hairdresser, was 19 when he entered the 3rd County of London Yeomanry and became a tank driver. In 1942 he was posted to North Africa as part of General Montgomery's 8th Army 'The Desert Rats' where he drove across North Africa and later took part in Landings in Sicily and Italy. Returning to England his unit crossed to Normandy on D-Day plus 1 (June 7 1944) and fought in all the major land battles until the Nazis surrender. At the end of the war he recounted that he was one of only 4 combatants out of 200 men in his unit who survived the war unscathed.

Jack, his younger brother saw service in India and the Malayan peninsula as one of the famed 'Chindits'. When demobilised, he married his cousin Renee Chisick, (father Harry Chisick and Grandfather Abraham Chisick). They acquired a newspaper tobacconist shop in the Edgware Road, changed their family name to Benson and raised two sons, Jeremy who was born in 1953 and Timothy in 1959.

My own war years from the spring of 1941 were spent in safety in Lent Rise, where apart from rationing and the war news, we were barely affected by the terrible daily air raids, and bombing that took place in London and other industrial towns and cities. Once every week, I would travel by train into London and was horrified by the devastation that the Germans inflicted upon innocent people and property. Amongst countless other women, I endeavoured to play my part in the war effort, by knitting gloves and scarves and such like for soldiers. I seldom saw Anne other than on the occasional weekend. Her work had increased many-fold, as H L Cabinets opened a further factory, 'Lazgil Aircraft Company', in Hampton Wick specifically manufacturing parts for Spitfires and other warplanes.

During the hostilities we had no idea what was happening to our families in France and Poland, but at the end of the war, after many weeks of frantic enquiry through the Red Cross and other agencies, we discovered bit by bit the awful truth. All but one in Poland had perished in the holocaust. In France my husband's brother Lev and several other members of our family had been deported to concentration camps and were murdered. Those few who had escaped to the Vichy controlled south of France survived in hiding, but were totally impoverished. We attempted to send them money, which proved exceptionally difficult with the currency exchange controls introduced, in the harshness of the post war economic period.

Chapter 12

1945

"Boobah, why are you crying?" enquired, Michael, my youngest grandson, who now ten years old was attending his first family wedding.

"No it's Grandma." I sniffed, wiping my eyes for the umpteenth time with my crumpled, white linen handkerchief. "I keep telling you, to call me Grandma."

"All right, Grandma, why are you crying?"

"It's because I'm so happy."

"But if you're so happy, why aren't you laughing and smiling? Even Aunty Essie's crying. You're hiding something. What's wrong?"

"Tuttelah, there's nothing wrong."

"There has to be something, and you're not telling me because you think I'm a child. I'm really old enough to be told the truth. You're all crying, and there has to be something that's not right."

The organ was playing the last chords of the Mendelssohn wedding-march. The congregation dressed in their best clothes, many of the young men in military uniform, was filing out of the Dunstan Road Synagogue in preparation for the group photograph on the steps outside. But my young grandson persisted.

"You're still crying Grandma! Why?"

"All these questions. Tuttelah darling, I've told you it's because I'm so happy."

"Michael, be a good boy and do leave Grandma alone. She's already told you she's happy. One day you'll understand that it's at times like this that we're reminded of past events that sometimes make us a little sad. Just give Grandma a kiss and wish her *muzzletov*, (congratulations, good fortune.) then we'd best all hurry outside, or we'll miss the group photographs on the steps."

My youngest daughter Becky, or Betty as she preferred, had just married an infantryman in the Canadian army, Private Issie Glick. We hurried outside and were just in time for one last photograph. On that freezing January day nobody was prepared to hang around for very long. We then briskly walked the short distance from the synagogue to Harry's spacious Hodford Road home, where the food for the wedding reception had been prepared and set out in the billiard room on their full sized billiards table. There was no music that I recall, if for no other reason than this was just after the last German offensive called the 'Battle of the bulge' early in 1945, and the war was still in progress.

It was a stand up buffet lunch, where expenditure on catering had been restricted by the wartime maximum of five shillings a head. Crockery and cutlery had been scrounged from every family member, none of which matched, but even so the meal was particularly sumptuous by wartime standards, with cold roast chicken and varieties of different salads, while the family was full of bonhomie.

In spite of all the camaraderie, I sensed that there were undercurrents, no matter how cheerful everyone appeared to be. Even my younger grandchildren listening, like mice, silently scurrying, unnoticed in almost every corner and alcove, or hidden behind furniture, supped piecemeal on every snippet of information. They gleaned it bit by bit, no matter whether the adults spoke in hushed tones, whispers, or in Yiddish, so that these young people might neither hear nor understand.

My grandchildren then gossiped amongst themselves, laughing and giggling with siblings and cousins, often arriving at outrageously mistaken conclusions, but somehow on this occasion they sensed that my daughter Anne and I had contrived, for entirely different reasons, to ensure that Becky should find a man who would marry her.

I believed at the time, though there was no confirmation that Becky might be crossing into her menopause. Though she might not have entered this loathed phase of older maturity, Anne and I knew that it might be imminent. In fact we knew, and had heard of women of similar ages in their late thirties who had entered that horrible change of life, with its depression and hot flushes.

Personally I had never experienced any menopause difficulties although the mere consideration of such feminine weakness in my daughter's life caused me great anxiety. As her mother, I realised only too well, that once unable to bare children the likelihood of marriage would be even more remote. Without a husband, Becky would one day be left to look after herself on her own as a lonely spinster, in what was shortly to become a very precarious post war world. And worst of all, I would have failed in my duty as a parent.

Anne, on the other hand, found that while her younger sister was a financial responsibility she could comfortably afford, she could no longer tolerate the presence of a sibling whom she considered to have become an irksome embarrassment.

Ever since leaving school as a 14 year old, Becky, had at every opportunity repeatedly borrowed her older sister's cosmetics and clothes. She knew full well how this infuriated Anne, especially in later years when many gowns were the latest, couture creations, but chose to ignore such matters. She had few friends of her own and in Anne's opinion didn't appear to have matured in habit or intellect beyond the nurturing East End years of her youth. Although 37 years old, she continued to live at home with me, as an unmarried woman, accepting board, and lodging provided indirectly by her sister. All these things caused repeated arguments between my daughters. This was bad enough, but Anne could no longer tolerate her sister mixing amongst her friends and colleagues. Anne claimed repeatedly that this was one burden, which was now too much for her to bear.

In 1936 Anne had purchased a flat on the fourth floor in a chic, expensive apartment block in Park Lane, with magnificent views of Hyde Park. Even in war time the fairy tale view overlooking the park was one of the finest anywhere in London. Most Friday evenings she would journey by train from Paddington to Taplow Station, where she would take a taxi to Lent Rise. There she would spend the weekend with her sister, Clara and me in 'Anneville', the modest 4 bedroom detached country house, which she'd acquired in the second year of the war.

By coincidence this was about a mile from the sumptuous Thames-side home of Cliveden where Nancy, Lady Astor, a charismatic American socialite and the first woman member of parliament, lavishly entertained. Subconsciously she may also have fleetingly daydreamed of a similar life style amongst the smarter set.

In preparation for the Sabbath Friday evening meal I would travel regularly by train each Thursday morning to Petticoat Lane. Arriving there armed with four or more stout empty shopping bags and usually assisted by my faithful, Clara, I would make all the kosher food purchases for the following week. I would then entrain that same afternoon from Paddington back to Taplow station and then walk more than a mile back to my home laden down with all those arm-wrenching shopping bags, full with every imaginable provision.

There, under my supervision Clara, would spend hours assisting me in the preparation of our many culinary delights, until all was ready late on Friday afternoon.

Since I never complained about the work involved in *shlepping* (carrying a heavy load) and cooking, Anne appeared completely oblivious of the physical effort required. She also seemed indifferent to the hours spent in careful preparation; of the food that she liked that had been cooked to perfection for her and her guests to enjoy over the weekend. That scarcely mattered since I regarded my efforts as a labour of love for my special daughter. Of course I also enjoyed making the rounds of the innumerable small East End shops where surrendering money and ration coupons I could banter and talk in Yiddish, exchanging gossip with shopkeepers I'd known for so many years.

Gregariously, Anne would invite any Jewish serviceman she met, who was away from home, to Lent Rise for Friday night dinner with Becky and me. Amongst those invited she displayed a particular partiality for those from the New World. One advantage of inviting these overseas guests was that they would often arrive with small gifts of chocolate or foodstuffs that were only available with ration coupons, if at all. Those invited for a repeat dinner, would frequently turn up with canned foods and other unobtainable delicacies, which were only available to US servicemen through their PX stores.

One such overseas guest was Issie Glick, who was a temporary patient in the Canadian Hospital in Taplow. Anne and Betty had been seated in the railway compartment when a Canadian serviceman had entered and sat opposite. As the train proceeded, he became aware of them talking and sensed they were discussing whether he was Jewish.

"Yes ladies, I'm Jewish. Let me introduce myself. My name's Issie Glick and I'm a serviceman in the Canadian army."

In response, they promptly invited him to join them for Friday evening dinner.

When invited back with a repeat invitation, he arrived with a wealth of otherwise unobtainable foodstuffs. Following his second dinner invitation he invited Betty out on a date to visit a cinema in Maidenhead. Whether there was a mutual attraction or this was a good deed in response to a sense of gratitude for a pleasant Friday evening dinner away from home, I don't know, but they dated again and soon became close friends. A little later they became engaged.

Issie was a good-looking, happy go lucky private in his mid twenties, from Montreal. Betty was a slim, smartly dressed manicurist who was shrewdly able to conceal her true age, effectively removing almost one third of her years in the process. My family and I, relieved at the prospect of seeing her wed encouraged her in this minor deception surrounding her age. A policy of silence, stronger than any introduced during the war to keep information away from the enemy, surrounded any hint or mention of her age to Issie, before the nuptials.

Anne was the happiest person of all that her sister was to be married and especially to somebody, who would carry her many thousands of miles away from London.

I carried out my usual investigations, into the suitability of my daughter's proposed husband, as best I could. Before military enlistment the groom had been employed as a modestly small cog in the Montreal garment industry making buttonholes. Apparently he had no other skill, nor any prospect of achieving a better position, without further training, once he returned to postwar employment. This wasn't at all to my liking, but the necessity of securing a husband for my daughter far outweighed all other considerations.

I knew that with the generous dowry that I'd long ago put aside for Becky, at least once married they'd be able to establish a comfortable home, but the problem remained and gnawed into my bones, making my rheumatism worse, of how they were going to maintain a reasonable standard of living after that.

It went through my mind that the newly-weds might be encouraged to settle in London, since I didn't want to see my youngest daughter journey to what seemed like the other side of the world, where I might never see her again.

"I'd rather have Becky stay home with me and take her chances of some day finding a Londoner, than have her disappear with some native Canadian into the forested wilds of Canada with its snowdrifts, bears, and wolves, where I'd never hear from her from one year to the next."

Anne seemed, reluctant to listen to my arguments.

"Mother, where do you get these strange ideas? Montreal is a major city, where the only bears and wolves you could find would be in a zoo. It's not some little *shtetle* (small Polish township) in the middle of a forest. If we don't find a husband for Becky now, she'll be left high and dry, with only me to support her.

She's engaged, so she's going to be married. This could well be her last chance of marriage. She's got to be married. I wouldn't care if Issie Glick were the bloody milkman, with a peg leg, and a patch over one eye, like Long John Silver or a hook for an arm like Captain Hook; she has to marry him. I'll do my best to help support them, but you've a duty as a parent to see her married. If you oppose the marriage then it will be your fault entirely that she'll live the rest of her life as a very miserable and lonely old maid. So far as I'm concerned, the sooner she's married the better; and the further she lives from London, better still."

Over the years I'd grown used to accepting Anne's opinions and advice on most matters. Consequently and perhaps foolishly, I ignored Issie's lack of employment prospects, particularly with Anne's repeated assurance that she would provide Becky with a monthly allowance and assist her husband in obtaining a job with better opportunities through her friendship with a business associate, Isaac Wolfson, managing director, of the General Universal Stores. With this assurance I encouraged the match and a date was speedily set for the wedding.

While we were constantly worried that the groom might discover the bride's true age, and call the whole thing off, or simply get 'cold feet', the groom for his part was certainly carried away by the relative affluence of the bride's family. Added to that was the guarantee that Anne and I would each provide a generous dowry.

Within weeks of V.E. day, (Victory in Europe, the cessation of hostilities in Europe) Becky found herself as a G.I. bride ensconced with hundreds of other young women from every conceivable background boarding a transatlantic liner in Southampton. It had earlier been fitted out as a troop carrier and in spite of the poor accommodation, the food was far better than the rations endured in England since late 1939, and the mid summer journey to New York proved to be an exciting experience.

In New York there was a brief stopover, punctuated by welcoming speeches and an official dinner. The Canadian contingent then proceeded onwards by train to Montreal. On arrival there were more speeches and a welcoming dinner followed by interviews by a war brides' reception committee. The committee was made up of a government sponsored group of ladies who had volunteered to assist the young women, many with young babies, to find suitable accommodation and adjust to life in Canada until their husbands joined them, once they were demobilised.

Becky enlisted the help of a real estate agent and located a modestly comfortable two-bedroom apartment. Using the larger portion of her dowry, she furnished it with expensive modern furniture, failing to conserve her resources for the future. Following this extravaganza, she diligently utilized the remainder of her months as a housewife to conscientiously fritter away the remainder of her capital while awaiting the return of her warrior husband from Europe, without any thought of seeking employment, or discovering those market places where she could shop more economically for provisions.

Within weeks of her husband's demobilisation, Becky found herself pregnant. In March 1946, for the first and only time, she gave birth to a child. Naming him, Russell, this was to be my ninth and last grandchild. Issie meanwhile had resumed his pre-war occupation, with its former salary, which was barely adequate to provide for a wife and child.

In the spring of 1947, braving flooded roads, I escaped from the worst winter weather experienced in the UK in living memory. I made my transatlantic crossing in the Cunard line's luxury Queen Elizabeth, from Southampton to New York, where Solly was a senior ship's steward. Although only my second ocean crossing it was a far cry from the one I'd experienced on that first occasion more than 40 years earlier, which had filled me with such a dread of ships and oceans.

Arriving in New York, I continued my journey by train to Montreal to spend three months with my daughter and newest grandson, papering over the financial rifts that had started to appear in Betty's marriage. I then returned to the scarcities of postwar England, having spent a small fortune on presents for each member of my family. Passing through the customs and immigration hall, I put on my best performance. I collapsed against a table announcing I felt faint and needed water. In no time at all I found myself seated regally in a wheel chair, propelled together with my uninspected luggage past the customs officers. The railway officials ignoring my third class ticket placed me in a first class compartment on the train bound for Victoria station and immediately provided me with a cup of tea.

Later in the year Becky returned to London with Russell, but without her husband, her fare paid for by me. They stayed with Essie and Titch in Overlea Road, for all her relatives to admire her infant son. After a month's vacation they returned to Montreal, loaded down with baby gifts, and what was to become an increasingly isolated married life for Betty.

Betty continued to rely upon her elder sister's financial support, without any sense of embarrassment and repeatedly appealed to Anne to help Issie secure a change of employment with a better salary.

Anne responded by requesting her business friend Isaac Wolfson to assist her. Wolfson created a job opportunity in one of his GUS stores in Montreal and as a consequence Issie became a warehouseman, after which promotion prospects would depend on the employee's aptitude.

Shortly afterwards, a protracted correspondence ensued over many years, with Becky remonstrating with her sister over her husband's poor salary and the lack of promotion opportunity. No amount of complaint on Becky's part, and she certainly knew how to grumble, could secure any improvement in her husband's job prospects within that company, which left one sister embittered and disillusioned and Anne completely exasperated.

Chapter 13

1945

Once the war was over I saw far more of my grandchildren who would visit Grandma in the country for days on end. My children, apart from Steve and Becky would regularly visit on weekends and appeared to get on well together with many of the old rivalries, a thing of the past, although whenever Anne and Mark met there was invariably a disagreement followed by a brief pyrotechnic shouting match, when sparks would fly.

From 1945 onwards, Anne was the only one of my children who remained single. In many ways she was the most successful if one measured success by career achievement and money, but I would have given my all to see her settled down and happily married.

Anne left school in 1917, when she was just 14. My husband and I arranged for her to attend Pitman's Secretarial College, for a shorthand and typing course, which was the best we could afford. With the war still in progress there was a great shortage of workers and she found any number of employers willing to employ her in spite of her lack of experience. She changed jobs from time to time gaining commercial skills by working for a good many different employers, until she obtained a job with the Lazarus brothers. They were a successful furniture manufacturer in Tottenham.

She joined the secretarial pool where she was one of more than fifty young typists. Pay and employment conditions were good and she worked there until there was a major disagreement between the brothers who then decided to separate, creating two new companies.

As a young, inexperienced furniture manufacturer in partnership with his older brother, Hyman Lazarus had many years earlier attended an auction. He'd been carried away in the bidding and purchased a huge consignment of veneers. Although he'd purchased them at a very advantageous price he admitted that he'd bought sufficient to last them to the end of the century; As a consequence he became something of a laughing stock in the furniture trade, but later, this error was to make him a small fortune.

The war had then intervened and veneer facing that had been used to give furniture a more luxurious finish went out of fashion. When Hyman Lazarus split up with his brother, he'd been told that since the veneers cluttered up valuable floor space, he could keep them, at no cost, providing he removed them to his new Tottenham premises, in Brentwood Road.

The veneers were moved by the truckload to be stored in his new factory warehouse, where, dry and gathering dust, they remained largely forgotten in the intervening years.

When Hyman Lazarus moved to his new factory he gave Anne the option of joining his new organisation 'H. Lazarus Cabinets' manufacturing bedroom furniture suites. As an incentive he offered her a more senior post in the typing pool, which meant more responsibility and a larger pay packet. Anne accepted.

She had inherited much of my ambition and drive, and by the time she was twenty-seven she had been promoted to head the typing pool. There she was responsible for nearly fifty women, many of whom were far older than her. It was some time after that when chance took a hand.

In the early 1930's there was a change of fashion and furniture with a veneer finish became the rage. Veneers were once again used in the manufacturing process but the increase in demand had not been anticipated and there was a tremendous shortage of this wafer thin timber covering. One of Hyman Lazarus' largest competitors 'H. L. Furniture' known as Lebus, had been experiencing difficulty in acquiring the veneers essential for the manufacture of their latest range of furniture. That morning Anne had received a telephone call from the purchasing department of Lebus enquiring whether H. L. Cabinets wished to dispose of any veneer that was surplus to requirement. Anne immediately spoke to her boss.

"Mr Lazarus? Anne Podguszer here sir. I've just taken a phone enquiry from Lebus, who wish to acquire any surplus veneer we may have available. They sounded quite desperate; I recall that we have a warehouse full. Would you be willing to sell any to them and if so, what quantity and at what price?

"Miss Podguszer, from the typing pool?

"Yes Sir."

"Why didn't the enquiry go to sales?"

"I tried to have them accept the call but they refused. Said they weren't interested because we only sell finished furniture and not timber. I remembered seeing stacks of veneer in the warehouse some time ago and I thought that this was the sort of situation that might be of interest to the company sir."

"Of course it is. We've hundreds of thousands of linear feet of the stuff that I've been anxious to off load for years. It's a fire hazard and takes up valuable floor space. I'd like to get rid of it at almost any price."

"I told them I'd call back straight away and if you give me a price, I'd be pleased to negotiate for the company."

"Well I purchased it almost twenty years ago. Can't remember what I paid and we wrote it off our balance sheet long ago. Since it only costs us storage space I'd suggest that you sell it at the best price you can get, say thru-pence a veneer. Do you think you can handle it?"

"I don't see why not sir. I'll do my best. Is there any limit to the quantity you wish me to sell?"

"No. It's only a temporary shortage, so sell the lot if you can. I'll be glad to get rid of it. We could always use the space it frees up."

Anne called H. L. Furniture back and announced that Mr Lazarus had a quantity of veneer for sale should they be interested. By the end of the day she had sold the entire stock of veneer.

Just prior to home time she phoned Mr Lazarus and announced.

"Anne Podguszer here, Mr Lazarus. I've sold all the veneer apart from what we need for our own production over the next three months."

"Miss Podguszer, would you mind coming to my office right now please."

On arrival at the office she knocked and entered.

"Miss Podguszer, would you mind if I call you Anne. This as I think you know is Mr. Banks our finance director. I've told him of your earlier conversation and I've asked him to sit in at this meeting.

"At what price were you able to sell our merchandise?"

"Sir, you gave me a figure of three pence, so I offered it at five pence, knowing that there was a shortage and they would attempt to negotiate a lower price."

"And what happened?"

"I sold it at four pence."

"Did you hear that Banks? We've made an unanticipated fortune. Four-pence a veneer. Well done Anne."

"No sir. I sold it at four pence a linear foot and they're responsible for haulage."

"I can't believe it. You've committed highway robbery and without a gun. That's absolutely fantastic.

"Anne, could you explain to us how you knew what our production needs would be for the next three months and how it is that you sold our entire stock? "

"It was a simple matter of arithmetic and common sense. In the typing pool we know the precise number of units sold each week, since we handle the documentation for the sales department. I simply went onto the shop floor and asked how many feet of veneer are used for one suite of furniture. Nothing could have been easier."

"That's remarkable. I wish more people in this organization could display the same common sense. Now tell us how you sold the whole stock? Surely Lebus didn't want it all?"

"No they didn't, but they seemed so grateful at having sourced a supply that I decided to use my initiative to find other buyers. I gave one of the girls a list of our competitors and had her find the phone numbers in the telephone directory. I then spoke to the purchasing departments and in what appeared to be no time at all I'd sold the lot at five pence a foot to anybody who needed it. The production director at Lebus was so grateful he even asked for my name, and an hour later I received a bouquet of flowers.

"Well I think you richly deserved it. What you achieved was phenomenal. You showed tremendous initiative. We're having a little celebration at the Savoy tomorrow evening to celebrate the tenth anniversary of this company. My wife and our directors will be there. If you'd care to join us then, I'm certain that Bessie would appreciate having another lady present."

"Thank you very much sir. I've never dined at the Savoy and I'd love to join your party."

"I'll have my driver pick you up at seven tomorrow evening."

And that's how it all started. Anne received a fantastic bonus and within a few weeks had been appointed a company director with her own office and a huge increase in salary. Her sole conversation revolved about her work and co-directors. She now referred to her employer as Hyman and then it was Hymie this and Hymie that. I met her employer and his family and was delighted to see with what ease Anne moved in an environment of wealthy and important business people. She frequently had business meetings, dined out until late and periodically had conferences that took her all over the country and even abroad with Mr. Lazarus who called her his right hand man. I never remotely suspected anything untoward until Anne moved out of our family home and took her own apartment.

Ginsy and Harry were the first to open my eyes, telling me what was going on and there was absolutely nothing that I could do about it.

Anne and Hymie Lazarus had become lovers. Although they were discrete, even Bessie Lazarus and her family knew what was going on. It seems that as her mother, I'd been the last to know.

The family rumourmongers commented that Anne received her promotion by sleeping with her employer, which infuriated me. In their jealousy they ignored the fact that although she never had the benefit of a college education, she was a highly motivated intelligent woman. She was always a self-assured child who took great care of her appearance. As she matured she earned the respect of her colleagues through her own merit, helping Hymie Lazarus develop a very successful public company. Amongst her family there wasn't a single person who hadn't cause to be grateful for her financial help or good counsel at some time or another.

Those she helped somehow resented the necessity of having needed her generosity. Not to her face, of course, but behind her back. They would infer that she required that they side with her in any family dispute and to agree with her during any discussion or disagreement. In addition they made up stories about her, some of which could be frankly libelous. Fortunately she remained largely unaware of the manner in which certain of her sisters in law and others vilified her.

Once she became a successful career woman, she established her home in Park Lane with a housekeeper. At the end of her day's work she would return home and after a shower would immediately hold court with family, or friends who were either invited round, or dropped by.

In elegant clothes, with her short bobbed hair, rimless glasses and slim figure she would sit in her lounge and entertain. In one hand she held in tapering fingers with those exquisitely manicured fingernails a measure of single malt whisky in a thistle shaped Waterford crystal glass, while in the other a cigarette, often in a long cigarette holder, from which she would inhale intermittently as she spoke. Seldom was it possible on these occasions to express an opinion contrary to hers before she would heatedly dispute the point, verbally battering her would be opponent into submission with force of argument and the occasional display of our Chisick temperament.

One of the stories that were whispered about and which I later discovered to have been true, concerned Anne's relationship with Hyman Lazarus. Anne had established a pattern of dining alone with Hymie several times each week at various smart West End restaurants. In the spring of 1935, at the start of their meal she announced.

"I've missed my period."

"Does it happen often?"

"No. In fact I've missed two. I saw a doctor last week who arranged some tests. I saw him again yesterday and he's confirmed that I'm pregnant."

"Oh my heavens. That does put the cat amongst the pigeons doesn't it."

"I've been sick with worry. What should I do?"

"It's what should we do. It's as much my problem as yours."

"Thank you. I knew that would be your attitude."

"While Bessie has known of our relationship for some time, I've also got Lisa and Leon to consider. Leon's just started at Eton and there's no way I could think of a divorce at this time."

"I'm not suggesting for a moment that you divorce Bessie. To embark on those sort of proceedings would take two to three years at the very least and would serve no useful purpose with my present predicament. We're not teenage lovers. We went into this with our eyes open and we've suddenly been caught out. There's nothing I would have wanted more than to be your wife and bear your children, but I accept that's never been an option. The question is what should I do now?"

"You can't ruin your career and the rest of your life with the stigma of a child born out of wedlock. If you elect to have our child then you would have my full support, but you would need to disappear from your family and associates for at least six months and then make your decision whether to have the baby adopted or to foster it."

"I couldn't possibly disappear for months on end. Even if that was an option and I had the child I could never give our infant away just like that."

"Then what do you want to do?"

"I just can't have this baby and furthermore I daren't go to some back street abortionist with all the attendant risks."

"Heaven forbid."

"Then for heaven's sake how do I go about ridding myself of this pregnancy?"

"I'm not exactly an authority on such matters, but I do know that you could visit a clinic in Switzerland where, with the right money, an abortion can be performed hygienically and safely, by a qualified doctor, with no danger to your health. Just give me a few hours and I'll obtain all the information necessary, after which you and I can travel abroad on business for a few days, to put this problem behind us."

Following a number of discrete phone calls, arrangements were made to consult a gynaecologist in Basel. Air reservations were made and Anne revealed that she and Hymie were flying from Croydon airport to Basel in Switzerland with the intention of negotiating the purchase of a large quantity of timber. Hymie returned to London three days later while Anne took the opportunity of extending her stay by a further few days for a little sightseeing.

Their personal and professional relationship flourished until Hymie became sick in 1945, and was diagnosed with a cancer of the stomach by Professor Henry Cohen, Liverpool's most eminent diagnostic physician (later Lord Cohen of Birkenhead). Over more than three decades, seldom did an Englishman of any affluence or importance ever surrender his hold on life until Dr. Cohen had been consulted. He would never render a fee for any patient seen outside Liverpool, thus avoiding a very onerous level of income tax, but would make a charge for travel expenses of one guinea a mile, as he journeyed in his chauffeur driven black Rolls Royce limousine.

Sir Stanford Caide, the fashionable Polish surgeon from Westminster Hospital operated and managed to keep him alive for a little over seven years, which was the time required to pass his assets to his family without incurring any estate duty.

Hyman Lazarus died on 15 Mar 1952, and while devastated by her loss Anne found some comfort in the £30,000 fortune bequeathed to her in his will. (in excess of £2,000,000 in 2008)

She continued working to assist Leon Lazarus, the incoming managing director, Hymie's son, but the joy and happiness had gone out of her life and after a few months she retired. Like a sailing ship entering the doldrums, Anne simply drifted aimlessly entering a period when she appeared to exist without any seeming purpose.

Some months later she was introduced to Jack Veronique, a pipe-smoking bachelor in his early 50's, at a dinner party given by some friends. Calling himself Vincent, he lived in a magnificent home in Totteridge with an elderly housekeeper. Shortly after the war he had developed his own imported fabric furnishing business, which he had built into a successful enterprise with a remarkable showroom and warehouse just off Regents Street.

He escorted her over his showroom and invited her to accompany him on visits to elite restaurants, the theatre, and opera and to all the social events and activities that might make an impression on a lady. Gradually Anne's depression lifted. She joined Vincent in a box at the races, visited the Chelsea Flower Show and accompanied him to numerous social and charitable events where she witnessed his generous charitable donations. In short she was becoming rather impressed with this man who sent her flowers every week and gladly accompanied her each Friday evening when she dined with me, Harry and Ginsy, at my flat in Bronwen Court.

It came as no surprise when Vincent proposed marriage. Anne accepted and they resolved that after their marriage, that they'd live in Anne's apartment with her Italian housekeeper, Rosa, still in attendance and would sell Vincent's property in Totteridge.

The marriage was celebrated just prior to Anne's fifty first birthday with a reception and afternoon tea at the Dorchester Hotel, following which they left for a three-week honeymoon.

After their honeymoon they returned to Anne's apartment where an unexpected surprise awaited her- numerous unpaid bills for the wedding reception and gifts that Vincent had given her during the past weeks of their courtship. Confronting her new husband, he admitted that he was a little short of money and would appreciate her paying the bills. Upon further questioning that ultimately turned into a veritable interrogation, Vincent revealed that he was broke and his moribund company was verging on bankruptcy, owing the Inland Revenue almost £50,000. He had misled her concerning his financial status and the precarious state of his business. Anne was mortified. She'd been deceived and completely taken in.

Vincent had somehow mismanaged his business affairs and was penniless. Anne realised that part of her attraction for Vincent was that she was a wealthy spinster who could solve his financial problems. An argument ensued and she told him in no uncertain terms to leave her flat immediately.

She then phoned me.

"Mother?"

"Hello Anne. Welcome home. Did you find the kosher food parcel I left in the fridge?"

"I don't know what to tell you, but my marriage is over."

"What are you talking about? How can your marriage be over? What on earth's happened?"

"It's finished. I've discovered that Vincent's broke I've sent him packing because he's a lying scoundrel who just married me for my money and hasn't got a pot to piss in. I intend to speak with my solicitors in the morning and have them start divorce proceedings."

"Don't say another word. I'm coming straight over. You're probably over reacting to a lover's tiff. Don't do anything rash, that you'll be sorry about later."

"There's nothing for me to regret. The man's a two-faced rogue who deliberately deceived me and married me for all the wrong reasons. I want nothing more to do with him."

"I'm putting my coat on and I'm coming over straight away. I'll call Harry to come over and we'll talk this thing over and help you sort things out."

"I don't want to talk to anyone. I feel so ashamed that I've been taken in like this and I know if I see that man again I'm likely to murder him."

"Make some tea for us. I'll be with you in a few minutes."

A little later once Harry and Ginsy had arrived, the four of us sat round the dining room table and talked long into the evening. As Anne's temper cooled, we were able to discuss the problem more rationally. Once again I was the head of my family.

"Anne you're fifty years old and if you thought it was difficult to find a partner when you were a spinster, it'll be many times harder as a divorcee."

"You're absolutely right. There's still a terrible stigma associated with divorce. The whole process will be more costly than you can ever imagine and it'll certainly take two or three years," explained Harry.

"I don't care. I want nothing more to do with the bastard."

"Of course you're angry and upset. The man's deceit wasn't that he's been womanising, or doing anything criminal. He was hard up and he felt ashamed of admitting it." I explained.

"He knew he was broke and he deliberately set out to ensnare me for my money. If I'd been poor, he wouldn't have been interested."

"Forget the money for a moment. You wouldn't have married him had you not loved him. You found certain qualities that you admired."

"Yes, but mother…"

"But nothing. Had you been an old hag of ninety, Vincent wouldn't have married you even if you possessed all the tea in China, would he?" I continued.

"Well?"

"Then what we're really talking about is love as well as money. So let's talk about the money. In my opinion the man probably doesn't realise that he needs your help far more than your money. He claims to have a good business and it's failing. If I were you, I'd go into his office first thing tomorrow. Find out what's gone wrong and help him to put it right. Show him like I found with your father, ova sholom, that a married couple can work together successfully and also have a good marriage."

"Mother's right. As you calm down and think more logically you'll see that you've nothing to lose. Work together. Give it a few weeks and then reassess everything. If it doesn't work out, then you can think of divorce and revenge. It's always been said that revenge is a meal best served when cold." advised Ginsy.

"What about all these unpaid accounts?"

"Easy. Damn the bills. Negotiate with the taxman and do a deal. Pay what you must and return everything else," said Harry.

"I'm emotionally exhausted and I've got to get some rest. I'll go into Vincent's office tomorrow at seven and he'll wonder what's hit him. Meanwhile please don't breathe a word to anybody. If news of this ever gets out, I know I'll die of shame."

Next morning, true to her word, Anne went into Vincent's showroom long before he arrived. She spent three hours sorting out a confused mess and by the time Vincent showed up at ten expecting his usual cup of coffee he was greeted by Anne who escorted him into his office, closed the door and then proceeded to lay down the law for a number of essential ground rules.

"Vincent, if we're to stay married we must put yesterday's sordid mess behind us. Do you agree?"

"Of course I do. I love you and I want to stay married with you as my wife."

"Very well. The first thing is that we need this business to succeed so that you can maintain your self-respect and don't have to ponce on your wife. Arriving at ten each morning and leaving early your staff have been short-changing you for years with the hours they work. It's small wonder you're going broke. As the boss you must lead from the front. Is that understood?"

"Of course."

"You must always be the first to arrive each working day. The next rule is that you or I will always lock up and be the last to leave. That way we set an example, which the staff has to follow."

Within weeks the business was flourishing and two years later they invested in purchasing the freehold of their showroom and warehouse. Only a small group of my family knew about Ann's initial problems. None ever mentioned the matter again, permitting the embarrassing start to her marriage to be soon forgotten.

Too old to have children, Ann and Vincent became grand companions and the marriage and their business proved to be a great success. They gave generously to a number of charities while Ann continued to support me, and Becky, in Canada.

In the summer of 1956 Anne and her husband were taking a weekend away from work by visiting Normandy. They stayed in Deauville and while lunching in one of that town's many fine restaurants entered into conversation with a middle aged French couple sitting at the next table. Throughout their meal they chatted amiably using a mixture of languages. At the conclusion of lunch while waiting for the waiter to appear with their bill, Anne took a visiting card from her handbag, bearing the name Anne Veronique with her address and handing it to their new acquaintances invited them to contact her should they visit London. The French gentleman reciprocated the invitation and as they were preparing to leave, handed Anne his card stating that if M. and Mde. Veronique ever visited LeHavre to be certain to contact them. Anne looked at the name on the card, Julian and Georgette Podguzer. In great surprise she exclaimed that Podguzer had been her maiden name. A few minutes of animated conversation followed as they discovered that although they'd never met previously, their late fathers had been brothers and they were first cousins, Julian being Sylvain's youngest brother.

With all my children happily married I considered this to be a measure of my success as a parent. The post war years were generally a happy period for me in spite of the post war power cuts and shortages that persisted into the early 1950's.

The war broke England economically and Britain in turn frustrated all legal attempts to settle the survivors of the holocaust in Palestine.

Worse still, Ernest Bevin, the labour foreign secretary contrived to have any immigrants caught attempting to enter the mandate imprisoned in detainee camps in Cyprus and then returned to concentration camps in Germany. Armed resistance occurred in Palestine while world public opinion veered in favour of the survivors of Nazi persecution being allowed entry. During 1947, the United Kingdom beset with difficulties of every kind at home, in India and in many of her colonies, handed the problem to the United Nations stating that all British forces would be withdrawn from the Mandate in mid May 1948.

A successful vote was passed in the UN recommending partition of the country, even though the Arab states voted against the resolution. But then that was to be expected, since most of them had sided with the Nazis during the war, which the British preferred to forget, since we were heavily dependent on the Middle East for our oil.

On May 14th 1948, David Ben Gurion announced the formation of the new independent State of Israel within the partitioned territories agreed by the UN. We were ecstatic with joy. We helped raise money in support of this new land but suddenly the euphoria vanished as Arab armies invaded from all sides. Weeks of fighting resulted in loss of life and territory but the fledgling state survived.

In England the Nazi movement lived on. Oswald Mosley, who had been interned during the war, was released from prison and was again leading a group of thugs under the titles, British Nationalists and British League, who stirred up vicious racial hatred against Jews and later, the newly arrived coloured immigrants. His fascist rabble would hold rallies in areas of London, particularly in the east end where a larger proportion of Jews still lived and worked. Jewish citizens in the vicinity were frequently beaten up and local residents were intimidated. Under the guise of freedom of speech they were always given police protection and in 1946 some 40 fascist meetings were held in London every week.

Having risked their lives defeating Hitler and his Nazi followers, a group of Jewish exservicemen, led by Gerry Flamberg, a decorated war hero who in 1944, had been parachuted into Arnhem, were determined to oppose these fascists by any means possible. They created an organisation known as 'The 43 Group', named from the number of exservicemen who attended the first meeting in 1946, which rapidly expanded to several hundred members.

These spirited young men, working in organised groups, broke up every fascist meeting and over a period of five years completely routed Mosley and his Nazi ruffians and agitators, driving them from the streets. The 43 group managed to infiltrate two of their members into the fascist head office. Without being detected they were able to provide advanced information, for years, about every meeting that the fascists were going to hold.

Fists and missiles of every kind were used, but never knives or firearms. I was particularly proud of Harry's sons in their stand against these gangs and told them so and encouraged them, in much the same way that Mark and Harry had opposed the fascists in the late 1930's.

Maurice and Murray both appeared in court as a result of their activities with the 43 Group, but were always found to be innocent.

In November 1948 Murray pleaded not guilty in Old Street Magistrates court to a charge of throwing a brick and injuring Jeffrey Hamm, a rabidly fascist senior member of Mosley's group, who like his boss had been interned for years during the war.

Hamm was the speaker at a union movement meeting in Stepney, and was making a virulently anti-Semitic speech standing on what the movement called an 'elephant van'. The van had been gifted to the fascists by a well-wisher and unknown to Moseley the donor was a member of the 43 group who used this ploy to infiltrate the fascist movement. These defamatory speeches were delivered mainly in Jewish neighbourhoods with the object of inciting racial hatred and violence against the Jews. The union movement always had groups of rowdy thugs present to defend their speakers, and Murray was one of a phalanx of 43 group members who attempted to stop the meeting. Police were always present to protect the individual's right to freedom of speech and to prevent the resulting violent confrontation.

The prosecution presented two union members who alleged that they had seen Mr Podro throw a brick at the speaker. Mr Hamm claimed he'd been knocked unconscious by the brick but did not see who'd thrown it. Murray denied throwing a brick and two members of the audience supported his claim. John Platts Mills Q.C. defended Murray and the case was dismissed through lack of evidence.

Murray later confided to me,

"Grandma, I never carried a weapon or threw a brick. I looked down and at my feet, just by chance, there happened to be this lump of concrete, as big as a fist. The speaker was spouting such vile anti-Semitic lies that I bent down picked it up and hurled it at him, in order to stop him. It was one of those lucky shots and somehow it struck him, sending him crashing to the ground. The police intervened and stopped the meeting, while Hamm was carted off to Bethnal Green Hospital.

"You know I don't believe in violence, but these Nazi's are so dumb that you have to knock the message into their heads with something really hard. It's the only way we can help them remember."

"Murray I'm proud of you. These were the anti-Semites who forced me to leave Poland. They killed my family in Poland and France and millions of others. What else do they want? The speaker must have been brain damaged before you knocked him down and now he's had a shock to his head perhaps he'll be able to think a little straighter."

Murray's second court appearance required him to give evidence for the defence. Two senior members of the 43 Group, Gerry Flamberg and John Wimbourne were charged in December 1947, with the attempted murder of John Preen, Oswald Mosley's fascist deputy. The case was heard at the Bow Street Court with David Maxwell Fyffe defending the accused. It was alleged that they had used a pistol to shoot a bullet at Preen through the open window of their car when he sat in his car parked in Paddington. The shot missed him and he claimed he immediately chased after his assailants car. He caught up with it recorded Flamberg's number plate and recognised the accused. Remarkably the police gave credence to the unlikely tale of an unarmed man at the receiving end of an assassination attempt being able to start his car and pursue fearlessly after armed assailants who had sped away in a rapidly moving vehicle.

On the second day of the trial Mr Robert Churchill, a gunsmith and ballistics authority was called as the expert defence witness. He clearly demonstrated that there was no trace of a bullet or any chemicals from the discharge of a firearm in either the accused or defendant's car indicating that there had never been a gun fired. The case against the accused was dismissed and the evidence that Murray was to have given proved unnecessary.

Both of Harry's boys had joined the 43 group after completing their national service. Once demobbed, Murray started his own leather goods manufacturing company and Maurice who had spent two years in the RAF, joined his parents in their leather handbag business.

When Mark's sons were demobilised Peter entered his father's millinery accessory business, while his younger brother Maurice entered teacher's training college and became a teacher, but following his marriage in 1951 he left teaching for a career in advertising when he started an advertising company assisted by his younger brother Michael.

Mark had been providing me with work for many years, which he regularly delivered and collected. He insisted on paying me and I was indebted for the recreational therapy this provided and I even taught Clara how to join in the fun and help me. We were fastidious in ensuring that Ann could find no trace of feathers or any of my work at her weekend visits, yet suddenly the cat was out of the bag once more. The Inland Revenue made an investigation to enquire why Ann was claiming a tax deduction for her mother as a dependent when her mother was employed and deriving an income that was not being reported. Suddenly Ann and Mark were at it hammer and tongs once more.

It took weeks of negotiation to settle the problem and again I was bored to tears without my therapy. As before, Ann was never able to appreciate how I was to resolve my boredom without working.

It was in early 1954, two years after Hyman Lazarus passed away that Anne decided to sell her house in Lent Rise and arranged that I would move back to London. Essie and Titch occupied Anne's house in Stamford Hill where I'd formerly lived, so she acquired a two bedroom flat in Grove End Road in St. John's Wood into which I moved with Clara. I recall this was the time that Ginsy had all her teeth extracted by a dentist because of dental caries and Harry, with strong healthy teeth foolishly had his removed, as he explained it, "I needed to keep her company."

I had experienced one or two falls, tripping over small obstacles in the street and at home, which caused me to feel a little unsteady and nervous when I walked. I was determined to maintain my mobility, so I decided to use a walking stick, it might even help in reaching any of the higher branches when fruit picking, although I suspected those days were now over. It vaguely crossed my mind that it might prove a useful deterrent if any thief attempted to snatch my handbag. Somehow I didn't think that rushing briskly at two hundred yards an hour crying out 'stop thief!' would enable me to catch many would be robbers, nor would my shaking the stick vigorously at them act as any great disincentive, unless they were to fall to the ground laughing.

My new home in Bronwen Court had no garden to speak of and I never again had the same benefit of walking in the countryside as I'd had living in Lent Rise. The main advantage was that my children and grandchildren could now visit me throughout the week. However the worst of my problems at this time was that from out of the blue, after twenty years as the most loyal companion, Clara became unwell and needed to retire. I'd only ever had a couple of real friends. They had both passed away and Clara had become my friend and confidante. It's said that nobody is indispensable but when one has a good friend who leaves, one can't but help missing them terribly.

A succession of housekeepers followed. In my opinion they varied only in their degrees of incompetence and deviousness. Some remained several months, others no more than a few weeks, or days. Somehow I couldn't adapt to these new interlopers and life was never the same without Clara, who I missed dreadfully.

In 1960, Anne decided that there had been such a rapid turnover of housekeeper companions that I would be better off living in a hotel. I imagined initially that this would be something like a suite of rooms in Claridges, or the Savoy, in the centre of London. I felt this might be the thing to rejuvenate me, so I hardly opposed the idea.

But Anne was married and doubtlessly Vincent had a say in the money she spent, even if it was her own. Once I'd given up my apartment I discovered that I was to be housed in a residential hotel in the 'velteran' (the wilderness) miles from anybody I knew. The term residential hotel was a euphemism for something that I soon learned was akin to a smart doss house filled with nothing but old people who were waiting. Waiting for their next meal, waiting for a visitor, or simply waiting and not comprehending what they were waiting for, or doing there.

Certainly this wasn't for me. I felt young and fit even though when I saw my reflection in the mirror staring back at me I knew I was deluding myself. My legs could barely carry my weight unaided and I convinced myself that it didn't matter that much since I had no partner with whom I could go dancing even if the opportunity presented itself. I wasn't like one of those old fogies and I wasn't going into a nursing home or residential hotel. I did the only thing that I was able. I rebelled at every opportunity.

Chapter 14

Mark's Story II

1922 to 1963

Ann and I wished to be married, yet at every turn we were thwarted by only one thing, or more correctly one person; my mother's intense opposition. Ann then hit on the only solution. Since we were both over 21, we could secretly marry in a registry office and then present my parents with a fait accompli. There was no way in which we could involve any member of my family, nor could we reveal this plan to Ann's parents who were certain to disapprove.

I posted the marriage bans in mid October and made an appointment to appear with my bride to be before the Whitechapel registrar for marriages three weeks later, on Monday afternoon November 6th 1922, with Ann's younger brother Sam Cohen and eldest sister Bloomah Goldstein as our witnesses.

The low key civil ceremony went without a hitch and we made a vow with our witnesses that apart from confronting my parents with our secret marriage, no other person was ever to be told of the duplicitous tactics we'd been compelled to employ.

The following evening as we were dining, I confronted my parents with my wish to become engaged to Ann, followed by an early marriage. Once more there was the same tirade from mother as she voiced her total opposition. At that juncture I produced our marriage certificate.

There was a stunned silence followed by mother letting out a shrill cry.

"Oh my God! Moisheka! Children! Did you hear? He's ruined his life!" and just sat and wept. As she sobbed she then wailed in the most intense anguish as she cried out:

"You foolish boy, whatever have you done? How could you do this to your parents, whose one concern has always been your well-being? You've married a working class girl, a mere nobody without a shred of ambition, with parents who can't help you in any way to establish yourself. Why did you have to marry her when you could have done so much better for yourself? With your brains and your good looks you could have had your choice from a score or more girls with dowries that could have made life so much easier for you. Why have you wasted your opportunities by marrying this poor 'frum', (orthodox) girl?"

"We may have a factory and a bigger home, but we're just as working class as she is."

"Children, just listen to your stupid brother! Moisheka, tell him how for years we've worked our fingers to the bone so that we could be middle class and he can't see the difference.

"Mother, there is no difference. So far as I'm concerned, Ann's parents are no more working class than us."

"When you have a business, like uncle Abraham or us, you're middle class, but if you're a wage earning tailor like Mr. Cohen then you're working class."

"I don't care a brass farthing for your class nonsense. I married Ann for the same reasons that you and father married, because I love her and I can't contemplate, even for a minute, going through life without her. We'll make our way in the world just as you've done, through our own endeavours, with hard work and in time we'll become even more middle class than you could ever wish. I'm sorry it had to be like this, but there was no way I could ever make you see or understand my point of view."

"Those are very fine words young man, but you'll discover the realities of life with a rude awakening soon enough. Had you followed my advice things could have been so much better for you."

The ordeal appeared to be at an end as Mother's tirade stopped, but I soon discovered that it was only the eye of the hurricane. I seized my opportunity to escape during the lull.

"We'll see. Now I'm going out to see Ann's parents to ask them to arrange a 'shule' (synagogue) wedding."

"You can marry this woman as many times as you wish and in as many shules as you please, but I'll not be there." Mother shouted.

"What do you mean?"

"Precisely what I intend. You've made your bed so go lie in it, but don't expect me to condone your foolishness and be a party to your deception. You do whatever you wish, but I don't have to be there to go through this charade."

Father who said so little in mother's presence stood up.

"Your news has left us a bit bewildered, to say the least, so give us a little time to adjust to what you've done. You go and see Annie Cohen's parents and let me have a talk with your mother."

All my mother's plans and cherished dreams to arrange a marriage of her choice for me had failed. Deep down she considered that Ann had schemed to ensnare the boss's son to improve her working class status and would forever blame her for thwarting her ambitious arrangements for my future.

I visited Ann's parents and asked a somewhat sceptical Mr. Cohen once again for permission to marry his daughter. Without revealing that I had already secretly married her, I had some difficulty convincing him that I was now a serious suitor for his daughter's hand in marriage. He finally consented and it was agreed that we could announce our engagement, but would wait until the early summer to be married. Meanwhile arrangements would be made for my parents to meet them.

Mother made the time we were engaged one of the unhappiest periods of my life and I did my best to shield Ann from the malevolence she exuded.

I could only believe that mother behaved this way in the hope that she could break our engagement and somehow have our marriage annulled. Not only did she persist in her refusal to attend our synagogue wedding, but she also refused to send out any of the invitations that Ann's father provided for our family and friends. Fortunately father made mother see sense, just in time, and in so doing helped to avoid the rift that was bound to have followed.

The marriage was booked at the Philpot Street Synagogue for Wednesday June 6th. 1923, which coincided with Derby Day. I travelled with father on one of his business trips to Paris where I purchased a full-length white wedding gown for my bride. The celebratory dinner dance held at the Crown Hall in Redman's Road, was a splendid affair and I learnt later that the hire of the hall with a four-piece band cost twelve pounds ten shillings, which was far more than a worker could earn in a month. I was pleased to see that in spite of her initial opposition, mother behaved impeccably towards my bride and her parents although I later learned that she'd told all her guests that she had paid for the wedding, since I'd married such a poor working class girl.

We set up home in a two room flat in Stoke Newington, where we retired after our marriage. Ann's parents had given us a generous wedding gift of a mahogany bedroom suite of twin beds a dressing table, wardrobe and tallboy, but somehow my parents overlooked the need to provide a celebratory marriage gift for a recalcitrant son. There wasn't much of a honeymoon, as next day it was back to work as usual, with no exception, even for the boss's son and his bride. We did have a honeymoon four days later, when on Sunday we took a railway day return to Westcliff on Sea.

I didn't expect that the truce between mother and my wife would last long. In fact it was a surprise that it lasted the few days that it did. In less than a week, mother succeeded in quarrelling with Ann, who left the factory in tears, vowing never to return.

My loyalty now belonged to my wife and I had no option but to resign. There was no premeditation. We had to earn a living and the only trade either of us knew was the manufacture of artificial flowers, hats and hat accessories. I purchased materials for Ann to make into samples, had stationery printed and within a couple of days I was on the road taking orders for our merchandise, manufactured by the 'Ostrich Feather Manufacturing Company', the business we had just set up.

Within days customers started buying our goods and we had more work than Ann could cope with in our small apartment. We urgently needed helpers for Ann and space. Ann's parents provided us with the use of a large room on the second floor in their home until such time as we could afford to pay rent for a small factory. With these premises, we acquired an assistant milliner to help Ann and then within a few weeks two further workers. During those summer months everything seemed to be progressing without a hitch. The orders rolled in faster than Ann and her helpers could produce and I could deliver our goods, so I used my spare time to construct my own 'cat's whisker', an early radio, with which to tune into the early BBC. My parents in law thought it a magical device when I first let them listen.

Unfortunately, there followed a period in the autumn of 1923 when my mother believed, without foundation, that I was poaching her clients and endeavoured to sabotage our fledgling enterprise.. She became particularly vindictive and sadly this adversely affected the relationship with my younger brothers and sisters who sided with mother. Fortunately her attempts were unsuccessful, but the acrimony resulted in our severing all contact with my family.

Almost two years elapsed before we saw my parents again, when a family friend helped bring us together to heal our rift and my parents saw their first grandchild when he was almost a year old. Matters then improved slightly, but it wasn't until some time after my mother retired from work that a really cordial relationship was resumed; although my wife found it difficult to forgive all the unwarranted hurts she had received from Sophia over the years.

Shortly after our first child, Peter, was born in April 1924, we negotiated a lease from the Ironmonger's Guild on premises at 117 Old Street on the corner of Ironmonger Row.

The ground floor provided a spacious area for a factory, while two upper floors gave us ample living accommodation in which to raise a family. In addition to the factory, we also started a confectionary and tobacconist shop, which fronted onto Old Street.

At about this time there was a great change in ladies' fashions. In 1922 Howard Carter, an explorer excavating in Egypt's Valley of the Kings uncovered the intact tomb of Tutankhamen who ruled in Egypt between 1334 and 1325 BC. The public and in particular the fashion industry appeared to be caught in a design frenzy to copy ancient Egyptian artifacts found there. Radical changes in fashion and style materialised almost overnight. Trends in ladies dresses, coats, shoes and hats, hairstyles and jewellery echoed the style of the ancient pharaohs. American architect Frank Lloyd Wright even introduced Egyptian themes into his designs. The flapper years had arrived and these dramatic changes provided us with fashion opportunities that we were able to exploit as our small company grew.

We had a large group of outdoor workers who worked in their own homes and in 1925 it became necessary to acquire a motor vehicle. My first car was a Morris Cowley, which I learned to drive following five minutes instruction from the car salesman, since no driving test, or license was required at that time.

In May of 1926 we experienced the General Strike. Every form of public transport was affected and during that emergency I volunteered for the role of a special policeman, and for ten days settled into becoming a bus driver. The strike organised by the Trades Union Congress in support of coal miners pay lasted nine days and failed in its challenge to the Conservative government of Stanley Baldwin.

In November of that year my father died in his fifty third year following an emergency hernia operation in the Middlesex Hospital. Born with a placid temperament, he was always able to calm my more highly-strung mother. He had a delightful lyrical tenor voice and sang every week in the synagogue choir. His main hobbies were singing and cooking and it was through him that I acquired my lifelong interest in opera and my brothers and I became very competent cooks. In my opinion his greatest quality was to have appreciated his wife's better commercial skills and to have given her the opportunity to build and develop a business, when Edwardian attitudes considered that a woman's role was in her home as a housewife and mother and was always subservient to her husband.

A severe economic downturn followed the Wall Street crash of October 1929. During the 1930s there was recession and unemployment in Britain, while in Germany the Nazi party acquired power and we witnessed the rise of a virulent anti-Semitism. The communists were the only group that appeared to oppose them and consequently for a time I became a supporter of that party and actively participated in opposing Mosley and the fascist party.

In 1934, in a home birth, Michael, the last of our five children arrived, although two years later Ann had a miscarriage at six months.

Apart from a difficult but brief period of personal bankruptcy in the early 1930's, the Ostrich Feather Company prospered under the joint efforts of my wife, who owned all the shares and myself.

Following the German 'Kristall nacht' (night of broken glass) in November 1938 the British government relaxed their immigration controls to permit 10,000 Jewish children under 17 years of age to enter the U.K. The children were sent by their parents in a desperate attempt to escape the Nazi tyranny under which they lived and since the immigration rules were not relaxed for adults, it meant the children were unaccompanied by any grown ups and most of them never saw their parents again.

At that time Harry and I were members of a committee that had been created to meet these young Austrian, Czech and German Jewish children arriving by train at Liverpool Street Station. Called the 'Kinder transport'. We provided these children with food and hot drinks and assisted them in finding homes with foster parents, while my sister Anne generously provided funds to support us in this aid programme.

That same year I acquired a television set with a miniscule eight inch screen and a Phillips record changer that could play up to six twelve inch records, stacked one upon the other, without needing to interrupt a classical music performance.

On September 3rd. 1939, Britain was suddenly again at war with Germany and the following day all of our children were evacuated. Peter and Maurice with Cowper Street school and Gloria, Arnold and Michael, were sent with their school into Cambridgeshire. Too old for military service, I enlisted as a 'fire watcher' and spent days hanging blackout curtains at home and helping others to ensure that no lights shone out from my own or any neighbours' windows at night. A period ensued termed the phoney war in which there were no hostilities and four of our younger children returned home. Since there was no schooling in London, Maurice and Arnold were again evacuated, this time to Mousehole, a quaint Cornish fishing village.

I visited Paris at least twice every year, purchasing merchandise and visiting my Podguszer cousins. I made my last visit in March 1940 and was unable to return until 1946. At the time of my last trip, I managed to help two cousins, Sylvain and his cousin, Max, escape from France on the last ferry from Calais to Dover and felt a bit like the Scarlet Pimpernel in the process.

When London came under its severest aerial bombardment from the summer of 1940 until mid 1941, I rented a house in Newlyn, Cornwall, a fishing village south of Penzance, where Ann, with Gloria, Michael and Ann's mother and a number of her sisters and their children stayed.

With Ann and the children away, I employed a young woman to assist with incoming telephone calls and housekeeping, since I couldn't run my business and attend to these tasks without help.

The following week Ann received a phone call while in Newlyn from my brother's wife, Ginsy, gleefully telling her that I'd installed a mistress in her absence. Ann appeared next afternoon, without warning having taken the morning train from Penzance to Paddington and promptly, unceremoniously ejected my helper. There were no accusations, but she never left me to manage on my own at home again.

During the war years with clothing and fabrics strictly rationed, it became impossible to create artificial flowers until I found an alternative source of supply. The government made rolls of a stout thin translucent material that could be used in covering window frames where bomb blast had shattered windows. This was made available to the public and no clothing coupons were required. I discovered that this material could be dyed, cut and machined into appropriate floral and leaf shapes. Colouring barber's cotton wool could simulate the stamens that I had previously brought over from France and with these improvisations, I could manufacture artificial flowers for the public who in drab, war-torn England needed something cheerful to brighten their homes.

In the summer of 1941 I acquired a four bedroom semidetached home some ten miles from the centre of London, in Heddon Court Avenue, Cockfosters, an area relatively safer from air attack than central London, although our home was damaged in an incendiary bomb raid in 1943 and V1 doodle bug bombs landed close by in 1944. This was to be the first and only home that we ever owned.

By 1943, all our children who had been evacuated had returned home. The younger ones to attend local schools while my elder sons were conscripted into the armed services when aged eighteen. By this time apart from Essie and my mother our family had all adopted new surnames, which were changed by deed poll.

We visited my mother, who lived near Maidenhead, on most Sundays, where we also met my sister, Anne who tended to stay there during the weekends. Being a little overweight I had been told that I had high blood pressure and apart from advice to lose weight, there was little more that could be done. Peter was demobbed from the army and came into our business, while Maurice, following his military service, entered the teaching profession.

Having moved to Cockfosters, consideration had been given only to the relative safety of the area from air raids. There were no facilities for religious education for our children and so with a number of like-minded people I helped found a local Synagogue where I remained chairman for ten years.

At the earliest opportunity, my cousin Sylvain Podguszer made arrangements to return to France. Since the family in France was destitute he endeavoured to circumvent the currency regulations, which restricted each person to £25 when leaving the United Kingdom. He attempted to smuggle considerably more, stuffed in a loaf of bread. His attempt was discovered, the money confiscated. Avoiding a custodial punishment, he was denied entry into this country for many years.

From 1947 onwards, we hosted fund raising meetings and all rejoiced at the miracle of the re-establishment of a Jewish state in May 1948 after nearly two millennia.

In the first years after the war the Labour government headed by Clement Attlee and the nation were mired in difficulties associated with shortages of every kind, made worse by some of the worst winter weather imaginable in 1946 and 1947.

Between 1946 and 1948 there were problems in Palestine as Britain turned immigrant holocaust survivors attempting to enter Palestine away returning them to camps in Cyprus and Germany. Under the terms of a British government regulation enacted in 1938, by Prime Minister Neville Chamberlain, known as 'The White Paper', Jewish immigration into Palestine was restricted to 10,000 persons a year and forbade Arabs to sell land to Jews.

Prior to the end of World War I the British and French governments had arranged to split up the defeated Ottoman Turkish Empire between them. In 1923, under the League of Nations the United Kingdom separated Palestine into two areas. An independent kingdom of Trans-

Jordan was created in the east and in the west, a Palestine mandate, with the intention of providing a Jewish homeland in part of that territory, honouring a pledge given in the 1917 Balfour declaration.

While there had always been a Jewish presence in Jerusalem and the surrounding territories since Roman times, the majority of the land was owned by absentee Arab landowners. As European Jews settled, bought land and commenced the process of draining swamps and reforestation they developed communal settlements, known as kibbutzim. Groups of Arabs under a Nazi agitator who styled himself, 'The Grand Mufti of Jerusalem', instigated civil unrest and riots when many defenceless Jewish settlers were murdered. Periodically more of these riots occurred and kibbutzim were compelled to acquire arms and train in self-defence. As a consequence of these disturbances the British introduced their 'White Paper', thereby denying groups of European Jews the opportunity to escape their Nazi persecutors. During World War II, the Grand Mufti lived in Berlin and the allies had to contend with large numbers of his Arab Nazi sympathizers in the Middle East. After the war, The Labour government under Clement Attlee reneged on the 1917 promise to help establish a Jewish homeland, and restricted Jewish entry into the area. A state of civil unrest ensued and in 1947 the dilemma of a thirty-year failed mandate with all its problems was handed over to the United Nations. The U.N. voted on partition and the Jewish state of Israel re-emerged in May 1948.

The first outward sign of anything untoward in my health came in September 1949, when I suddenly found myself in the London Clinic with an acute urinary retention and was advised that I needed a prostatectomy. While there, I developed pneumonia and remained in hospital for three weeks, during which time my symptoms of retention abated and the operation was postponed. One year later I was again rushed into hospital with the same urinary problem and had to undergo a prostatectomy under Mr. Dickson-Wright, a general surgeon from St. Mary's Hospital.

In June 1951, my son Peter was married to Doreen Jacobs in Leicester, while in October 1951, immediately prior to Maurice's wedding to Yetta Kahn I was rushed to hospital, with a suspected brain tumour. In St. Mary's Hospital Lindo Wing, again under the care of Mr Dickson-

Wright, I underwent surgery, where it was discovered that I had a subdural haematoma, a blood clot, most probably caused by some minor trauma to my head. Over several weeks I made an excellent recovery except that I was never quite as robust in my walking and experienced an increasing nominal aphasia where I found increasing difficulty, much as my mother did, in remembering names.

In April 1952, our first grandchild arrived and was named Philip after Ann's youngest brother who had been killed in a 1941 London air-raid when he'd failed to take shelter.

Ann and I were completely beguiled by this infant. We would never have believed it possible that mature adults could become so utterly obsessed with a child. Peter took a more prominent role in the Ostrich Feather Company during my illness, while Maurice left teaching to start his own advertising company. Gloria relinquished her work as a florist due to a skin allergy and retrained to become a secretary. Arnold commenced his studies at medical school and Michael was employed in advertising intending later to join his brother Maurice in partnership.

In 1954 my sister Anne, who we long believed to be a confirmed bachelor, was at last married. Her marriage did however experience some difficult teething problems when she discovered that her husband had concealed that his fabric business was in a chaotic state and was verging on bankruptcy. My son Maurice and his wife were expecting their first child in the autumn and our happiness seemed never ending when the following year my sister Essie's only daughter Betty Defries married Ralph Levy, an Edinburgh University medical student. It was at her wedding at the Brent Bridge Hotel that my mother's illusion of family unity finally disintegrated.

At the reception, childish insults were hurled at my wife and me by my brother Harry over some trivial matter relating to a pair of stockings belonging to Peter's wife that had been left for repair in Harry's shop the previous week. Almost akin to a reflex, the Chisick family temperament asserted itself. Blows were substituted for words, and pandemonium ensued.

The family unjustifiably took sides against me, as Anne and Essie allied themselves with Harry, against Solly and me, with my mother in the middle, unable to mediate to make her children see sense. Regrettably this split in the family proved irreconcilable and I never again saw, or spoke with Harry, Anne, or Essie.

In April 1959 Gloria, the last of our children was married. Prior to that I had been particularly distressed that both my younger sons were married leaving my wife and I with an unmarried daughter in her late 20's, reminiscent of the problem experienced by my mother thirty years earlier.

I had first met Anne Moss and her late husband in the mid 1920's when I branched out for a brief time into the fish and chip business. I had acquired a shop in Dalston and obtained my fish from the same wholesaler who supplied a fish and chip shop a couple of hundred yards away owned by them. After half a year I sold the company with a modest profit. A little later following the arrival of their first and only child the Moss's also disposed of their business and acquired a confectionary and tobacconist shop in a location next door to the Gaumont cinema in Wood Green.

I next met Anne Moss in the summer of 1957 when she recognised me in the local newsagent's shop. I learned that she was a widow and had recently retired and now lived in Heddon Court Avenue, not 200 yards from where I lived. I invited her for tea that Sunday, where in the comfort of our lounge over tea and cheesecake, which was one of my wife's specialties, we chatted. She told us that her only son Ivor, had qualified as a doctor in Guy's hospital and was in general practice. A bachelor in his early 30's, he still lived at home and she admitted that long ago she had despaired of his ever finding a wife. We explained that our daughter was unmarried and arranged for her son to meet her when she returned from New York next month. To help encourage Anne Moss to think more favourably of a possible union I explained that Gloria had a substantial dowry, which was more than sufficient to purchase and furnish a substantial home in the area.

When Gloria returned to London, she and Ivor had the opportunity to meet and with encouragement from both families they were married some months later.

Gloria's dowry had been in the form of a £5,000 endowment insurance policy in my daughter's name, which matured when she was aged 25. Unknown to me, the policy had been paid directly to her and she had spent every penny travelling to New York and extravagantly living there for more than two years in an apartment in Gramacy Park. I discovered this fact just before her marriage and then had the dilemma of replacing the money that had been earmarked to pay for a detached house being constructed for the newly weds, just off Beech Hill, in addition to providing the finance for her wedding at the Porchester Hall.

My Edwardian philosophy had always been to provide an education for my sons, who would one day need to support a wife and family, saving the bulk of my finance to endow my daughter with as generous a dowry as possible. With hindsight, I should have been more equitable towards my sons. My attitude had been that the parents of the young woman my son was to marry would behave as generously as I intended towards my own daughter, but sadly this was seldom the case.

When my youngest son Michael married Myra Samuels in 1958, her father had promised that he would provide his daughter with a dowry of one thousand pounds. This represented a substantial deposit, which with a mortgage, would enable them to acquire a home and Michael purchased a house in Oakwood in anticipation of these funds, but some weeks after the wedding his father in law presented him with a cheque for 39 pounds explaining that this was his daughter's dowry minus the cost of the wedding expenses. He had concealed the fact that he intended that the dowry was to pay for a costly wedding.

In early summer 1962, unaware of the silent atheromatous plaques of cholesterol that had slowly been obstructing my arteries, I suddenly collapsed. Days later when I recovered consciousness in Guy's Hospital I discovered that I was unable to move my right arm and leg. Even worse was the discovery that I was bereft of speech and unable to make any verbal communication. I'd had a hemiplegia (stroke) due to a blocked cerebral artery. My family encouraged me as best they could and I lacked the ability or courage to ask them to do something, anything, to put me out of what I perceived as a humiliatingly debilitating illness from which there was no hope, or possibility of recovery.

In spite of my illness I never heard from Harry, who when we were younger had been my best friend, or my sisters. Only Steve maintained any contact. My mother was incommunicado in an old peoples home and worse still, Peter had not only embarked upon a divorce, which at the time was socially abhorrent, but indicated he was about to compound his folly. Foolishly he intended to marry Helen Brown, the divorcee 'friend' who had schemed to destroy his marriage and there was nothing I could do to thwart his intentions.

In March 1963 my younger sons, Arnold and Michael, arrived to tell me they had just returned from my mother's funeral at the Edmonton Federation cemetery and to wish me long life. I cried and sobbed unashamedly as I had never cried since I was a little boy.

In anguish, I wept for my shortcomings as a son and the harsh words spoken over the decades in anger, wishing that I might turn the clock back, just momentarily, to retract, apologise and make amends. I wept for my indifference to her problems as she aged. I wept for the manner in which my illness had humbled me to childlike impotence. And finally I wept in self-pity for my inability to be present, as was my duty, at her interment.

Less than three months later, Arnold's wife, June gave birth to a daughter, a pretty, fair-haired child with blue eyes, who they named after my mother. This gave us our ninth grandchild, six boys and three girls.

On the morning of Monday November 18th I was awakened by an intense discomfort in my chest, which rose into my neck and throat. I called out to Ann as best as my stroke would permit. Somehow she heard me as she was dressing and came running down to where I had a bed on the ground floor to see what was amiss. As she arrived she anxiously enquired.

"Mark, whatever's wrong?"

The discomfort had progressed rapidly into a pain in my chest of such severity that I could do no more than gasp out. "Ann!"

Her look of anguish as she rushed to the phone silently conveyed more than any words, as the pain ruthlessly crushed me. I heard her urgent plea.

"Dr Hyman, Please come quickly. It's Mark.."

Then there was that intense bright light in the tunnel.

Mark died from a blocked coronary artery and was buried the following day in the Reform Cemetery in Hoop Lane. His siblings Harry and Anne attended, the internment but declined to attend the traditional shiva in his home.

Chapter 15

March 1963

*I*t was late Thursday afternoon when Anne Veronique's office phone rang, with a call from the nursing home.

"Mrs. Veronique, matron here. I'm calling to let you know that your mother has developed a touch of bronchitis and to be on the safe side we feel that she should be looked after in our nursing wing."

"Is it anything serious?"

"No, not at all, it's no worse than a bad cold. She's no temperature and her pulse is normal. It's just so that we can observe her more closely."

"Has she seen the doctor?"

"No. I don't think a little bronchitis warrants disturbing the doctor."

"Maybe so, but I'd prefer that you arrange for him to see her."

"It's been a particularly severe winter and the doctor's been rushed off his feet. He's terribly busy and I don't think…"

Never one to brook any nonsense Anne interrupted her in mid sentence.

"I'd like you to tell him that I'm requesting a private consultation and that I'd like her to be seen as soon as possible please."

"As you wish Mrs Veronique. I'll call you once he's seen her."

The following morning Anne telephoned the home.

"Good morning matron. I'm phoning to enquire how my mother passed the night?"

227

"She's very comfortable and had a good night. The doctor has only just examined her. He's confirmed, as we suspected, that she's a touch of bronchitis and he's prescribed a cough linctus."

"Does he think there's any need for a chest x-ray?"

"We discussed that very point Mrs Veronique and he's of the opinion that the upset of moving your mother to the hospital would be far worse than the benefits of that investigation. He said he'd call again on Monday to review the situation and if there was no improvement he'd then consider an x-ray."

"Thank you. Now my husband and I have to be present at a trade fair where he's one of the exhibitors. It lasts two days and we have a very busy schedule today and Saturday. I shalln't be able to visit until Sunday and I'd be grateful if you could tell mother that I send my love and will see her Sunday morning."

Late that evening the night nurse recorded in her observations:

'10.30 p.m. Mrs. Morris restless. Reluctant to take fluids and appears confused at times.'

Having written her report, she 'phoned the doctor who agreed to attend the following day. Next, Mrs. Veronique was called and a message was left with the housekeeper, Rosa, requesting that she inform Mrs Veronique that Mrs Morris was not so well.

Suffering a head cold, Rosa, retired to bed early before her employer had returned home but left a hand written note stating that the Home had telephoned. The Veronique's returned home late and tired that evening and failing to see Rosa's penciled message went straight to bed.

Soon after 1 p.m., the duty nurse found that the patient's breathing was more rapid and she was rambling incoherently. Without any sign of a fever the patient's pulse was weaker and it was clear that her condition had deteriorated. Less than an hour later her breathing was more laboured and she could no longer be roused, by which time the nurse had been able to contact Mrs. Veronique who said she'd be over as soon as possible.

In the small hours of the morning, Sophia woke from her sleep, a constricting feeling in her chest. She felt breathless as though she'd run up a flight of steps, although with her rheumatics she hadn't attempted anything so energetic in years. In the austere ward the colourless silvery moonlight coming through her bedroom window cast unfamiliar shadows no matter where she glanced. Feeling clammy and cold she suddenly discerned in the half-light a recognizable short tubby figure silently approaching the foot of her bed. Even in the absence of her hearing aid, she would still have expected to hear some sound, but there was none, apart from the intermittent rasp of her own breathing.

Wondering if this were a dream or whether there might be some one else in the room she called out.

"Who's there? Who is it?" as fumbling she reached out on her bedside locker to retrieve her glasses, which in her haste she then placed askew on the bridge of her nose. She then attempted to locate her hearing aid, the earpiece of which she always found difficult to attach, when she distinctly heard a familiar voice.

"Zlata. Don't be frightened, it's only me."

"Good heavens, am I dreaming? I don't believe it! Is that really you Moisheka? "

"Of course it's me, darling. Who else would be calling at this time of night?"

"I thought I recognised you, but I couldn't believe my senses. Nobody's called me darling like that in years."

"Well that's a husband's prerogative."

"Moisheka, wait a few moments while I organise my hearing aid."

"Don't worry and fuss about hearing aids, shmearing aids. We haven't much time and you seem to be hearing me just fine."

"You're right I can hear you perfectly. In fact I haven't been able to hear so well in ages. These national health aids are worse than useless most of the time and sometimes I wonder why I bother with one."

"What's this national health you mention?

"Oh it's a free health service the government introduced after the war, which they couldn't afford then and can afford even less now. I've got this sharp pain which catches in my chest every time I take a deep breath."

"Then call someone to give you something to ease it."

"No, I've had it for a couple of days and the nursing staff've been giving me some medicine but it doesn't seem to make any difference. In fact it's getting worse and I don't need to be a doctor to know that."

"That's nonsense. If it's hurting, then you should call one of the nurses."

"Moisheka, I rang the bell only a few minutes ago but nobody comes. You ring to summon someone again and again, and then you can call until you're blue in the face and still no one responds. The place could burn down and they wouldn't notice, let alone call the fire brigade. When we're old they treat us as though we're young children. In fact at times I think they'd even treat animals better."

"I said you should call the nurse if you're not feeling well."

"It's always the same when you want some one. They're probably yachnaring (gossiping) or shloffing (sleeping). Whenever they arrive, their excuse is always the same. 'We're rushed off our feet; we've been so busy. We're always so short staffed we've no time even for a tea break'.

If you complain, and heaven forbid you should do such a thing, I've heard them say; 'The old girl's confused, particularly at night, and doesn't know what she's talking about. She's old and becoming senile, poor thing.'

If only I were a few years younger, I'd show some of these khorvas, a thing or two that'd make them buck their ideas up a bit. Once when I rang my bell at night and there was no response I crept round to the office and found two of them, each with their legs up on an armchair, asleep. Girls who are paid to work and sleep for a living whether they're in a uniform or not are whores."

"They're nurses and they're tired, but not whores. You mustn't say such things."

"Moisheka you know me, I don't beat about the bush. I call a spade a spade. These girls, always painting their nails and putting on lipstick are only interested in men. On Tuesdays and Wednesdays they talk about 'Roll on Friday' and on Thursday and Friday they talk about where they're going with their men friends. On Mondays they're recalling their romantic fantasies about what happened Saturday and Sunday night and can hardly stay awake. I know what they're up to and I know a khorva when I see one.

I remember that time I was in Paris visiting your family just after the second war. I was walking back to the hotel one night with two of my teenage grandsons Arnold and Michael, Mark's youngest boys, when we came across a small group of those French tarts, all dressed up to the nines. They started calling out to the boys and teasing them.

'How'd you two boys like to have a good time with us?'

I should have ignored them but I was angry and called out.

"Leave them alone. They're children."

'We like 'em young, they're more fun than some of the older farts.'

"Go away." I shouted back.

'You come with us boys! Don't listen to the old girl. We'll show you a few tricks to remember.' One of them called and the other laughingly said. 'I slept with your old man last night. We had a right old time of it and he told me all about you being a frigid old cow.'

"You should only sleep where my husband is." I yelled back as laughing, we walked out of earshot. And you tell me I can't recognise a tart when I see one.

"What is this place and what are you doing here?"

"It's an old people's home, but to me it feels more like a prison. A couple of days ago they put me in the nursing wing because they said I had a chest infection and they could keep a better eye on me. Can't say I've noticed any difference."

"What about your pain? Shouldn't you call someone?"

"It'll be better soon when I get back to sleep."

"Well if you say so. How long have you been in this home?"

"Questions, questions! You can see I'm not feeling so good, but I'll tell you. I've been here far too long and there's no escape, no matter how hard I try, and believe me I've tried. Everything would have been all right but like a fool I let the children persuade me first to give up the business and then my home."

"I don't believe you. Why on earth did you let that happen?"

"I was bamboozled, that's why. They talked me into letting them look after me. They're good children with lots of fine intentions, but when you get old, you'd best watch out. You should never give up your independence.

They said. 'Mother, you can't possibly manage on your own. No matter who we employ to help you, you're so difficult they won't stay. So we've arranged for you to stay in a nursing home where you'll be safe and looked after properly.'

An institution where you're looked after and can't leave when you want has always been a jail in my book, no matter what else they call it."

"Sophia, were you as hard to get on with as they claimed?"

"Of course not. In my own home I wanted things done my way and in that situation any person would want the same thing. Maybe the younger people couldn't conform to my ways, but that wasn't my fault. Naturally they'd claim that I was being difficult in order to cover up their own incompetence, wouldn't they? My hair may be grey and my skin wrinkled, but I still have a mind of my own. So what if I can't manage stairs with the arthritis in my knees and I can't move faster than a three legged tortoise, that's no reason for throwing me into a home with all these alte kakas."

"Using all this bad language, you're lucky they don't arrest you. You shouldn't say such things about people. You should just have told the children you wanted to return home."

"I tell them every time I see one of them, which isn't often, but they say I haven't a home anymore and I'm better off in here, where I can be supervised properly in case I fall or if I'm unwell in the middle of the night. They should only know. The girls here are so sex-crazed they can't even keep awake at night. I know because I listen to what they're saying when they think I'm asleep.

Let me tell you, Moisheka, it's not a great thing to grow old. As I've aged I've had to endure the curse of loneliness and it's a blight even money can't remove. I don't have any more friends. You remember Mrs Levine? She was the last of them and she passed away, ovasholom, nearly fifteen years ago. I've got grandchildren, but apart from two or three, I haven't seen them since I came in here. Anybody would think I've got something contagious like leprosy."

I suppose there just comes a time when we've lived long enough, and then it's really time to go."

"I don't know about such things, I was just 53 when I passed on."

"Have you seen anything of my parents since you've been on the other side?"

"Darling when you die you don't see anything or anyone. Doesn't matter what anybody tells you, its just emptiness. Whether you've been good or bad there's nothing more, just a great zilch."

"That's ridiculous, you're here. You're seeing me. Everyone tells us there's a better life in the hereafter and people have been saying that for thousands of years. It has to be true."

"It's all wishful thinking. No matter how many people yearn to believe that nonsense and I admit that I was one of them, there's no heaven, Garden of Eden, or angels. There's no afterlife with God, not even hell. There's just the one life here on earth, so you'd best make the most of it."

"But we're told that we have a spirit and a soul that lives on forever and only the body dies."

"At one time everyone, without exception, believed that the world was flat, but that didn't make it true. If it makes you happy believing in God and accepting these fairytales, go ahead and believe. There's no real harm in it, I used to. The soul that we talk about is only the memory people have of you. Once you're gone then poof! Like a candle flame it goes out."

"Moisheka, I can't accept what you're telling me. You went to synagogue every week of your life and you sang regularly in the choir sometimes two or three times each week. We had a kosher home and we did all these things because we believed in God. Are you telling me you don't believe anymore?"

"Yes and no. Going regularly to shule and singing in the choir was a way of life. I enjoyed it and met some fine people. It taught me a wonderful code of ethics. Studying the Torah (Old testament) and the comradeship of those who did likewise were part of my very being and I admit that in spite of what I now know, I would do the same again. It gave my life a unique purpose and inner comfort, which I also wanted for you and our children.

All I can tell you is that providing you've lived a good life you're given one solitary concession. You're allowed a brief visit to see whomever you wish just before they depart this existence. That's why I'm here. I chose to see you darling.

You know it seems like only yesterday that my father, ovasholom, came to see me in the hospital after my operation in 1926."

"Are you telling me that you're only here because my life's ending?"

"Yes, I wouldn't be here otherwise. Regardless of whether you feel comfortable about it, everything and everyone has a limited life span."

"I know, I'm not a complete idiot, but when's this thing supposed to happen?"

"I don't know exactly, but very soon; imminently."

"I don't believe you. You're talking rubbish. I remember eleven years ago when Mark was desperately ill and the surgeons were going to operate on his brain. I went to the Rabbi and had his name changed to *Chaim* (life) so the angel of death wouldn't find him. What they said was a tumour turned out to be a blood clot. The operation was a success and he recovered. One of my children could do the same for me."

"Zoshia, I just explained and perhaps you didn't understand me. There are no angels or demons. Changing a name won't enable you to live any longer."

"But the rabbi told me it would make all the difference and it did. I witnessed it. Believe me, it was a miracle. I saw it with my own eyes."

"There are some very fine rabbis, and holy men of every kind who genuinely help people. The Catholics have Saints who performed miracles all the time, as easily as you made your artificial flowers, but nonetheless the truth is there are no Gods and no afterlife. Were the world's population to accept this, then there would be so much unemployment amongst priests and those connected with religion, and even more distress to the people they serve, that it's better that none of them should know. Voltaire was absolutely right when he said 'If there weren't a God man would need to invent him.'"

"Moisheka, you could be wrong. You said 'any moment', long ago and nothing's happened."

"Darling if you want to believe in Santa Claus, the tooth fairy, elves, goblins, God, or any of this hocus-pocus nonsense, that's up to you. It really doesn't matter anymore. The only thing that's important now is to realise that I'm here to help you. I loved you more than anyone else and I've been given this one opportunity.

"You mean it's so soon that I might never have the chance to see the spring primroses as they come into flower again?"

"That's the way it has to be. Very soon you'll be gone and in no time at all you'll merely be a fading memory in the minds of anyone you've known."

"Moisheka, couldn't you try to use a little influence to give me just another day or two, so that I can see the buds on the trees breaking into leaf just once more."

"Zoshia my love, it's not within my power to extend your time here."

"Moisheka make one last try, just for me. All I want is a couple more hours for a few last goodbyes and to enjoy one last sunrise, and maybe hear the early morning birds calling to each other."

"I can't help you even by a few seconds let alone a few minutes. Anyway I thought you were fed up with your life living in this place."

"I am, but however much of a dump this is, and however seldom I see my children, this is the only life I have. Although it's not been much fun all alone in recent times, what's left of my life's still very precious to me.

Listen to me Moisheka. I've got to tell you something important that I've never told anyone. I made so many mistakes as I went along. I know that I was downright wicked at times, but somehow I just couldn't help myself. When I arrived in this country with my three little ones and just the clothes on my back, I was so anxious and frightened. Life was such a struggle and I had this burning need to succeed. Not for myself, but to give our children a better start in life than we had when we were youngsters, to make something of themselves. I felt that if you and I worked hard as a team we could really make it happen, and we did. From nothing, all our children now own homes, drive cars and have a comfortable life, with things that we couldn't even imagine when we were young. But now after a lifetime's work I've been discarded by my children so that I'll be leaving with less than when I arrived in England."

"Don't fret darling. We all make mistakes and in the end we all leave with nothing, no matter who we are."

"At least with you holding my hand, I don't feel lonely any more."

"There's not much time left, tell me about what's happened since I left you. It'll occupy your mind while we're waiting."

"I still think you're mistaken, but if that's the way it's to be then I suppose I shouldn't complain. We had some fine years together and a few good laughs didn't we Moisheka?

"Of course we did, but it was really hard work in those early years as we tried to establish ourselves."

"I wasn't complaining. I think it was worth the effort, but I'm finding it a bit difficult to talk so much. When you died I no longer had any friends who could share memories with me of the happy times when we were young. The years passed so quickly, where do they all go? Life's like a well. When it starts to run dry that's the time you realise how precious the water is.

"When this thing happens Moisheka, is it painful? Will I have an opportunity for a few goodbyes?"

"Zoshia darling, when it was my time I recall Solly waking me up in the hospital. I sat up and said 'Hello,' and as I did so I noticed a large fly buzzing round my head. I had this terrible pain in my chest and throat and suddenly I couldn't catch my breath. I started to think how silly it was with this bluebottle-buzzing round and I couldn't breathe, then out of the blue my father appeared at the side of my bed. He didn't stay long; I don't even recollect what we talked about. I know he smiled at me just like when I was a little boy and I felt an inner calm. I remember looking at him and he seemed to be moving away, getting smaller and calling for me to follow him and not to get lost as he moved away from me towards a very bright light at the end of what seemed like a tunnel; then nothing.

"What happened after I died? How did you feel?"

"I was so hurt and angry. I kept asking myself what had I done that you should treat me so abominably? Not a good bye, no last kiss, just nothing but a huge great emptiness. My heart was broken into tiny little pieces and I felt I could never forgive you. You took my whole life away without any warning."

"Zoshia. It was an illness. I had no choice."

"Stop! You were my closest companion; my best friend and you betrayed me. It was worse than discovering you had another woman."

"Don't be so foolish. You know I would never have done anything like that to you."

"I know, but you asked me how I felt at the time and I'm trying to tell you. It's seared deep in my memory as though it was yesterday. And then I just felt a total numbness. Everything was as though I was in a dream world. Family, the children and even friends cuddled me, tried to comfort me.

I know they felt awkward not knowing what to do for me and I felt so alone and just couldn't stop crying. No sooner did I stop then some word or thought started it off again, and I continued to go through the motions of living as best I could. I was so jealous of any other woman I saw who still had a husband and selfishly I kept asking myself why did this have to happen to me and not perhaps to one of them. It was wicked and wrong, but I just couldn't avoid those thoughts.

The children and I missed you terribly at first and to be truthful I still do, although I think the children hardly give you a thought other than when they light a Yartzeit (remembrance) candle. It's nearly 37 years and I can tell you, that while the pain of your death gradually faded over the years it's always been a lonely life sentence for me."

"I'm so sorry darling, but I was never given an option. Look we're becoming a little too morbid. I don't know how long we're permitted to chat like this, so let's be a bit more cheerful. Tell me what happened to the children after I left? Are they happy and well?"

"That's a difficult question to answer. Our children are middle-aged people, all older than you were when you passed away and I hate to tell, but most of them don't speak to each other. They prefer to argue and row over the most trivial matters just like when they were youngsters. It's as though there's a part of each of them that's never grown up.

"Mark hasn't been to see me for nearly a year. He and Annie Cohen used to visit once every week, regular as clockwork. Nobody tells me why they haven't been to see me, or at least 'phoned. They say he's been very busy. They must think I'm soft in the head. Something must be wrong but I don't know what. In spite of all my foreboding he and Annie Cohen have had a good marriage. They've four boys and a girl. You remember Peter the first one; well after him the next boy was named Maurice after you. Then they had a daughter, Gloria named after my mother Geitle. Their youngest son, a sweet boy, they called Michael after my brother who went to America. Another of his boys they called Arnold. He became a doctor and recently returned from Canada with two children. He and his wife, June, just visited me, the first time in years. When I noticed she was pregnant, she said she was expecting in May and I'd love to know what she's going to have. Apart from Peter and last week Arnold, none of their children have visited me since I've been here.

Harry and Ginsy I see regularly. They've two lovely boys. Murray is the elder and the youngest is also called Maurice, after you. He's in the leather business with Harry. Annie did very well for herself. She changed her name to Anne Maurice but married too late in life to have children. Essie is happily married and of all the children she looks most like you. Short, a bit overweight, she has your temperament, and can sing so sweetly. Her husband Titch is one of the kindest men and they have just one daughter, Betty. A pretty girl, but like her mother a bit overweight. She married a doctor and they've two daughters. Becky lives in Montreal with the Canadian soldier she married. They have one son called Russell and although I haven't seen her in 11 years, she writes regularly. From what she writes, her husband isn't too good a provider and Annie has to keep sending money. Solly's been a good boy although he could have done so much better if only he'd have taken my advice. He's been married and divorced and married again but has no children. He works as a steward on a transatlantic liner and lives near Liverpool, so I rarely see him."

"It's a great pity they don't get on well together. Are there any great grandchildren?"

"Yes. I think there are nine or ten. I see them once and never again. The grandchildren who I idolised when they were young now rarely visit me as they grow older and start their own families. It's as though I become more invisible to them as I age. I think I could die a contented woman, if only I could believe they'd remember the good times we had together. I was unable to see my parents and grandparents once we were forced to leave Warsaw and I remember how it broke my heart, but somehow the young seem too busy these days and don't seem to care about older people."

"Zoshia, you're feeling a bit miserable at the moment so you're exaggerating. I'm sure they're really good caring youngsters."

"You're probably right, but Moisheka, this pain is getting worse and I can hardly catch my breath any more. I feel like I'm drowning; yet there's no water. I think the well I just spoke about has dried up completely."

"Zoshia darling, I wouldn't be here if the end wasn't close. It's been my one bonus. I've been permitted to return just to tell you how much I loved you and to comfort you as you go into the beyond. We'll never meet again after this."

"Don't be so foolish, of course we'll meet. I'm convinced of it no matter what you've said.

"I'm going to call the nurse again, for all the good that'll do. You know last week Mrs Levy in the next bed died. She fell out of bed and broke her hip. They left her there ignoring her calls for hours. They said she died from the fracture, but let me tell you that lying there unattended for hours, she died mostly from exposure and shock. Moisheka, it's lucky none of us can see how we're going to meet our end. It would make everyone so depressed they'd probably all go in search of a moving train and there'd be people standing in a queue waiting in turn to jump in front of it."

"What a morbid sense of humour."

"Moisheka, could you sing to me and then I won't feel so lonely. It was your lovely singing voice that first attracted me to you."

"Was that all?"

"Well that and your lovely blue eyes. It's strange that only Essie and Mark's boy Peter inherited your voice. Somehow, they both also look more like you."

"It's been such a long time; I don't think I could sing."

"With you here I don't feel so frightened and so alone. Please don't leave me again."

"Sophia, have you forgotten so soon? I told you I'm here to help you."

"I felt so alone before and now I'm with you I have a real companion again. It makes a wonderful difference.

If only I could have made Anne understand me better. Of all my girls she's the one who was most like me, with drive and ambition.

Moisheka I can see that light at the end of the bed you were telling me about. It's small and very bright and getting brighter. It's getting much closer. I'm frightened. Take my hand. I can hear you calling, but the light is so intense it's blinding me and I can't see you. Not so fast, let me take your hand again Moisheka. I'm coming with you this time, but I'm not as agile as I used to be. I don't feel frightened any more, but wait for me....."

When the night nurse next made her round she checked Sophia. There was no pulse, no respiration, only her intense blue-grey eyes to be closed and that once determined chin to be supported. Momentarily she paused and thought how sad that so many of the old folk died alone. Then she hurried back to the telephone to inform the doctor of his patient's demise. He readily agreed to attend as soon as possible to confirm that death had taken place and to provide a death certificate. Normally this could have waited until the morning but this after all was a private patient and the next of kin would shortly be on the scene. The nurse then recorded in her notes that her patient had passed away peacefully at 2.30 a.m.

Anne's arrival coincided with that of the doctor who explained that in the elderly a bronchopneumonia might often go undiagnosed but that such a circumstance was often to the benefit of all concerned since it saved the costly indignity of prolonging life by no more than a few hours with numerous tubes pushing oxygen, fluid and nutrients in and taking waste away. Of course the elderly patient was never given the choice to express an opinion, nor to query the lack of investigation that might have prolonged her life.

With what he considered were his words of comfort, he wrote out the statutory death certificate. Three days later his account appeared in the mail and was settled promptly.

Sophia was interned at the Federation Cemetery in Edmonton on Monday, March the 21st, where she was laid to rest alongside her husband Morris in a shared grave.

Her son Mark, severely incapacitated by a stroke was unable to attend.

Although he frequently argued with his mother and to the casual observer appeared most intolerant, he cried like a child when informed of her demise. Neither Becky in Canada and Solly in mid ocean on a Cunard liner attended. Shiva was held that same day, for half of one day at Anne's Park Lane home, short-changing the elderly matriarch yet again.

Following Sophia's passing, a great granddaughter was born ten weeks later on May 28th 1963, who was then named after her.

Chapter 16

The reader might be curious to learn what happened to Sophia's six children.

Mark, the eldest, had been diagnosed in 1945 with high blood pressure and in the absence of any specific medicine for that ailment, had been advised to lose weight and avoid any excess intake of salt.

In the early summer of 1962, he was suddenly disabled by a severe stroke from a blood clot in an artery on the left side of the brain, which resulted in a complete loss of power in his right arm and leg, and also affected his speech. In November the following year, he succumbed to a coronary artery thrombosis. His widow, Ann, developed a stroke in 1990, which impeded her speech. She entered Springview, a care home in Enfield, where she remained and enjoyed the remaining years of her life and where her sister in law, Ginsy, later became her immediate neighbour. She died in Oct 1993, aged 96, following a further stroke.

Harry, her second son, had been a smoker and developed a cancer of the tongue, which was successfully treated. Later a cancer of the prostate gland was diagnosed and he died in hospital in December 1979. His widow, Ginsy, entered Springview residential care home in 1992, where she remained until her demise from old age in 1995.

Over many years, Harry and Ginsy, dined with Anne and Vincent every Friday evening. Their youngest son, Maurice, had separated from his wife, and commenced divorce proceedings in the early 1970's. In no uncertain terms, Anne expressed her strong disapproval of her nephew's course of action, which so intensely upset, Harry and Ginsy, that it caused a permanent rift in their relationship and they ceased dining with each other, from then onwards.

Unaccompanied by Vincent, Anne, attended her nephew, Russell's wedding, which took place in New York, in April 1973, and was the sole representative of Becky's family.

Anne and Becky argued and soon fell out. The cause of their disagreement was yet again over clothes. Ever since childhood there had been repeated squabbles relating to garments borrowed without consent. Anne was an immaculately dressed woman who wore clothes that were always in the height of fashion. She had chosen to wear a smart black cocktail dress for the occasion. Becky felt that however elegant, black was entirely inappropriate for a wedding. She criticised her sister's choice of colour claiming that it was more suitable for a funeral than the celebration of her only son's marriage and demanded that she change.

Nobody told Anne what to do or wear and certainly not her younger sister. The sisters quarreled vehemently and Anne, as was her custom, was never prepared to give way on any point about which she felt strongly. The outcome was that Anne left the celebrations in a huff. The sisters never communicated with each other again, and Anne's parting shot was:

"If your son's old enough to marry, then he should be prepared to shoulder the financial responsibility of helping his parents." Following which Anne withdrew all financial support. There had been an acknowledged belief that Russell, Anne's youngest and for a time favourite nephew, might join the Veronique fabric business with a view to inheriting it from his childless Aunt but following the fall-out at his wedding no offer ever materialized, and like his mother, he was likewise cut off without a penny. Becky retaliated by cutting up and destroying every photograph of her English family in her possession.

Anne was generous with money, but often lacked tolerance where her family was concerned should they fail to agree with her on any principle. In the last two years of her life she had little contact with her family apart from her niece, Betty and her nephew, Arnold. She developed a cancer of the Pancreas and after an increasingly painful year-long illness died in hospital in 1978.

Just three days prior to her death Becky flew from Montreal to visit her terminally ill sister. Vincent, steadfastly and most unreasonably refused to permit Harry or Becky to enter the hospital sick room to see her, and immediately after the funeral Becky returned to Canada. Anne left a considerable estate, dividing her assets between her husband and donations to various charitable organisations. Nothing was left to her sister, who was in need of financial help, or any family member. Vincent never invited any of Ann's family to the stone setting, stating that he didn't want any fuss and broke off all communication with them. He died in his late 90's of old age, in a care home.

Becky developed a bone tumour in her left upper arm and received treatment for this painful problem for many years. She passed away in Montreal from cardiac failure. Following her sister's demise, Becky frequently communicated with her older brother's wives and both regularly sent her money. Issie spent his last year in an old person's home, regularly visited by his son Russell, a radio journalist, and died of old age in 2007, shortly after the marriage of his only granddaughter Stephanie.

Steve was hospitalised in Birkenhead with a pelvic tumour, most probably a cancer of the prostate gland, where he died in 1967. The only members of his family to attend his funeral were his older brother Mark's widow and her four sons.

Essie, the kind vivacious daughter who was the first of the Podguszer children to be born in England, succumbed to Alzheimer's disease and died in Brighton in 1968 where her husband Titch had cared for her.

At the time of Sophia's passing, there were nine grandchildren, and later 20 great grandchildren, amongst whom only brothers Philip and Jonathan Powell are still connected with the millinery trade.

Dedication:

My grandmother, Sophia Podguszer, who preferred to be called Zoshia, was a well-built woman, about 5ft 5ins tall, with a fantastic mop of hair and blue grey eyes, which sparkled with playful good humour. She spoke English with a middle-European accent and had a dynamism and personality that was both serious and high-spirited. Driven by an ambition to succeed she schemed and worked to improve the lot of her family. While the word failure might never have been a part of her vocabulary, chutzpah certainly was.

Outwardly she always projected an appearance of, sweetness and innocence, and with an abundance of zeal was invariably able to charm and outwit those civil servants, petty officials and others of influence whose path she periodically crossed. To observe her using all the wiles and acting skills of a Sarah Bernhardt, to appear in some way naively blameless, or incapacitated was a lesson to all who knew that this was simply a performance to ensure the success of the enterprise on which she was embarked. Her children often suggested that had she chosen, she would have made her name as a dramatic actress on the stage. She was a character!

She knowingly made my mother's life particularly unhappy, since she considered that she had ensnared her son into marrying beneath him and in her latter years undoubtedly paid a heavy price for alienating the one woman who ultimately could have cared for her in the twilight years of her life.

The nursing and care facilities of fifty years ago, in the 1960s, have evolved and fortunately most no longer bear comparison with the antediluvian facilities, which were then common place. The standard of accommodation is infinitely better; the care provided is more professional, with daily recreational activities and far stricter licensing regulations, which are constantly monitored, although there is always room for improvement, particularly since those seeking care are often considerably older and consequently frailer than in years past.

Full of a mixture of guilt and love I dedicate this story in gratitude to a woman who greatly influenced the lives of all her grandchildren and encouraged me when I was of an age when such things were important.

In conclusion I wish to thank the family members who have assisted me in recalling stories of which I was unaware, or had forgotten concerning Sophia, in particular my brothers Maurice and Michael Powell and my cousins Murray and Maurice Podro, Russell Glick and Yvonne Arbesfeld. In addition I would like to extend my great appreciation to other family members; son in law Michael Williams, cousin Ronald Goldberg, Balcombe cousin Jan Porter who have been of inestimable help in proof reading and editing and grandson Tristan Balcombe with his I.T. assistance. I wish to recall my gratitude to cousins Claire Glovin and Jan Porter, who read the early proofs and were so encouraging.

Lastly and by no means least I would like to thank June, who has had to contend with the long hours I spent in writing this biography, who has read and reread my chronicle and without whose love, patience and encouragement this book might never have seen the light of day.

Should I have inadvertently upset or offended any family member with this book's contents, it has been unintentional and I apologise unreservedly.

Arnold Powell
London April 2010

About the Author

Arnold Powell was born in London the fourth of five children and graduated from Sheffield University faculty of medicine in 1957. His experiences since then have included medical practice in Baltimore Maryland USA and Saskatchewan Canada, before settling into general practice in North London in 1963. Seven years later he and his wife, June, established Springdene Nursing and Care Homes, which has grown to provide first-rate care and accommodation for a large number of senior citizens in four modern London nursing homes.

He retired from primary health care in 1996 and subsequently began a second career as an author. He and his wife have lived in East Finchley for almost forty years, while close by live their three children and nine grandchildren.

His first published novel was 'In Search of Henry', followed in 2007 by 'Raging Against Time', an autobiography.

This, his third book, 'A Touch of Chutzpah', is biographical and is in reality two books woven into one. The first conveys the story of Sophia, an assertive woman, who worked tirelessly to raise herself and her family from crushing working class poverty to middle class affluence within a few years of arriving penniless and pregnant in England with three pre-school age children, the eldest of whom was the author's father. There followed thirty years in retirement, when she became increasingly reliant upon her children. As Sophia aged, she spiralled slowly into an unacceptable decline, shedding her independence along the way, until finally and against her wishes she was compelled to live in a nursing home where she later died.

Lightning Source UK Ltd.
Milton Keynes UK
01 April 2010

152196UK00002B/42/P